THE DEBATE ON *POSTCOLONIAL THEORY AND THE SPECTER OF CAPITAL*

THE DEBATE ON
POSTCOLONIAL THEORY AND THE SPECTER OF CAPITAL

EDITED BY ROSIE WARREN

VERSO
London • New York

First published by Verso 2017
The contributions © The contributors 2017
The collection © Verso 2017

3 5 7 9 10 8 6 4 2

Verso
UK: 6 Meard Street, London W1F 0EG
US: 388 Atlantic Ave, Brooklyn, NY 11217
versobooks.com

Verso is the imprint of New Left Books

ISBN-13: 978-1-78478-695-3 (PB)
ISBN-13: 978-1-78478-696-0 (LIBRARY HB)
ISBN-13: 978-1-78478-697-7 (US EBK)
ISBN-13: 978-1-78478-698-4 (UK EBK)

British Library Cataloguing in Publication Data
A catalogue record for this book is available from the British Library

Library of Congress Cataloging-in-Publication Data
Names: Chibber, Vivek, 1965– author.
Title: The debate on postcolonial theory and the specter of capital / Vivek
Chibber.
Description: Brooklyn, NY : Verso, 2016.
Identifiers: LCCN 2016033498 (print) | LCCN 2016036372 (ebook) | ISBN
9781784786960 (hardback) | ISBN 9781784786953 (paperback) | ISBN
9781784786977 ()
Subjects: LCSH: Postcolonialism. | BISAC: POLITICAL SCIENCE / History &
Theory.
Classification: LCC JV51 .C47 2016 (print) | LCC JV51 (ebook) | DDC
325/.301 – dc23
LC record available at https://lccn.loc.gov/2016033498

Typeset in Minion Pro by Hewer Text UK Ltd, Edinburgh
Printed in the United States

Contents

Introduction

The Chibber Debate

Achin Vanaik

From time to time a few books have so wide an impact, eliciting such a large and varied range of responses that are completely or in part laudatory, hostile, and mixed, that one comes to realize that the original text has become a significant intellectual event in its own right. Vivek Chibber's *Postcolonial Theory and the Specter of Capital (PTSC)* is one such event which deserves to be paid the tribute of being followed by a volume—*The Debate on Postcolonial Theory and the Specter of Capital*—comprised of select commentaries on that original work along with authorial responses to them. This is not the first critique of either the theoretical trajectory of Subaltern Studies or of postcolonial theorizing. So why has it had such an impact? And why have published responses to it been far fewer and academic reception to it quieter in India than elsewhere, even though in many ways Chibber's book carries a special importance for Indian academia given the direction "critical studies" in India's social sciences is currently taking? What, more generally, is the importance of the book?

From the mid-1980s onwards, there have been numerous works that criticized the theoretical pretensions of Subaltern Studies as a distinct school of historiography, especially after its alignment with the cultural turn associated with postmodernist, poststructuralist approaches. This gave rise to postcolonial forms of theorizing whose principal bugbear is the "epistemic violence" done by the use of Eurocentric conceptual categories (including much of Marxism) to try and understand what was once called the Third World and even the global history of modernity(ies), for which an "epistemic parity" of sorts is presumably required between European and non-European thought frames. The body of criticism of this turn—in which there has often been an admirable defense of a modest universalism of categories and a theorization of modernity where the identification of causal mechanisms leans more strongly toward changes in political economy than cultural resiliencies—has targeted both Subaltern Studies and postcolonial thought. If *PTSC* has made waves by making similar critiques, this is partly because the wider political context has been conducive to its favorable reception but more so because of the distinctive and undeniable virtues of the text itself.

CONTEXT AND TEXT

The 1960s and 1970s were a period of such worldwide ferment that revolutionary transformations in which socialism would transcend capitalism seemed possible. These hopes faded in the 1980s and 1990s, particularly after the collapse of Communism, which brought no solace even to those currents on the Left that had been hostile to Stalinism and opposed to Maoism, regarding them as obstacles to the development of a genuinely democratic socialist order. For many disillusioned radicals the subsequent global ascendance of capitalism was accompanied by the narrowing of progressive political possibilities to the achievement of bourgeois liberal democracy now no longer even to be deemed "bourgeois." Class struggle was no longer central; struggles against oppression of other identities besides class became more prominent. The material circumstances for encouraging both the fragmentation and academization of a progressive radicalism in thought and practice had emerged. Being a post-Marxist seemed better than being an ex-Marxist; the former implied a more benign forward movement, while the latter connoted regrettable wastefulness and stupidity in adherence to past loyalties.

However, the invasions in West and Central Asia and in North Africa by the US and Europe in the first decade of the new millennium, backed directly or indirectly by an expanding alliance network that now includes India, changed all this. Coupled with the biggest and most generalized capitalist crisis (2007/8–12) since the Great

Depression (with negative consequences that have endured long past the crisis), these military endeavors threw the effects of a universalizing capitalism and state-backed manifestations of imperialism, not easily explained in cultural terms, into the spotlight. This is the context in which *PTSC* appeared.

In constructing his study of Subaltern Studies and postcolonial thought, Chibber rejected the use of a wide fish-eye lens. Instead, he analyzed in microscopic detail particular Subaltern Studies texts that sought to provide the theoretical framework for undertaking historical sociological studies of contemporary societies, and which have undoubtedly shaped much of the discourse in postcolonial studies. Postcolonial studies made its mark first in cultural studies but had a greater initial impact on historical sociology, and more specifically the historical sociology of contemporary capitalism and modernity. Subaltern Studies theorization became something of a standard-bearer for how such studies should be carried out. Chibber's focus on these studies was therefore quite fruitful; never before had key theoretical propositions emerging from the stable of Subaltern Studies that had aimed for and achieved wide influence in postcolonial studies been subjected to such intense scrutiny.

Chibber exercises scrupulous care in laying out the key arguments of the three major figures—Ranajit Guha, Partha Chatterjee, and Dipesh Chakrabarty—whose work he chooses to interrogate. He makes the most charitable interpretations where ambiguities exist: the opposing cases are as coherent as possible and his refutations that much more persuasive. His framing of opposing views and his arguments in response are presented with great clarity of expression, avoiding any linguistic or grammatical obscurity. You may agree or disagree with what he is saying, but you will not be confused by it. Michael Schwartz, a contributor to this volume, has even suggested that those seeking to understand the methodological and theoretical presumptions that claim to make Subaltern Studies a distinctive historiography may well turn to *PTSC* in the future, rather than to the relevant Subaltern Studies texts themselves.

Finally, it is the *comprehensive* character of Chibber's challenge to this theorizing that has made his work stand out and has, in a sense, raised the stakes in the subsequent debate that emerged over his book.

Some have read *PTSC* as a "no-holds-barred knockout" aimed at certain forms of postcolonial theorizing; unsurprisingly, this view has provoked dismissive and sharp responses, even though *PTSC* itself was careful never to substitute rhetorical flourishes for sustained argument.

This introduction will eschew the common practice of providing brief summaries of the various chapters that make up this volume. Chibber, in his detailed responses to the first three interlocutors featured here and his reply to those who contributed to a symposium on *PTSC*, makes the main arguments of his original work amply clear. Attempting a summary of the chapters in this book would take up too much space, introduce unnecessary repetition, and detract from the intellectual excitement to be gained from reading these exchanges with fresh eyes. Therefore, having described the context for the book's distinct reception, I now turn to the questions posed in the very first paragraph of this introduction: why has the book met with such a muted response in India? And what, more generally, is its importance? It will become obvious that I have a strongly positive assessment of both *PTSC* and of the way in which Chibber has answered his interlocutors in this volume.

But before proceeding along that path, a few brief and general comments on the other contributions in this volume may not be entirely amiss. Chatterjee and Spivak see no merit in *PTSC*, whereas the other contributors, for all their disappointments, reservations, and criticisms, acknowledge the book's strengths and register some degree of appreciation for it. Unsurprisingly, there is a certain sharpness of tone in the exchanges between Chibber, Chatterjee, and Spivak; both sides recognize the high theoretical stakes involved in this tussle over the validity of the Subaltern Studies/postcolonial thought alignment.

But Chatterjee and Spivak are dismissive of Chibber's argument in different ways. The former defends not only his own work but that of the other two Subaltern thinkers as well. His principal line of defense, regarding Guha's foundational (for Subaltern Studies theorizing) argument for "dominance without hegemony" in the East, is not a detailed and systematic dissection of opposing arguments à la Chibber, but an elaborated accusation that Chibber has simply failed to understand Guha's purpose, and that therefore his criticism on that score is utterly misplaced. Similarly, conceptual failures on Chibber's part to properly understand capitalism (and Marx on "abstract labor") as well as the implications of the non-disappearance of the peasantry underlie Chibber's failed caricatures of his own and Chakrabarty's work. What Chibber makes of all this can safely be left to the discernment of the careful reader.

But while Chatterjee does engage, in his own way, with Chibber's text, it is far more difficult to know what to make of the Spivak piece. Here, dismissal arrives through literary flourishes, an attempt at a kind of "intellectual outmaneuvering" rather than any direct confrontation with what Chibber is saying. Spivak's rebuttal is replete with linguistic obscurities and periodic references to other writings that presumably sustain her point of view, though their links to the framework of her immediate critique are left largely unelaborated. Certainly, one major criticism of postmodernism and its influence in postcolonial thought is that obscurity of presentation tends to find a more honored place there than elsewhere.

In the contributions of subsequent interlocutors and the exchanges that follow, a more productive and thoughtful debate emerges. The problem of infinite cultural regress is cited. History 2's "conjunctural contingent causality" is not incompatible with the "powers, tendencies, structures" identified by Marxism. By "hegemony," does Gramsci mean the absorption through habitus of certain ways of reacting/accepting/consenting which are pre-reflective rather than meaning the active organization of consent? For all the virtues of Chibber's "ruthless rationality," does he subscribe to a version of "soft rational choice theory"? And how tricky might this be for the case he makes? What about the planetary dangers immanent within History 1 of *Capital* and our possibility of transcending this not just through class struggle but through technological advances to end scarcity? In short, there is much rich fare waiting to be consumed.

AN INDIAN SPECIFICITY

Though there is an Indian edition of *PTSC* which has certainly sold well, it has not created a comparable stir to that which took place in the

Anglophone countries. Apart from the text by Partha Chatterjee, who spends part of the year teaching at Columbia University in New York City, there are no other texts in this latest compilation from scholars based in India. This is not because *PTSC* has gone unnoticed—far from it. But despite having its supporters and detractors, the compulsions to defend Subaltern Studies in the light of Chibber's assault have been considerably weaker. When the Subaltern Studies project first appeared in the early 1980s, it was much discussed in India but not in the West. The project was born in a dissident Left milieu influenced by growing disillusionment with existing Communist states and orthodoxies, the outburst of Marxist-influenced peasant and tribal insurgencies of the late 60s and 70s, the euphoria generated by the end of Mrs. Gandhi's Emergency Rule (1975–7), and the general impact of Thompsonian social "history from below" reinforced by Thompson's own visit to India in 1976–7.

It was really after the imprimatur given to Subaltern Studies by Edward Said and Gayatri Chakravorty Spivak in the late 80s that it embarked on its meteoric career in that part of Western, especially American, academia concerned with "Third World Studies" and "Colonial Discourse Analysis." For those working on Indian colonial history, the emphasis on studying subaltern groups resulted in the emergence of a host of micro-studies. Many were of high quality and did what good history from below does—explicate popular forms of behavior and follow local meaning systems in ways which also illuminated broader processes of change, thus providing wider and deeper insights. Many more practitioners than in the West saw this emphasis on studying the oppressed merely as an acceleration of a preexisting tendency in the field. Theorizing Subaltern Studies as a profound methodological break was more often perceived as a form of pompous self-aggrandizement. After all, the mainstream tradition in post-independence history writing was strongly anti-colonial and certainly aware of if not always immune to problems posed by colonial complicity in Western scholarship. Effectively consigning all or most of Indian historiography before Subaltern Studies into the dustbin of the "colonized mind-set" seemed far too dramatic and unnecessary to many.

Given that the birthplace and focus of Subaltern Studies was India and that the specific works of Guha, Chatterjee, and Chakrabarty were part of a field of study to which many other knowledgeable practitioners belonged, there was bound to be a more critical evaluation of their respective contributions than in the social science and humanities departments of Western academia. But here is where the backlash emerged. Postcolonial thought does have a growing and powerful attraction for Indian scholars in the various disciplines of history, sociology, politics, and international relations that comprise the social sciences today. Therefore the absorption of Subaltern Studies theorizing within postcolonial thought has become highly pertinent, only this time under the sign not of the "Subaltern" but of a "Different Indian Modernity"! Chibber's *PTSC* finds itself part of the arsenal in the intellectual-political face-off between the defenders of a cross-cultural universalism and their opponents, among whom are newer adherents from India.

THE SPECTER OF MARXISM: THREE PROPOSITIONS

As the title of the text that initiated this debate makes obvious, the specter of capital is most prominent within the discussion launched by Chibber's book. But even though Chibber did not attack his three Subalternists in *PTSC* for "not being Marxist enough" or for being the "wrong kind of Marxist"—indeed he makes no appeal to the supposed authority of "hallowed texts" as a tool for challenging arguments—the specter of Marx and Marxism does hover over his critique. Insofar as he defends the view that capital's universalizing (but never homogenizing) drive in the non-West is a much more causally relevant factor in shaping those societies than the Subalternists (or postcolonial thought) claim, he is defending the strengths of a particular paradigm of Marxist provenance for the investigation of the specificities of capitalist development in the poorer countries. It defines his characterization of capitalism as market dependence for exploiters and exploited in any society of increasingly generalized commodity production where labor power too is a commodity.

Marxism is not a theory of everything. Yes, there are other fruitful approaches to understanding various aspects of human existence and societies. Chibber would be the first to declare this obvious truth and he himself has pointed to what he considers to be certain flawed propositions within orthodox Marxism. But like any major research agenda, Marxism has the capacity to learn from the outside, to develop its analytical tools, to expand its scope of operation, and to deepen its insights and perspectives. The message then is to tread carefully and honestly. Do not ignore the strengths of Marxist studies at their best. Do not dismiss the capacity for internal correction and development within the Marxist tradition. Above all, do not underestimate the power of Marxism as a general approach to historical sociology, and certainly not its power as a specific theory of capitalism. Otherwise one may end up with a framework that is "post"-Marxist in the very worst sense of the term—not any kind of advance but a bad retreat or detour.

There are in fact three basic and crucial propositions that flow from currents within the broad Marxist tradition, endorsement or rejection of which does constitute a dividing line in the exchanges that make up *The Debate on Postcolonial Theory and the Specter of Capital* between those who on balance come out in broad support of *PTSC* and those who do not. Both explicitly and implicitly, they shape the various contributions to this volume. They are: 1) Capitalism's emergence creates a historically distinctive separation between the economic and the political. 2) Capitalism is inescapably characterized by uneven and combined development. 3) Regardless of cultural diversity, there exists a modest but vital universalism of the human condition that provides a weak foundation for a collective project of human advancement.

By separating the economic and the political, a capitalist mode of production permits the emergence and consolidation of a new kind of civic and political equality in law and practice that we have come to know as liberal democracy. Since it permits but *does not enable* this, it is not axiomatic or automatic that capitalist development promoted by capitalists will establish a regime that is identifiably on the side of liberal democratic rather than non-democratic forms of class rule. Neither will it automatically produce a system with the basic ingredients of the political culture associated with liberal democratic regimes, namely a political culture of values that can be traced to the Enlightenment. There is great flexibility in this respect; historically, it is struggles from below that have been crucial to the formation of such political regimes and the institutionalization of such values. This feature is central to the discussion about the differences between the bourgeoisies of the West and East and about the nature of social relationships and political orders in these different societies. Testimony to the variant possibilities provided by this separation of the economic and political is actually given by the reality of today's world. In Iran a theocratic state rules over a capitalist economy; a tribal state controlled by around 7,000 families rules over an extractive capitalist economy in Saudi Arabia; among the newly industrializing countries a "soft Islamic" state prevails in Malaysia and a "soft Buddhist" state in Thailand; there is a "hard Jewish" state in the high-tech capitalist economy of Israel; authoritarian regimes (civilian and military) in a host of countries pursuing a capitalist path of development; a weak secular state under pressure from Hindutva forces in a fast-growing capitalist India; and, irony of ironies, a Communist state in China presiding over the fastest-growing capitalist economy in history!

Trotsky's theory of uneven and combined development would also have provided a better understanding of the peculiarities of the political-economic matrices of the countries mentioned in the preceding paragraph. For some reason the key theorists of Subaltern Studies and others who remained loyal to the existing Left parties in India never felt tempted to resort to Trotsky's insights in the way they willingly turned to Gramsci. It is not unreasonable to believe this had something to do with their past or continuing alignments with Stalinist and Maoist traditions. Whatever the undoubted merits of Gramsci's work, he has always been in the Indian context the safer political option. One can be a Gramscian without having to repudiate one's present or past association with Stalinism or Maoism. Appreciating Trotsky will never in the same way represent a purely intellectual choice, for he and his stream of supporters carried the burden of belonging to the Marxist and International Left tradition, the great political enemy of Stalinism in thought and practice and by extension a Maoism that earlier looked to Stalin's Russia for foreign policy support and also pursued the vision of building "socialism in one country." Even the reputational cost to be paid in moving away from Stalinist and Maoist doctrines as the bearers of a Marxism that needed to be transcended—that is, drifting toward the "post-condition"—was much less if one could keep silent or ignore the long-standing alternatives presented by the Trotskyist and other anti-bureaucratic traditions within Marxism.

The tragedy, however, is that uneven and combined development is actually a very powerful analytical tool for developing a global historical sociology suited to our times. In postcolonial thought the non-West is said to require postcolonial categories if it is to be properly understood. Here it is "hybridity" that reigns supreme; the most important source for this "Difference" with a capital D is, supposedly, cultural particularities rooted in the distinctive pasts of the social entities concerned. Understanding these postcolonial entities thus requires using newer postcolonial categories, in the search for which there is the tendency to veer close to nativism and ahistorical cultural essences even as many pursuers of this approach insist they are not nativist or essentialist—for doesn't hybridity imply non-essentialism? But uneven and combined development, where the unevenness is both inherited and created and where the combination operates at all levels—the sociological, economic, technological, political, ideological, cultural, and moral—creates a much more complex set of juxtapositions, re-articulations, interactions, and combinations of the old and new. Here hybridity is not simply the result of cultural factors and sensibilities (inherited and persistent) making each social entity distinctive from all others.

From the time when capitalism took flight on its universalizing mission, hybridity should have never been understood in static terms. Its reproduction has itself become much more dynamic. One must talk of the shaping power not just of "distinctive cultural sensibilities" but of "changing cultural sensibilities." And those elements responsible for this dynamism will owe much more to capitalism and capitalist-related infusions than to the more static/enduring mechanisms of the pre-capitalist past. A capitalist modernity creates *common processes* that unify *and* differentiate as never before. Capitalism eliminates/preserves/distorts/limits/combines/originates and therefore, as Perry Anderson has pointed out, *all* modernity is necessarily hybrid because there is always a simultaneity of different and alternative social, economic, cultural, and political realities and of future trajectories.[1]

The preoccupation with "difference above all" has expectedly resulted in the declaration that there are multiple modernities. The advocates of multiple modernities acknowledge that there is a special kind of "newness" about modernity as compared to passages of change in the past that justifies it being seen as a distinctive kind of change; hence it is "modern." And yes, they would accept that there is a common core across differences relating to institutions (mainly economic and political) created by the history and legacies of European colonial expansionism across the world even if these function in ways different from their operation in the West. There are of course a range of disagreements about how much today's modernity(ies) has/have changed or sped up in the past centuries. However, multiple modernities advocates would not accept that there is anything like a *profound* rupture between modernity and pre-modernity in that the rate, depth, and scope of change in modernity is qualitatively of an incomparably greater order. That would then focus attention on determining the new entity that would explain this, for which the strongest candidate by far is capitalism.

Rather, the temporal differentiation from the pre-modern past is taken as necessarily less than the spatial differentiation between civilisational-cultural clusters, i.e., the cultural-civilisational continuity *within* each cluster is *the* key to explaining the very fact of multiple modernities. Logically enough this leads to a search for those long-standing essences or characteristics that are indigenous to that culture/civilization/society/nation or however else one may wish to describe it. This then is the direction being taken by a small but increasingly influential minority within Indian academia that sees itself as critical and radical and therefore hostile to the mainstream discourse, and wishes to contribute along with counterparts elsewhere to the fashioning of a post-Western wisdom across the social sciences.[2] This is a lineage that can in part be traced back to Subaltern Studies. Moving from misunderstanding the subaltern to misunderstanding Indian society, postcolonial thought became applicable for studies of a much wider range of aspects of India, from secularism to IR to political activity to social relationships to elite discourses, and so on. You no longer have to be some kind of anti-capitalist radical to adopt postcolonial thought or even to side implicitly or explicitly with the subaltern. The hallmark of the newer radicalism is a conceptual rejection of Eurocentrism.

What now of the standoff between universalism and cultural particularism? That people are shaped by culture is an undeniable "universal" truth. But how far down do culture and cultural particularity go? Bruce Robbins, a contributor to this volume, has asked if there is a problem of "infinite regress." There will always be something even more local than the localism many would deem necessary for understanding the shaping effect of culture on a chosen collective entity. Or as William Sewell Jr., another contributor, has suggested, postcolonial historians should view Europe not as a "provincializing" entitity but as one that contains many provinces, each with different histories—the implication being that these historians might embark upon provincializing the provinces in an ever-diminishing direction. What then becomes of the "generalized" statements, claims, and narratives to which even postcolonial thought must resort?

The belief that culture is our nature is equally problematic. The claim here is that different cultures create different natures and mentalities through socialization; therefore neither a universalizing discourse nor the themes emerging from an Enlightenment-inspired universalism can properly make sense of the non-Western world. The point is, as many Marxists and non-Marxists have pointed out, that culture is *of* our nature. It is only against a shared background of common reference that we can meaningfully talk of difference. Sharing the same species-based bodily dependency for a long period after birth, we cannot survive without *nurture*—the term that connects nature and culture—which is of course always culturally constituted. There is always mediation by cultural codes. But no matter what the subjective clothing, objectively constituted needs, aspirations, and capacity will express themselves in resistance to exploitation and oppression everywhere and in all times, just as innate capacity for speech and second-order reflection leads to personal and social self-correction, and artistic creativity can be found in all human collectives, big and small. Our human similarities of *minimal common* rationality/needs/instincts/capacities/emotions provide enough resources for cross-cultural learning and behavior, or at least a weak but real foundation for working together to fight common oppressions in a universalist project.[3] This has now become more necessary than ever before.

PRIME UNIVERSAL NECESSITIES

For the first time in human history, the species itself is threatened by possible mass devastation through dangers humanly created. Now more than ever there is a need for a response that subordinates our differences to what we collectively share as global dilemmas. Even as there exist the most obscene and historically unmatched levels of wealth concentration and inequality, "Basic Needs" (which now go well beyond nutrition to include health, education, leisure, respect and personal dignity, and freedom from fear) for so much of the world's population are and will remain unmet. This is not because of a scarcity of resources but in spite of the fact that for some time now the age of such global scarcity is finally over! Ecological limits of various kinds are in the process of being crossed with profoundly negative consequences for the delicate metabolism that connects humans with nature. The cloud of a nuclear conflagration and nuclear winter looms constantly over us even as it shifts its geographical positioning.

These three great and universal evils are intimately connected to a globalizing capitalism. In the case of the first two, this is obvious enough and would alone call for the urgent need to overthrow capitalism. Insofar as capitalism requires a mechanism of coordination and stabilization, that unlike the principle of competition is not inherent within its universalizing drive, this can only come from the protections provided to ruling classes from the nation-state as the dominant political unit, and also from the system of nation-states requiring some mechanism of stabilization to prevent competition between the more powerful nation-states (and their ruling classes) from getting out of hand. The fact that some of these states are armed with nuclear weapons adds its own dose of acute tensions. Indeed South Asia is probably the most dangerous zone in this regard. The implication here is that the struggle to transcend the most deadly forms of militarized nation-state rivalries may require challenging the capitalist ballasts of the nation-state system itself.

In these times, surely, a non-controversial and, yes, universal value must act as our principal lodestar for radical thought and practice—a cross-cultural and *secularly* grounded notion of "human flourishing" whose precondition, of course, must be the survivability of humans everywhere. By analytically downgrading the importance and power of capitalism in shaping our contemporary world order, Subaltern Studies/postcolonial thought acts more as a diversion than as support for a task that an earlier global radicalism saw much more clearly. Capitalism itself must be transcended because its inner dynamics are incompatible with the achievement of an equitable and ecologically sustainable world order, and may even be necessary for a nuclear-free one to emerge. The historical name given to the pursuit of this earthly transcendence has been socialism. This remains a universalism worth fighting for. One hopes that *The Debate on Postcolonial Theory and the Specter of Capital* can help persuade more people to accept this simple truth.

How Does the Subaltern Speak?

An Interview with Vivek Chibber

In recent decades, postcolonial theory has largely displaced Marxism as the dominant perspective among intellectuals engaged in the project of critically examining the relationship between the Western and non-Western worlds. Originating in the humanities, postcolonial theory has subsequently become increasingly influential in history, anthropology, and the social sciences. Its rejection of the universalisms and meta-narratives associated with Enlightenment thought dovetailed with the broader turn of the intellectual Left during the 1980s and 1990s.

Vivek Chibber's 2013 book, *Postcolonial Theory and the Specter of Capital*, represents a wide-ranging challenge to many of the core tenets of postcolonial theory. Focusing particularly on the strain of postcolonial theory known as Subaltern Studies, Chibber makes a strong case for why we can—and must—conceptualize the non-Western world through the same analytical lens that we use to understand developments in the West. He offers a sustained defense of theoretical approaches that emphasize universal categories like capitalism and class. His work constitutes an argument for the continued relevance of Marxism in the face of some of its most trenchant critics.

This interview was conducted for *Jacobin* magazine by Jonah Birch, a graduate student in sociology at New York University.

At the core of postcolonial theory is the notion that Western categories can't be applied to postcolonial societies like India. On what basis is this claim made?

This is probably the single most important argument coming out of post-colonial studies, and this is also what makes it so important to engage them.

There has been no prominent body of thought associated with the Left in the last 150 years or so that has insisted on denying the scientific ethos and the applicability of categories coming out of the liberal Enlightenment and the radical Enlightenment—categories like capital, democracy, liberalism, rationality, and objectivity. There have been philosophers who have criticized these orientations, but they've rarely achieved any significant traction on the Left. Postcolonial theorists are the first to do so.

The argument really comes out of a background sociological assumption: for the categories of political economy and the Enlightenment to have any purchase, capitalism must spread across the world. This is called the "universalization of capital."

The argument goes like this: the universalizing categories associated with Enlightenment thought are only as legitimate as the universalizing tendency of capital. And postcolonial theorists deny that capital has in fact universalized—or more importantly, that it ever could universalize around the globe. Since capitalism has not and cannot universalize, the categories that people like Marx developed for understanding capitalism also cannot be universalized.

What this means for postcolonial theory is that the parts of the globe where the universalization of capital has failed need to generate their own local categories. And more importantly, it means that theories like Marxism, which try to utilize the categories of political economy, are not only wrong, but they're Eurocentric, and not only Eurocentric, but they're part of the colonial and imperial drive of the West. And so they're implicated in imperialism. Again, this is a pretty novel argument on the Left.

What made you decide to focus on Subaltern Studies as a way of critiquing postcolonial theory more generally?

Postcolonial theory is a very diffuse body of ideas. It really comes out of literary and cultural studies, and had its initial influence there. It then spread through area studies, history, and anthropology. It spread into those fields because of the influence of culture and cultural theory from the 1980s onwards. So, by the late 1980s and early 1990s, disciplines such as history, anthropology, Middle Eastern studies, and South Asian studies were infused with a heavy turn toward what we now know as postcolonial theory.

To engage the theory, you run up against a basic problem: because it's so diffuse, it's hard to pin down its core propositions. So first of all, it's hard to know exactly what to criticize. Also, its defenders are able to easily rebut any criticisms by pointing to other aspects that you might have missed in the theory, saying that you've honed in on the wrong aspects. Because of this, I had to find some core components of the theory—some stream of theorizing inside postcolonial studies—that is consistent, coherent, and highly influential.

I also wanted to focus on those dimensions of the theory centered on history, historical development, and social structures, and not the literary criticism. Subaltern Studies fits all of these molds: it's been extremely influential in area studies; it's fairly internally consistent; and it focuses on history and social structure. As a strand of theorizing, it's been highly influential partly because of this internal consistency, but also partly because its main proponents have a Marxist background and are all based in India or parts of the Third World. This gives them a great deal of legitimacy and credibility, both as critics of Marxism and as exponents of a new way of understanding the Global South. It's through the work of the Subalternists that these notions about capital's failed universalization and the need for indigenous categories have become respectable.

Why is it, according to the Subaltern Studies theorists, that capitalism's universalizing tendencies broke down in the postcolonial world? What is it about these societies that impeded capitalism's progress?

Subaltern Studies offers two distinct arguments for how and why the universalizing drive of capital was blocked. One argument comes from Ranajit Guha. Guha located the universalizing drive of capital in the ability of a particular agent—namely, the bourgeoisie, the capitalist class—to overthrow the feudal order and construct a coalition of classes that includes not only capitalists and merchants, but also workers and peasants. And through the alliance that is cobbled together, capital is supposed to erect a new political order, which is not only pro-capitalist in terms of defending the property rights of capitalists, but also liberal, encompassing, and consensual.

So for the universalizing drive of capital to be real, Guha says, it must be experienced as the emergence of a capitalist class that constructs a consensual, liberal order. This order replaces the *ancien régime*, and is universalizing in that it expresses the interests of capitalists as universal interests. Capital, as Guha says, achieves the ability to speak for all of society: it is not only dominant as a class, but also hegemonic in that it doesn't need to use coercion to maintain its power.

So Guha locates the universalizing drive in the construction of an encompassing political culture. The key point for Guha is that the bourgeoisie in the West was able to achieve such an order while the bourgeoisie in the East failed to do so. Instead of overthrowing feudalism, it made some sort of compact with the feudal classes; instead of becoming a hegemonic force with a broad, cross-class coalition, it tried its best to suppress the involvement of peasants and the working class. Instead of erecting a consensual and encompassing political order, it put into place highly unstable and fairly authoritarian political orders. It maintained the rift between the class culture of the subaltern and that of the elite.

So for Guha, whereas in the West the bourgeoisie was able to speak for all the various classes, in the East it failed in this goal, making it dominant but not hegemonic. This in turn makes modernity in the two parts of the world fundamentally different by generating very different political dynamics in the East and West, and this is the significance of capital's universalizing drive having failed.

So their argument rests on a claim about the role of the bourgeoisie in the West, and the failure of its counterpart in postcolonial societies?

For Guha, absolutely, and the Subaltern Studies group accepts these arguments, largely without qualification. They describe the situation— the condition of the East—as a condition in which the bourgeoisie dominates but lacks hegemony, whereas the bourgeoisie of the West has both dominance and hegemony.

Now the problem with this is, as you said, that the core of the argument is a certain description of the achievements of the Western bourgeoisie. The argument, unfortunately, has very little historical purchase. There was a time, in the nineteenth century, the early twentieth century, even into the 1950s, when many historians accepted this picture of the rise of the bourgeoisie in the West. Over the last thirty or forty years, though, it has been largely rejected, even among Marxists.

What's strange is that Guha's book and his articles read as though criticisms of this approach were never made. And what's even stranger is that the historical profession—within which Subaltern Studies has been so influential—has never questioned this foundation of the Subaltern Studies project, despite freely acknowledging that it's the foundation. The bourgeoisie in the West never strove for the goals that Guha ascribes to it: it never tried to bring about a consensual political culture or represent working-class interests. In fact, it fought tooth and nail against them for centuries after the so-called bourgeois revolutions. When those freedoms were finally achieved, it was through very intense struggle by the dispossessed, waged against the heroes of Guha's narrative, the bourgeoisie. So the irony is that Guha really works with an incredibly naïve, even ideological notion of the Western experience. He doesn't see that capitalists have everywhere and always been hostile to the extension of political rights to working people.

Okay, so that's one argument about the radical specificity of the colonial and postcolonial worlds. But you said before that there's another one?

Yes, the second argument is featured primarily in Dipesh Chakrabarty's work. His doubts about the universalization of capital are quite distinct from Guha's. Guha locates capital's universalizing tendency in a particular agent: the bourgeoisie. Chakrabarty locates it in capitalism's ability to transform all social relations wherever it goes. And he concludes that it fails this test because he finds that there are various cultural, social, and political practices in the East that don't conform to his model of what a capitalist culture and political system should look like.

So, in his view, the test for a successful universalization of capital is that all social practices must be immersed in the logic of capital. He never clearly specifies what the logic of capital is, but there are some broad parameters that he has in mind.

That strikes me as a pretty high bar.

Yes, that's the point; the bar is an impossible one. So if you find in India that marriage practices still use ancient rituals, if you find in Africa that people still tend to pray while they're at work—those kinds of practices make for a failure of capital's universalization.

What I say in the book is that this is kind of bizarre: all capital's universalization requires is that the economic logic of capitalism be implanted in various parts of the world and that it be successfully reproduced over time. This will, of course, generate a certain degree of cultural and political change as well. However, it doesn't require that all, or even most, of the cultural practices of a region be transformed along identifiable capitalist lines.

This is the theoretical argument you make in the book about why capitalism's universalization doesn't require erasing all social diversity.

Right. A typical maneuver of postcolonial theorists is to say something like this: Marxism relies on abstract, universalizing categories. But for these categories to have traction, reality should look exactly like the abstract descriptions of capital, of workers, of the state, and so forth. But, say the postcolonial theorists, reality is so much more diverse. Workers wear such colorful clothes; they say prayers while working; capitalists consult astrologers—this doesn't look anything like what Marx describes in *Capital*. So it must mean that the categories of capital aren't really applicable here. The argument ends up being that any departure by concrete reality from the abstract descriptions of theory is a problem for the theory. But this is silly beyond words: it means that you can't have theory. Why should it matter if capitalists consult astrologers as long as they are driven to make profits? Similarly, it doesn't matter if workers pray on the shop floor as long as they work. This is all that the theory requires. It doesn't say that cultural differences will disappear; it says that these differences don't matter for the spread of capitalism, as long as agents obey the compulsions that capitalist structures place on them. I go to considerable lengths to explain this in the book.

A lot of the appeal of postcolonial theory reflects a widespread desire to avoid Eurocentrism and to understand the importance of locally specific cultural categories, forms, identities, and what have you: to understand people as they were, or are, not just as abstractions. But I wonder if there's also a danger in their understanding of the cultural specificity of non-Western societies, and if that is a form of cultural essentialism.

Absolutely, that is the danger. And it's not only a danger; it's something to which Subaltern Studies and postcolonial theory consistently fall prey. You see it most often in their arguments about social agency and resistance. It's perfectly fine to say that people draw on local cultures and practices when they resist capitalism, or when they resist various agents of capital. But it's quite another to say that there are no universal aspirations, or no universal interests, that people might have.

In fact, one of the things I show in my book is that when the Subaltern Studies historians do empirical work on peasant resistance, they show pretty clearly that peasants [in India], when they engage in collective action, are more or less acting on the same aspirations and the same drives as Western peasants were. What separates them from the West are the cultural forms in which these aspirations are expressed, but the aspirations themselves tend to be pretty consistent.

And when you think about it, is it really outlandish to say that Indian peasants are anxious to defend their well-being; that they don't like to be pushed around; that they'd like to be able to meet certain basic nutritional requirements; that when they give up rents to the landlords they try to keep as much as they can for themselves because they don't like to give up their crops? Throughout the nineteenth and twentieth centuries, this is actually what these peasant struggles have been about.

When Subalternist theorists put up this gigantic wall separating East from West, and when they insist that Western agents are not driven by the same kinds of concerns as Eastern agents, what they're doing is endorsing the kind of essentialism that colonial authorities used to justify their depredations in the nineteenth century. It's the same kind of essentialism that American military apologists used when they were bombing Vietnam or when they were going into the Middle East. Nobody on the Left can be at ease with these sorts of arguments.

But couldn't someone respond by saying that you're endorsing some form of essentialism by ascribing a common rationality to actors in very different contexts?

Well, it isn't exactly essentialism, but I am endorsing the view that there are some common interests and needs that people have across cultures. There are some aspects of our human nature that are not culturally constructed: they are shaped by culture, but not created by it. My view is that even though there are enormous cultural differences between people in the East and the West, there's also a core set of concerns that people have in common, whether they're born in Egypt, or India, or Manchester, or New York. These aren't many, but we can enumerate at least two or three of them: there's a concern for your physical well-being; there's probably a concern for a degree of autonomy and self-determination; there's a concern for those practices that directly pertain to your welfare. This isn't much, but you'd be amazed how far it gets you in explaining really important historical transformations.

For 200 years, anybody who called herself progressive embraced this kind of universalism. It was simply understood that the reason workers or peasants could unite across national boundaries is because they shared certain material interests. This is now being called into question by Subaltern Studies, and it's quite remarkable that so many people on the Left have accepted it. It's even more remarkable that it's still accepted when over the last fifteen or twenty years we've seen global movements across cultures and national boundaries against neoliberalism, against capitalism. Yet in the university, to dare to say that people share common concerns across cultures is somehow seen as being Eurocentric. This shows how far the political and intellectual culture has fallen in the last twenty years.

If you're arguing that capitalism doesn't require bourgeois liberalism, and that the bourgeoisie didn't play the historical role of leading this popular struggle for democracy in the West, how do you explain the fact that we did get liberalism and democracy in the West, and we didn't get those outcomes in the same way in a lot of the postcolonial world?

That's a great question. The interesting thing is that when Guha wrote his original essay announcing the agenda of Subaltern Studies, he ascribed the failure of liberalism in the East to the failure of its bourgeoisie. But he also suggested that there was another historical possibility, namely that the independence movement in India and other colonial countries might have been led by popular classes, which might have pushed things in a different direction and perhaps created a different kind of political order. He brings this up and then he forgets it, and it's never brought up again in any of his work.

This is the road that, if he had taken it—and if he had taken it more seriously—could have led him to a more accurate understanding of what happened in the West and not just in the East. The fact is that in the West, when a consensual, democratic, encompassing order did finally emerge, slowly, in the nineteenth and early twentieth centuries, it was not a gift bestowed by capitalists. It was in fact a product of very long, concerted struggles on the part of workers, farmers, and peasants. In other words, it was brought forth by struggles from below.

Guha and the Subalternists miss this entirely, because they insist that the rise of the liberal order was an achievement of capitalists. Because they misdescribe it in the West, they misdiagnose its failure in the East. In the East, they wrongly ascribe its failure to the shortcomings of the bourgeoisie.

Now, if you want an accurate historical research project explaining the tenuousness of democratic institutions in the East and their veering toward authoritarianism, the answer does not have to do with the shortcomings of the bourgeoisie, but with the weakness of the labor movement and peasant organizations, and with the parties representing these classes. The weakness of these political forces in bringing some sort of discipline to the capitalist class is the answer to the question that Subaltern Studies poses. That question is: "Why are the political cultures in the Global South so different from the Global North?" This is where they ought to be looking: at the dynamics of popular organizations and the parties of popular organizations, not at some putative failure of the capitalist class, which in the East was no more oligarchic or authoritarian than it had been in the West.

You're obviously very critical of postcolonial theory. But isn't there something valid and valuable in its indictment of the postcolonial order?

Yes, there's some value, especially if you look at Guha's work. In all of his work, especially in *Dominance without Hegemony*, I think there's a very admirable criticism of and general contempt toward the powers that be in a country like India. And that's a tremendously positive alternative to the kind of nationalist historiography that had been in place for decades in a country like India, in which the leaders of the independence movement were seen as something akin to saviors. Guha's insistence that not only was this leadership not a salvation, but that it was in fact responsible for so many of the shortcomings of the postcolonial order, is to be lauded and endorsed.

The problem is not his description of the postcolonial order; the problem is his diagnosis of where those failings come from and how they might be fixed. I am entirely on board with Guha's general attitude toward the Indian elite and its henchmen. The problem is that his analysis of its causes is so wrongheaded that it gets in the way of an appropriate response to and criticism of that order.

What about Partha Chatterjee? Doesn't his work offer a serious critique of the postcolonial state in India?

Some aspects of it, yes. On a purely descriptive level, Chatterjee's work on nationalism, like Guha's, does show the narrowness of the nationalist leadership's concerns, their fidelity to elite interests and their suspiciousness of popular mobilization. All that is to be lauded.

The problem, again, is with the diagnosis. In Chatterjee's case, the failings of the Indian nationalist movement are ascribed to its leadership having internalized a particular ethos, and this is the ethos and orientation that comes with modernization and modernism. So for Chatterjee, the problem with Nehru is that he very quickly adopted a modernizing stance toward the political economy. In other words, he placed great value on a scientific approach to industrialization, to rational planning and organization—and that's at the heart of why, to Chatterjee, India is locked in a position of "continued subjection" in the global order.

It's fine to say that Nehru abided by a narrow set of interests, but to locate the deep sources of his conservatism in his adoption of a modernizing, scientific worldview seriously mistakes what the problem is. If the problem with the postcolonial elite is that they adopted a scientific and rational worldview, the question arises: how do postcolonial theorists plan to get out of the current crises—not only economic and political, but also environmental—if they're saying that science, objectivity, evidence, and concerns with development are to be ditched?

Chatterjee has no way out of this. In my view, the problem with Nehru's leadership, and with the Indian National Congress's leadership, was not that they were scientific and modernizing, but that they linked their program to the interests of the Indian elites—of the Indian capitalist class, and the Indian landlord class—and that they abandoned their commitment to popular mobilization and tried to keep the popular classes under very tight control.

Chatterjee's approach, while it has the trappings of a radical critique, is actually quite conservative, because it locates science and rationality in the West, and in doing so describes the East much as colonial ideologues did. It's also conservative because it leaves us with no means through which we might construct a more humane and more rational order, because no matter which way you try to move—whether you try to move out of capitalism toward socialism, whether you try to humanize capitalism through some kind of social democracy, whether you try to mitigate environmental disasters through a more rational use of resources—all of it is going to require those things which Chatterjee impugns: science, rationality, and planning of some kind. Locating these as the source of the East's marginalization is not only mistaken, I think it's also quite conservative.

But is there nothing to the critique that postcolonial theorists make of Marxism, as well as other forms of Western thought rooted in the Enlightenment—that they're Eurocentric?

Well, we have to distinguish between two forms of Eurocentrism: one is kind of neutral and benign, which says that a theory is Eurocentric insofar as its evidentiary base has come mostly from a study of Europe. In this sense, of course, all the Western theories we know of up to the late nineteenth century overwhelmingly drew their evidence and their data from Europe, because the scholarship and the anthropological and historical literature on the East was so underdeveloped. In this sense, they were Eurocentric.

I think this kind of Eurocentrism is natural, though it's going to come with all sorts of problems, but it can't really be indicted. The most pernicious form of Eurocentrism—the one that postcolonial theorists go after—is where knowledge based on particular facts about the West is projected onto the East and might be misleading. Indeed, postcolonial theorists have indicted Western theorists because they not only illicitly project onto the East concepts and categories that might be inapplicable; they systematically ignore evidence that is available and might generate better theory as well.

If it's Eurocentrism of the second kind that we're talking about, then there have been elements in the history of Marxist thought that fall prey to this kind of Eurocentrism. However, if you look at the actual history of the theory's development, those instances have been pretty rare.

Since the early twentieth century, I think it's accurate to say that Marxism is maybe the only theory of historical change coming out of Europe that has systematically grappled with the specificity of the East. One of the most curious facts about Subaltern Studies and postcolonial theory is that those who espouse them ignore this. Starting with the Russian Revolution of 1905 and on to the Revolution of 1917, then the Chinese Revolution, then the African decolonization movements, then the guerrilla movements in Latin America—all of these social upheavals generated attempts to grapple with the specificity of capitalism in countries outside of Europe.

You can rattle off several specific theories that came out of Marxism that not only addressed the specificity of the East, but explicitly denied the teleology and the determinism that Subaltern Studies says is central to Marxism: Trotsky's theory of combined and uneven development, Lenin's theory of imperialism, the articulation of modes of production, and so forth. Every one of these theories was an acknowledgement that developing societies don't look like European societies.

So if you want to score points, you can bring up instances here and there of some sort of lingering Eurocentrism in Marxism. But if you look at the balance sheet, not only is the overall score pretty positive, but if you compare it to the orientalism that Subaltern Studies has revived, it seems to me that the more natural framework for understanding the specificity of the East comes out of Marxism and the Enlightenment tradition, not postcolonial theory.

The lasting contribution of postcolonial theory—what it will be known for, in my view, if it is remembered fifty years from now—will be its revival of cultural essentialism and its acting as an endorsement of orientalism, rather than being an antidote to it.

All of this begs the question: why has postcolonial theory gained such prominence in the past few decades? Indeed, why has it been able to supersede the sorts of ideas you're defending in your book? Clearly, postcolonial theory has come to fill a space once occupied by various forms of Marxist and Marxist-influenced thought, and has especially influenced large swathes of the Anglophone intellectual Left.

In my view, the prominence is strictly for social and historical reasons; it doesn't express the value or worth of the theory, and that's why I decided to write the book. I think postcolonial theory rose to prominence for a couple of reasons. One is that after the decline of the labor movement and the crushing of the Left in the 1970s, there wasn't going to be any kind of prominent theory in academia that focused on capitalism, the working class, or class struggle. Many people have pointed this out: in university settings, it's just unrealistic to imagine that any critique of capitalism from a class perspective is going to have much currency except in periods when there's massive social turmoil and social upheaval.

So the interesting question is why there's any kind of theory calling itself radical at all, since it's not a classical anti-capitalist theory. I think this has to do with two things: first, with changes in universities over the last thirty years or so, in which they're no longer ivory towers like they used to be. They're mass institutions, and these institutions have been opened up to groups that, historically, were kept outside: racial minorities, women, immigrants from developing countries. These are all people who experience various kinds of oppression, but not necessarily class exploitation. So there is, as it were, a mass base for what we might call oppression studies, which is a kind of radicalism—and it's important, and it's real. However, it's not a base that's very interested in questions of class struggle or class formation, the kinds of things that Marxists used to talk about.

Complementing this has been the trajectory of the intelligentsia. The generation of '68 didn't become mainstream as it aged. Some members wanted to keep their moral and ethical commitments to radicalism. But like everyone else, they too steered away from class-oriented radicalism. So you had a movement from the bottom, which was a kind of demand for theories focusing on oppression, and a movement on top, which was among professors offering to supply theories focusing on oppression. What made them converge wasn't just a focus on oppression, but the excision of class oppression and class exploitation from the story. And postcolonial theory, because of its own excision of capitalism and class—because it downplays the dynamics of exploitation—is a very healthy fit.

What do you think about the prospects for postcolonial theory? Do you expect that it will be eclipsed within the academy and within the Left anytime soon?

No, I don't. I don't think postcolonial theory is in any danger of being displaced, at least not anytime soon. Academic trends come and go, not based on the validity of their claims or the value of their propositions, but because of their relation to the broader social and political environment. The general disorganization of labor and the Left, which created the conditions for postcolonial theory to flourish, is still very much in place. Plus, postcolonial theory now has at least two generations of academics who have staked their entire careers on it; they have half a dozen journals dedicated to it; there's an army of graduate students pursuing research agendas that come out of it. Their material interests are tied directly to the theory's success.

You can criticize it all you want, but until we get the kind of movements that buoyed Marxism in the early years after World War I, or in the late 1960s and early 1970s, you won't see a change. In fact, what you'll see is a pretty swift and vicious response to whatever criticisms might emerge. My sad, but—I think—realistic prognosis is that it's going to be around for quite a while.

Part I.
Debates

CHAPTER 1

Subaltern Studies and *Capital*

Partha Chatterjee

This is the text of a presentation made at the "Marxism and the Legacy of Subaltern Studies" panel at the Historical Materialism Conference at New York University on April 28, 2013. Partha Chatterjee is a founding member of the Subaltern Studies Collective and lives in Kolkata.

From the moment of their appearance in 1982, the series called Subaltern Studies and the work of scholars associated with it have come in for criticism from many quarters. Vivek Chibber's 2013 book, *Postcolonial Theory and the Specter of Capital*, is the latest in that line. It is a critical study devoted entirely to the early work of three Subaltern Studies historians: Ranajit Guha, Dipesh Chakrabarty, and Partha Chatterjee. I examine below Chibber's arguments against these scholars whose work he takes, rather inexactly, to be emblematic of postcolonial theory today.

DOMINANCE WITHOUT HEGEMONY

Chibber rejects Guha's criticism of the bourgeois democracy of postcolonial India as a dominance without hegemony[1] by arguing that no bourgeois revolution, not even the English Civil Wars of the 1640s or the French Revolution of 1789, was hegemonic in Guha's sense. Chibber's refutation of Guha is, however, based on a gross misunderstanding of Guha's claim. It should be obvious from a reading of Guha's longish essay that it was intended as a critique of liberal historiography and the liberal ideology it represented. It was not the historical sociology of European bourgeois revolutions that Chibber understands it to be. The short section entitled "The Universalising Tendency of Capital and Its Limitations,"[2] from which Chibber quotes extensively, was meant to draw out two major claims of liberal historiography: that capital has a universalizing tendency and that the revolutions of England and France established bourgeois hegemony in the sense of being able to "speak for all of society." Both claims, as Guha points out, are supported by Marx: the universalizing tendency appears in the *Grundrisse*, and the achievement of the English and French bourgeois revolutions in bringing about "the victory of a new social order" is described in the 1848 articles in the *Neue Rheinische Zeitung*. Taken in isolation from Marx's critique of capital in his larger body of work, according to Guha, these statements "would make him indistinguishable from any of the myriad 19th century liberals who saw nothing but the positive side of capital in an age when it was growing from strength to strength."[3] We know, of course, that Marx also suggests that capital must come up against limits it cannot overcome. More on that later.

Of Liberal Claims

The crucial point is that nowhere in the essay does Guha offer any propositions of his own that might be construed as a historical sociology of bourgeois revolutions in England and France. Indeed, he does not need to make any such sociological claims at all. All he needs is, first, an account of liberal claims that the new social order established by the bourgeoisie enjoyed the consent of all classes in society and was therefore hegemonic in its power. Second, he needs an account of liberal claims that British rule in India also enjoyed a similar basis of consent from Indian subjects. Third, he needs an account of claims by Indian liberals that India's postcolonial order was similiarly hegemonic to the European bourgeoisie because the Indian liberal bourgeoisie could legitimately speak on behalf of the entire nation. Finally, Guha needs to show that these liberal claims to hegemony for the colonial as well as the postcolonial regimes are spurious. That is what the essay is designed to achieve. He needs to make no claims of his own about the real history of bourgeois revolutions in Europe.

Consequently, Chibber's elaborate exercise of summarizing the real history of the English and French revolutions to show that the

English revolution was not anti-feudal (because feudalism in England had already come to an end), or that the French bourgeois revolution-aries were not capitalists, is entirely beside the point. This demonstra-tion does nothing to Guha's argument. All it does is assert that Marx's description of the historical character of those revolutions was inac-curate in light of the findings of historians writing at the turn of the twenty-first century upon whose work Chibber draws. Similarly, Chibber's charge that Guha holds a Whig view of history is also misplaced. The Whig view belongs not to Guha but, unsurprisingly, to historians of the Whig persuasion who are, in fact, the targets of Guha's critique.

Further, on the specific point about the French Revolution, it is clear that when Guha talks about the Indian bourgeoisie in the nine-teenth and twentieth centuries, he does not mean capitalists in particu-lar. In fact, he does not use the term "capitalist" to describe this group at all. What he means is the political-intellectual leadership of the liberal nationalist movement that came from the intermediate strata—the middle class—wedged between the traditional aristocracy and the lower orders of laboring people: precisely the bourgeoisie in the French sense of the word who comprised the bulk of the Third Estate. In contrast to Chibber's conclusion, nothing that Guha says about the Indian bourgeoisie is meant to apply specifically to Indian capitalists.

But Chibber's examination of the assumed counterfactual assumption of European bourgeois hegemony as opposed to Indian bourgeois non-hegemony sheds light on an interesting question regarding the method of historical comparison. Chibber's exercise requires the assumption that India's twentieth century shares the same historical time-space as England's seventeenth and France's eighteenth. How else could we map the constitutive elements of the French or English revolutions onto the field of victory of the Indian bourgeoisie in the mid-twentieth century and arrive at our compara-tive assessments? But this assumption is patently invalid, given that the justificatory claims of liberal ideology had permeated deep into the structures of rule in colonial India through the nineteenth century and were inherited by the triumphant Indian bourgeoisie in the mid-twentieth. British rule in India had to be justified before the British parliament and public as well as its potential Indian critics not by the standards of seventeenth-century ideology but by contemporary standards of nineteenth-century liberalism. If ruling India required deviating from some of those standards, the justification could not proceed by rejecting the universal validity of those liberal norms. Rather, arguments had to be constructed on why the specific situation in India warranted an exception to the universal norm. The colonial history of India is replete with such exceptions. As a consequence, when the Indian nationalist bourgeoisie rejected the allegedly exceptional status of colonial India and assumed power in the sovereign postcolonial nation-state, it too justified its rule not by the standards of seventeenth- or eighteenth-century Europe but by the highest standards of twentieth-century liberalism. The best proofs of this are the Indian Constitution of 1950, designed to meet the most advanced liberal constitutional standards available anywhere in the world, and the litany of pro-imperial historians who have described Indian independence as not merely a gift but indeed a fulfillment of liberal British rule.

POSTCOLONIAL STATE

Hence the non-hegemonic character of the Indian bourgeoisie is disproved not by the English bourgeoisie of the seventeenth century or the French bourgeoisie of the eighteenth, but by the bourgeoisie of the nations of Western Europe and North America after the Second World War. This is the test to which Guha subjects the postcolonial Indian state—a test that its liberal bourgeois leadership had itself welcomed, and that Guha concludes the Indian bourgeoisie has failed. Its hegemony is spurious; its rule is mere dominance in which the element of coercion far exceeds that of consent. It is also significant, though unnoticed by Chibber, that the whole essay is only a "preamble to an auto-critique." Returning to the theme of the universalizing tendency of capital, Guha notes in his concluding section that liberal ideology fails to see the intrinsic limits to capital's self-expansion and the points of resistance it can never overcome. Yet even anti-colonial historiography failed to perceive these aspects of capital, of which it had yet to launch a serious critique. For Guha, the fight against liberal historiography was thus only the first step in constructing an anti-colonial critique of capital.

Before leaving the theme of hegemony, one should also take note of Chibber's understanding, or rather misunderstanding, of it. Guha argues, echoing Antonio Gramsci, that a hegemonic bourgeoisie succeeds in representing its own interests as the universal interests of society. Nowhere does Guha make the argument that Chibber attributes to him: that the bourgeoisie managed to attain hegemony because "it incorporated the real interests of subaltern social classes into its revolutionary program."[4] It would be absurd for anyone following Gramsci's lead to say so. In fact, the hegemonic move on the part of the bourgeoisie is almost always a response to pressures from the subaltern classes—an attempt to preempt direct resistance and opposition. The hegemonic move is a feat of representation, often accomplished by a successful deployment of political rhetoric: it is constructed in and through ideology.[5]

ABSTRACT LABOR AND CAPITALIST PRODUCTION

Chibber roundly criticizes Chakrabarty for regarding formal equality and impersonal power relations as quintessential aspects of capitalist power. Where Chakrabarty reads the persistence, indeed the reproduction, of coercive methods within the industrial labor process and of the consciousness of religious, caste, and other cultural differences among the industrial working class as a limit that colonial capital has been unable to surpass, Chibber regards those features as entirely compatible with capitalism in general. Chakrabarty derives the essential conditions of capitalist production from a fairly conventional reading of Marx. Chibber, in rejecting this reading, offers an alternative account of capitalist production that does not have any recognizable relation to the Marxist tradition. The differences between the two approaches are striking and deserve attention.

Chakrabarty derived his understanding of the universalizing tendency of capital from Marx's analysis of the logic of capitalist accumulation. It is the dynamic of accumulation that pushed European capital to seek overseas territories where it could find raw material and labor suitable for employment in production. But capital encountered social forms of labor there that it could not transform into homogeneous abstract labor. Industrial production under colonial conditions thus posed, says Chakrabarty, an obstacle to the universalizing tendency of capital. Chibber offers an entirely different definition of the universalizing tendency of capital. "The universalizing process is under way," declares Chibber, "if agents' reproductive strategies shift towards market dependence."[6] In other words, as he repeats, "what is universalized under the rule of capital ... [are] the compulsions of market dependence."[7] Now, it is hard to understand how market dependence alone can be a sufficient criterion for the universalization of capital. For instance, one can imagine a system of simple commodity production by owner-producers completely dependent on the market but not employing wage labor and thus not engaging in capitalist production. Marx was emphatic that capitalist production could only take place when capital owned the means of production but sought a mass of wage laborers who had no means of production of their own. In other words, a so-called primitive or primary accumulation must bring about about the dissociation of a mass of laborers from their means of labor. Without this, there is no capitalist production.

It is only because of the emergence of free and alienable labor power that can be bought and sold like any other commodity that abstract labor can appear as the common measure of all concrete forms of labor employed in capitalist production. Abstract labor is not a meaningful category for anything but the capitalist form of production. While Marx's definition of abstract labor is a major pillar of Chakrabarty's argument, Chibber rejects it. Instead, he insists that abstract labor is a measure of the laborer's productive efficiency which is brought about by the competitive conditions of the production of exchange values.[8] Abstract labor, for him, measures the "socially necessary levels of efficiency" of the laborer.[9] Bizarrely, he invokes Marx's definition of socially necessary labor time as the canonical support for his argument.[10]

But how could the production of exchange values itself bring about an abstract measure of socially necessary levels of efficiency? Even in precapitalist modes of production where particular commodities may be produced for exchange in the market, there could exist socially recognized measures of efficiency in specific branches of the concrete labor process. Thus, in small peasant agriculture or crafts manufacture, there may well exist an accepted norm of average efficiency in, let us say, harvesting a specific crop or planing a log of wood. But how could there be a common measure of socially necessary levels of efficiency across all branches of manufacturing in an economy unless labor has been turned into labor-power—that is, a commodity that can be bought and sold in the market? How could capitalists or anyone else speak of "benchmark levels of efficiency" that apply generally to the manufacture of clothes, shoes, automobiles, missiles, and every other commodity unless there is first a common measure for labor as a commodity? That common measure, we know from Marx, is abstract labor.

Marx is so explicit and elaborate in explaining his concept of abstract labor, not only in *Capital* but in the *Grundrisse* and *Theories of Surplus Value*, that there can be little confusion about its meaning. Abstract labor is that common homogeneous element that enters into the production of all commodities by virtue of the fact that they are all products of the employment of labor-power as a commodity. Even though the concrete labor processes are heterogeneous, labor-power as a commodity is the same across all branches of production. Like all commodities, labor-power too has value which, like the value of all other commodities, is given by the value of the commodities required for its production. In the case of labor-power, this amounts to the value of the commodities required to reproduce for the next period of production the labor-power expended in the previous period. In short, the value of one unit of labor-power is the value of the subsistence goods required to reproduce that unit for the next period of production. Marx says that under capitalist production, there is an average labor-time socially necessary for its reproduction: "In a given country in a given period, the average amount of the means of subsistence necessary for the worker is a known *datum*."[11] In branches of production that require labor of higher skill or efficiency than average, the value of labor-time is expressed as multiples, or complex combinations, of simple or average labor-power. This means that it requires greater expenditure on subsistence goods to reproduce labor of higher or more complex quality; hence those providing higher-quality labor must be paid more.

What this means is that in capitalist production, there can be no independent determination of "socially necessary levels of efficiency" of labor; these levels can only be derived from the prevailing average value of labor-power in the economy—that is, from abstract labor as the common homogeneous dimension of labor-power as a commodity. Following this definition from Marx, the problem that Chakrabarty[12] poses is this: did capitalist industrial production in colonial Bengal succeed in establishing abstract labor as the common measure of labor-power? His evidence suggests, for instance, that the Brahmin worker in the jute mill claimed to need more subsistence goods than his lower-caste fellow workers because of the obligations of his caste. Others needed to keep the women of their families in the village because it was dishonorable for women to live and work in the urban slum. The role of the labor contractor or *sardar* in controlling, often coercively, the economic and social life of the worker, and the dependence of mill managers on these coercive controls, is a major feature of Chakrabarty's account. Finally, Chakrabarty details the way in which Calcutta jute mill workers in the 1930s and 1940s, even as they came together under communist trade unions in struggles against their employers, frequently broke into violent religious conflict among themselves on questions of political allegiance.

Chakrabarty interprets this as evidence of the lack of freedom of the industrial worker in colonial Calcutta. In other words, the worker here is not, strictly speaking, proletarianized: he or she still retains organic links with peasant production in the rural areas, and despite working for the most part in the urban factory, his or her subsistence needs for the reproduction of labor-power (which includes the reproduction of the family) are partly met by the rural peasant economy. Chakrabarty's point is that this situation cannot be assumed to be transitional, something that would in due time give way to the general sway of free proletarian wage labor. Rather, this structure of relations was systematically reproduced under conditions of colonial capitalism—hence Chakrabarty's claim that the jute worker's political culture did not split him into his "public" and "private" selves or relegate "all distinctions based on birth" to the sphere of the "private." Thus, "the jute-mill worker had never been 'politically' emancipated from religion."[13]

Chibber excoriates Chakrabarty for this statement, accusing him of all manner of crimes ranging from obscurity to orientalism, but does not notice that Chakrabarty is directly paraphrasing Marx's "On the Jewish Question," in which Marx set out the conceptual conditions for the emergence of the abstract citizen-subject of the modern state under the rule of capital. By contrast, Chibber does not find in Chakrabarty's evidence any reason to doubt the universalizing spread of capital, since, he claims, the persistence, reproduction, and manipulation of racial, ethnic, or religious divisions among laborers is fully consistent with capitalist production in general.

THE TROUBLE WITH THE PEASANTRY

The difference in perspective is brought out most sharply in Chibber's discussion of the question of peasant consciousness as viewed by historians of Subaltern Studies. Repeatedly, Chibber refers to their alleged claims, expressed most elaborately by Chatterjee, that "peasants and industrial workers in the East have a wholly different psychology from those in the West," and that the "political psychology" of Western workers revolved around secular conceptions of individual rights whereas those of Eastern peasants were motivated by community and religious obligations.[14] The peculiar fact is that, to the best of my knowledge, of the few million words that Chatterjee has published in the last forty years, he has not used the word "psychology" a single time, let alone the phrase "political psychology."

When historians of Subaltern Studies speak of peasant consciousness, the academic discipline they invoke most often is not psychology but anthropology. In fact, one of the achievements of their work is to bring within the field of Marxist discussion the remarkable body of scholarship produced by social anthropologists of South Asia since the 1950s. The empirical work of anthropologists has brought to light, for instance, the evolving institutions and practices of local power in the countryside from colonial times to the present, the manifestations of caste not as the doctrinal construct of religious or legal texts but as practised in actual social relations, and the changing political significance of religious practices. The overwhelming conclusion to be drawn from these anthropological studies is than an immense heterogeneity of practices exist, especially in rural South Asia, that defy conventional orderings imposed by Indological and colonial scholarship. This is the empirical evidence that Subaltern Studies scholars writing in the 1980s and 1990s sought to introduce into Marxist debates over the nature of the postcolonial state and the transition to capitalism.

Consequently, when Chakrabarty or Chatterjee speak about the consciousness of community among peasants or industrial workers, they take pains to situate that consciousness within specific, empirically described, historical contexts of space and time, precisely to avoid reducing the concept of community to some orientalist or romantic trope. Chibber expresses surprise that the story that Chatterjee tells of the Bengal peasantry "is a thoroughly materialist one."[15] Nonetheless, says Chibber, Chatterjee insists that "Indian peasants were motivated purely by their perceived duty to the group, with little or no consideration of their individual self-interests."[16] Chibber's attribution is completely wrong: nowhere does Chatterjee[17] say this. Had he followed more carefully what Chatterjee does claim about community consciousness, Chibber would not have been surprised by Chatterjee's materialist account.[18]

No one familiar with the Bengal countryside and its agrarian history would argue that peasants have little or no consideration for their individual self-interests. The sense of individual property was well developed in agrarian Bengal even before the colonial land settlements. The latter introduced stricter and more codified definitions of the respective rights of different grades of proprietors and tenants, almost always defined as individual persons. It was sometimes remarked in the early twentieth century that the sense of mutual cooperation and common property among peasant families in Bengal in the matter of agricultural production was relatively weak in comparison with the owner-peasants of southern India, not to mention the so-called tribal communities among whom individual property in land was almost nonexistent. It would have been absurd for Chatterjee to deny that individual self-interest was indeed functional, even prominent, among Bengal peasants.

"POLITICAL STRUGGLES"

Chatterjee's claims about the activation of community relates not to the social and economic transactions of everyday rural life, but only to what he carefully designates as "political struggles." By this he means the antagonistic confrontations, never very frequent, between peasants and the formal structure of state power represented by government officials and big landlords. These moments of confrontation were extraordinary events. Chatterjee's evidence suggested to him that while peasants may have pursued their individual self-interest in routine economic activities such as defending their plots, mobilizing family labor, selling or buying crops, taking or repaying loans, and buying or selling tenancy rights in land, they acted out of a sense of collective solidarity when defending their political claims against the colonial state and landlords. In eastern Bengal, where most peasants were Muslim small tenants facing big landlords and urban moneylenders, mostly Hindu, the political struggle quickly took on religious overtones. In the Southwest, where the pursuit of self-interest under favorable economic conditions had led to differentiation among the peasantry, there were conflicts between large farmers and sharecroppers, but these were suspended at moments when there emerged a political struggle between peasants and the colonial state.

The rhetoric employed in these struggles itself emphasized the distinction between the economic conflicts of self-interest and the political conflict in which community solidarity, described by real or imputed bonds of kinship, was expected to prevail. Chatterjee is indeed claiming that there was a discontinuity between the everyday and the extraordinary, the economic and the political, the domain of self-interest and that of community solidarity. The dynamics that prevailed in one did not pass smoothly into the other. Subsequent studies by Subaltern Studies scholars such as Gyan Pandey, Shahid Amin, David Hardiman, and Gautam Bhadra showed in much richer detail the moments of activation of community solidarity in peasant movements from different parts of South Asia. The pursuit of individual self-interest in ordinary times did not mean that the bonds of community were erased; they could be brought into play, sometimes with remarkable suddenness, at moments of political conflict with state power.

REASONS AND INTERESTS

Chatterjee's claim fits exactly with Chakrabarty's that the political consciousness of peasants, and of industrial workers who had not ceased to be peasants, was different from that of the bearer of abstract rights in civil society and the abstract citizen-subject of the bourgeois state. That difference is the ground for Chakrabarty's distinction between reasons and interests in the political sphere. Reasons are derived from beliefs, interests from needs. Chibber criticizes Chakrabarty for suggesting that reasons, not needs, are culturally constituted. Once again, Chibber ignores the solidly Marxist provenance of this distinction, derived from Hegel's analysis in *The Philosophy of Right* of civil society as "the system of needs," a domain in which the fulfilment of needs through economic self-interest creates abstract rights whose recognition within the laws of the state leads in turn to the constitution of the abstract citizen-subject. This is the understanding of civil society and the bourgeois state that Marx adopts and that both Chakrabarty and Chatterjee follow. But Chibber prefers to abandon Marx's view altogether and instead plumps for a wholly different conception of needs.

Chibber claims that there are certain basic needs that are understood in every culture, even though they may give rise to specific, culturally framed reasons; we may therefore interpret the expression of these reasons as evidence of these needs,[19] and conclude that there are "some needs or interests that are independent of culture."[20] Anthropologists may squirm at his mode of argument, but Chibber attributes the interested pursuit of basic needs to "a component of human nature."[21] Of such universal basic needs, he picks one, "the simple need for physical well-being,"[22] as most relevant in the political struggles of workers and peasants, and he does not stop there. Recounting the long history of struggles by workers in Europe to defend their political rights, Chibber announces that they follow "from the defense of a single basic need: to defend one's physical well-being."[23] This, he declares in bold capitals, is "the universal history of class struggle."[24]

The philosophical sweep and arbitrariness of these statements by Chibber are staggering. At one extreme, by deriving political actions from a single universal propensity of human nature, he aligns himself with an entire tradition of early modern philosophy that leads directly to the contractarian school of liberal political thought. At the same time, he invokes in his support the contemporary economist and philosopher Amartya Sen's concept of basic needs, completely forgetting that Chibber's own derivation of basic needs from universal human nature would put him squarely in the camp of what Sen[25] calls the transcendental approach and from which he scrupulously dissociates himself. At another extreme, the motivation to defend the universal need for physical well-being as described by Chibber is independent not only of culture but of modes of production, state formations, power structures, and all other historical configurations. Slaves, serfs, peasants, workers: everyone could be said to be defending this universal need. Indeed, if physical well-being is so universal a motivation, it is hard to see why the subaltern classes should be the only ones pursuing it; why are the non-productive classes not also engaged in defending their need for well-being? Finally, the pursuit of physical well-being emanating from human nature suggests a universal biopolitics. Or is it zoo politics, since animals are also known to pursue and defend their need for physical well-being? In short, Chibber's universal history of class struggle is materialist universalism run amok.

UNIVERSALITY AND THE UNCERTAINTIES OF HISTORY

Chibber clearly has little patience with rhetorical techniques such as irony. That is why he reads Chatterjee's statements on Reason as a Western imposition on non-Western nationalism as blatantly orientalist propaganda, little realizing that Reason with a capital R (which is what Chatterjee[26] consistently uses) is an obvious ironical play on Hegel's philosophy of world history in which Reason can properly belong only to the West. Chibber's suspicion about Chatterjee's orientalist sympathies is confirmed by the latter's argument that non-Western nationalism began by claiming sovereignty over an inner spiritual domain. Chibber's lazy reading leads him to overlook Chatterjee's specification that this is an early nationalist strategy before it begins its political contest over state sovereignty. Obviously, Chibber should not have expected to find any such spiritual claims in Sukarno, Nasser, or the Ba'athist leaders, all of whom were the political leaders of nationalism in the period of decolonization. Rather, he ought to have looked at the earlier history of religious reform, the creation of modern vernacular literatures, reform of the family, and other social movements in the Arab countries and Indonesia that produced these political leaders of the mid-twentieth century.

Chibber is perplexed that Chatterjee, even after dismissing Gandhi's anti-modern alternative as unrealizable, nevertheless criticizes Nehru for his state-led modernization plans. Surely, Chibber says, Nehru made "a rational response to real constraints."[27] Chatterjee, of course, had shown that without the anti-modern, anti-capitalist, anti-industrial maneuver by Gandhi, the peasant masses could not have been mobilized by Indian nationalism and Nehru's leadership subsequently established over a sovereign postcolonial state. In that case, either Gandhi's intervention was the greatest confidence trick in political history or, as Chatterjee argues, it must be justified as the mysterious workings of objective forces that bring about the universally destined result regardless of the ideological motivations of particular historical players. That is what Hegel called the Cunning of Reason and what Nehru, like all other postcolonial nationalist leaders, accepted as the real compulsion of the global system, as Chibber puts it. For Chatterjee, this is the prison house into which state nationalisms are forced, even though their political practices acknowledge every day the real presence of historical difference.

Chibber announces several times in his book that the historical differences pointed out by Subaltern Studies scholars are all perfectly compatible with the universalizing tendency of capital. Extra-economic coercion, consciousness of ethnic or religious identity among industrial workers, and cultural construction of reasons for political action can all be assimilated within the same universal history of capital common to both West and East. Hence the distinction between History 1 and History 2 is, for him, a non-problem. Indeed, he simply conjures away the problem by proposing a definition of capitalism so capacious that it would bring a blush even to the pale cheeks of Adam Smith.

We could, of course, turn Chibber's claim around and say that capital's journey in the East has at last revealed its true face, hitherto hidden from us by its liberal mythology. In Western capitalism we saw only a shy debutante; it is the confident maestro who now performs in the East. Were this true, it would be the sweetest consummation of the project of Subaltern Studies. Unfortunately, that happy ending is not to be.

The historical problem confronted by Subaltern Studies is not an intrinsic difference between West and East, as Chibber repeatedly insists. The geographical distinction is merely the spatial label for a historical difference. That difference is indicated—let me insist emphatically—by the disappearance of the peasantry in capitalist Europe and the continued reproduction to this day of a peasantry under the rule of capital in the countries of Asia, Africa, and Latin America. That is the crux of Chakrabarty's distinction between History 1 and History 2,[28] derived from Marx's own separation of historical conditions "posited by capital itself" and conditions that it merely finds. The difference is not as inconsequential as Chibber maintains. As Marx explains in *Theories of Surplus Value*, money, which long preceded capitalist production, is not a condition posited by capital. A credit system with a currency guaranteed by a central bank is.[29] When this happens successfully, it means for Chakrabarty the replacement and effective erasure of History 2 by History 1. His question is: has this happened in countries like India? A great deal hangs on the answer.

That is also why, despite the apparent similarities between the disciplines, Subaltern Studies could never have been carried out in the same way as History from Below in Europe. The recounting in the latter body of work of the struggles of peasants and artisans during capitalism's ascendancy in Europe was inevitably written as tragedy, since the ultimate dissolution of those classes was already scripted into their history. Should we assume the same trajectory for agrarian societies in other parts of the world? Does a different sequencing of capitalist modernity there not mean, as Subaltern Studies scholar Sudipta Kaviraj[30] has suggested, that the historical outcomes in terms of economic formations, political institutions, and cultural practices might be quite different from those we see in the West? Do those differences not imply, in turn, that the process of primitive or primary accumulation of capital has to be carried out in many Asian, African, and Latin American countries under conditions never encountered in the history of Western capitalism, as demonstrated by Kalyan Sanyal[31] writing in the trail of Subaltern Studies? That is what is at stake in Chakrabarty's distinction between History 1 and History 2. The implication is that, contrary to the historical method Chibber prefers, getting one's European history right is not the magic formula that will solve the problems of historical change in the non-Western world. The historical specificities of the political, economic, and cultural institutions and practices of those people, including their distinctive linguistic traditions, must be given primacy by the historian.

UNIVERSALISM

Nevertheless, Chibber's plea for continued faith in the universal values of European Enlightenment deserves a final comment. Universalism has been defended with far more subtle and sophisticated arguments than Chibber has mobilized in his book. One can only acknowledge that the debate between universalism and its critics continues and will not be resolved in a hurry. The choice between the two sides at this time is indeed political. The greatest strength of the universalist position is the assurance it provides of predictability and control over uncertain outcomes. It is the assurance that past history is a reliable guide to the future which leads Chibber to insist that capitalism and the struggles of subaltern classes must be the same everywhere. He says this even while acknowledging that the defense of political rights by workers all over the West has led to the "perverse result" of capitalist orders dominated by democratically unaccountable financial oligarchies.[32]

In the rest of the world, capital is engaged in battles it has never fought before, just as peasants and workers are resisting capital in ways that have never been tried before, because the historical conditions are unprecedented. The critics of universalism argue that the outcomes are unknown, indeterminate, and hence unpredictable. They accept the challenge of risky political choices, based on provisional, contingent, and corrigible historical knowledge. Since the early work of Subaltern Studies which Chibber dissected, the discipline has gone in several new directions, especially after important interventions by Gayatri

Spivak[33] and Gyan Prakash.[34] The historical practice of Subaltern Studies scholars does not rule out the rise of new universalist principles, but these, they insist, must be forged anew. What is certain is that the working classes of Europe and North America and their ideologues can no longer act as the designated avant-garde in the struggles of subaltern classes in other parts of the world.

Historians of Subaltern Studies have only attempted to interpret a small part of these struggles. And changing the world, needless to say, is a job that cannot be entrusted to historians.

CHAPTER 2

Subaltern Studies Revisited

A Response to Partha Chatterjee

Vivek Chibber

> *This is the longer version of an article that appeared in the* Economic
> and Political Weekly *on March 1, 2014.*

My intention in *Postcolonial Theory and the Specter of Capital* (hereafter *PTSC*) was to assess the theoretical framework generated by the Subaltern Studies collective. To do so involved three distinct tasks. First, I sought to distill from the key writings the project's essential arguments. Second, since these arguments were in large measure a critique of Enlightenment and especially Marxist theories, it was necessary to assess the validity of their critique on empirical and conceptual grounds. Lastly, I suggested that their own theoretical innovations were a failure, both as theory and as normative critique. To be sure, my verdict was not kind to the project. But I tried, in the book, to reconstruct the Subalternists' arguments as clearly and generously as possible, and to base my own alternative formulations on logic and evidence, not on appeals to authority.

In his response, Partha Chatterjee has decided to abjure all of these conventions. Instead of honestly trying to engage the arguments of *PTSC*, he either ignores them altogether or distorts them beyond recognition. He even manages to extend the same courtesy to the Subalternists' work, including his own. Both of these problems are remarkable in themselves, but even more so because, as I will show, the distortions are so clumsy that even a cursory reading of the texts is enough to expose them.

GUHA AND THE BOURGEOIS REVOLUTIONS

Chatterjee starts by taking up my critique of Ranajit Guha's *Dominance without Hegemony* (hereafter *DH*). I argue in *PTSC* that Guha's work is both foundational to the entire Subalternist project—hardly a controversial claim, since they insist upon this fact themselves—and fundamentally flawed. Its flaw is that it generates a set of contrastive claims about the Indian bourgeoisie and Indian capitalism that rest on a comparison with European achievements. The comparison fails because Guha quite dramatically misunderstands the European story. For Guha, the basic condition of Indian political culture is that the subaltern sphere continues to be separate from that of the elites, unlike the West, where the elite and subaltern worlds were integrated very early in their modernization. The reason that India differs so from the West has to do with the weakness of the Indian bourgeoisie. In the West, a vigorous and dynamic bourgeoisie overthrew feudalism and created an integrated political order in the aftermath of the bourgeois revolutions of 1640 and 1789 in England and France respectively; in India, the bourgeoisie drew back from this challenge during its own counterpart to the bourgeois revolution: the struggle for independence from British rule. I show in *PTSC* that Guha's understanding of the European experience is baseless. And when we compare the two records, it turns out that the European bourgeoisie was no more committed to an integrated political culture than was its Indian counterpart; moreover, political culture in the former was no more integrated after its bourgeois revolutions than in the latter in 1948. Hence, the case for a deep "structural fault," as Guha calls it, between East and West—at least on this score—is a failure.

Chatterjee responds with three assertions: first, that Guha never makes any claims about the classic bourgeois revolutions at all—his criticism is only of the historiography of colonial India and the comparisons that it makes with Europe; second, that when Guha uses the expression "Indian bourgeoisie" he is not referring to capitalists, but in fact to the middle-class leadership of the Congress; and third, that, insofar as Guha has any European referent in mind, it is the mid-twentieth-century British state, not the earlier vintage of the eighteenth or nineteenth century. These are quite astounding claims, and readers familiar with *DH* might wonder if Chatterjee is being face-tious. But he seems to intend for us to take him at his word. I will therefore respect his challenge and attend to his claims seriatim.

Before proceeding, we should make one observation about method. In *PTSC*, my critique of Guha's argument is carefully laid out over the course of three chapters, with one chapter devoted entirely to an expli-cation of his view. I present his case very elaborately, because, as I say in the preface to the book, I want readers to be confident that I am not setting up a straw man that can easily be knocked down. Toward this, I not only describe his position, but do so with the help of innumerable passages from *DH*, accompanying each claim with supporting cita-tions or quotations, and showing how they fit into the overarching structure of Guha's argument. Chatterjee is of course free to disagree with my reading of Guha. But even the weakest standards of scholarly integrity would oblige him to then provide some explanation for why Guha seems to be saying, in all the passages that I adduce, exactly the opposite of the view that Chatterjee attributes to him. If Chatterjee were at all concerned with the facts, he would go back to at least some of those passages and explain how it might be that when Guha says "France in 1789," he really means "England in 1945." What we get instead is a barrage of assertions, not backed up by any textual evidence, and without any engagement with the evidence that I adduce in support of my interpretation. Later in this chapter I will provide a suggestion as to why Chatterjee adopts this novel strategy.

Does Guha refer to the bourgeois revolutions?
Let us take up the first of Chatterjee's claims regarding Guha: that his argument is only about the historiography of colonial India, and hence he does not make nor need to make any substantive claims about the bourgeois revolutions. There are two distinct issues here: a textual one about whether Guha in fact makes claims about the bourgeois revolu-tions, and a logical one about whether he needs to for his argument.

It is of course true that *DH* is centrally devoted to a critique of liberal historiography, of which I make ample note in *PTSC*.[1] The issue is whether Guha rests his case upon any substantive claims about actual history of the West. Chatterjee says that he does not—"nowhere in the book," he announces, "does Guha make any claims" about the bourgeois revolutions.[2] All of Guha's factual arguments are supposed to refer only to the Indian experience. But here is Guha's own encapsulation of his argument, which I quote in *PTSC* and which Chatterjee could not possibly have missed when he read my book:

> Liberal historiography has been led to presume that *capital, in its Indian career*, succeeded in overcoming the obstacles to its self-expansion and subjugating all precapitalist relations in material and spiritual life well enough to enable the bourgeoisie to speak for all of that society, *as it had done* on the occasion of its historic triumphs in England in 1648 and France in 1789. Resistance to *the rule of capital* has been made to dissolve ideally into a hegemonic dominance.[3]

It is easy to see that this passage flatly contradicts Chatterjee's claims, and I will adduce several others in what follows. But the point is not to go hunting for quotations or to pile up instances where certain words are mentioned. It is, rather, to examine the structure of Guha's argument, so that we may appreciate the place that such references occupy within it.

The passage I have just quoted comes at the end of Guha's presentation of the essence of his view. He deems liberal historiography to be a kind of apologia for colonialism, and therefore ideological.[4] Historians working within the parameters of liberal ideology, according to Guha, are upholding the worldview and interests of a certain class—the metropolitan bourgeoisie. "A bourgeois discourse par excellence, [liberal historiography] helped the bourgeoisie to change or at least significantly modify the world according to its class interests in the period of its ascendancy, and since to consolidate and perpetuate its dominance."[5] Consequently, liberal scholarship "speak[s] from within the bourgeois consciousness itself."[6] The scholarship of colonialism that Guha is criticizing is therefore not only wrong but attached to the defense of bourgeois dominance as well. His project is thus one of ideological critique.

How, then, does one criticize such an ideology? According to Guha, one points to the contradiction between the claims it makes and the reality of the world. This is what the rising bourgeoisie did in Europe in advance of the great bourgeois revolutions: "The bourgeoisie itself had dramatized such decalage during the Enlightenment by a relentless critique of the *ancien régime* for decades before *the French Revolution* and anticipating it in effect."[7] This critique, Guha continues, was "true to the real contradictions of the epoch," that is, those central to feudalism, which was the economic system of the ancient regime, and which the rising bourgeoisie overthrew in 1789—or so Guha claims.[8] Just as the rising bourgeoisie based its criticism on the contradiction between reality and its ideal representation, so too, Guha argues, "the critique of the dominant bourgeois culture arises from the real contradictions of capitalism."[9]

Now we are approaching the heart of the matter. If liberal historians are the representatives of capital, then it follows that a critique of their work has to point to a gap between their claims and the actual course of events—the real contradictions to which Guha refers in the preceding paragraph. What are these? "One of such contradictions which serves as a basis for the critique of bourgeois culture in dominance relates to the universalizing tendency of capital."[10] On the one hand, capital does have a powerful universalizing drive—it revolutionizes social relations, replaces old institutions with those bearing its stamp, spills beyond national borders, and brings remote regions under its sway. But this drive is frustrated by its own limits. Here Guha turns to Marx for guidance. For Marx, the rise of the bourgeoisie to power and dominance in the early modern period was an expression of its universalizing drive—a drive that is real. But this drive began to run out of steam not long after the class achieved hegemony. Nowhere was this more obvious than in the revolutions of 1848.

Whereas the bourgeoisie had valiantly crafted an encompassing social coalition against the ancient regime and replaced it with a new order in the classical bourgeois revolutions, it turned away from any such undertakings in 1848. Guha observes that "the triumph of the universalist tendency was not obvious in bourgeois practice . . . The failure of the Prussian revolution of 1848 *to achieve the comprehensive character of the English and French revolutions respectively of 1648 and 1789*" inspired Marx to "write a series of brilliant but bitter reflections on this theme."[11] In these writings, "the performance of the nineteenth-century German bourgeoisie is distinguished . . . from that of their class in seventeenth-century England and eighteenth-century France in terms of their respective records in overthrowing the old order."[12]

This brings us to the nub of the issue. After describing how Marx drew up a balance sheet of the bourgeoisie's achievements in 1848 and set it against the record of their performance in the great bourgeois revolutions, Guha declares, "The relevance of this [i.e. Marx's] critique for the study of colonialism can hardly be overestimated." It presents, Guha suggests, a template for the analysis of capital's colonial venture. Marx overturned liberal apologies for the practice of the bourgeoisie in 1848 by showing that such apologetics endowed capital with ambitions that it no longer entertained. He showed that liberals ascribed to capital a universalizing commitment that it had in fact abandoned. So too, in the colonial setting, "the representation of the colonial project of the European bourgeoisie as a particularly convincing example of the universalist mission of capital has for a long time been a matter of routine in academic teaching and writing."[13] And just as Marx had shown that 1848 instantiated capital's abandonment of its universalizing drive, so too, Guha says, the critique of liberal historiography must show that the latter "has been primarily responsible for a serious misrepresentation of the power relations of colonialism."[14] It is at this point that Guha presents us with the encapsulation of his view, which I quoted above: the misrepresentation perpetuated by liberal historians is their assumption, similar to that of liberal apologists in the mid-nineteenth century, that capital is motivated by the same revolutionary commitments that it supposedly had in 1648 and 1789. This is the contradiction—the real anomaly—that anti-colonial critique points to as ideological critique.

Guha's method of critique is derived from Marx's "brilliant but bitter" reflections on the failure of capitalists in 1848. He follows Marx on this count very faithfully. Marx accepted the story about bourgeois heroism in 1648 and 1789, and so too does Guha. In the section of the book where he lays out the basic premises of his argument, Guha comes back again and again to the reality of their achievements in the early stages of capitalism, when it was, to him, a truly revolutionizing force and embodiment of a universalizing drive, and its later career, when this drive was abandoned. Just as Marx condemned the Prussian capitalists for turning away from the ambitions of their predecessors, so does Guha. He complains about the Indian variant, "the indigenous bourgeoisie, spawned and nurtured by colonialism itself, adopted a role that was distinguished by its failure to measure up to the heroism of the European bourgeoisie in its period of ascendancy."[15] What was this period of ascendancy? It is abundantly clear that Guha has the bourgeois revolutions in mind. No one who reads the crucial opening sections of *DH* can miss the architecture of the argument, nor the significance of Guha's references to the bourgeois revolutions. He builds it systematically and very lucidly in the first twenty pages of *DH*, making it impossible to misunderstand him. It is quite remarkable that Chatterjee tries to suppress this obvious and quite uncontroversial fact.

My account also enables us to see why Guha feels compelled to draw a contrast with the bourgeois revolutions. *Pace* Chatterjee, he does not develop his argument as a simple refutation of the liberal description of British rule in India. Guha is not content to simply show that colonialism was despotic. His ambition is to analyze colonialism at a deeper level: as an instance of capital in its global venture. For Guha, liberalism misrepresents the true nature of colonialism because it is unable to see the mutation that capitalism undergoes as it expands into the colonial world. It assumes that capitalists in a colonial setting are motivated by the same goals and ambitions that drove the Western bourgeoisie in its "period of ascendancy," as Guha describes it. Liberal historiography assumes that capital strove to integrate the subaltern sphere with the elite sphere, that it built a consensual social order and secured its social hegemony, giving it the authority to "speak for all the nation." It assumes, in other words, that capital retained its universalizing drive.

The entire structure of *DH* is built around this idea—that in its colonial venture, capital abandoned something it possessed in 1640 and 1789. Chatterjee clearly avoids this basic fact about Guha's book, because to understand Guha's central argument in this way is to appreciate the book's intrinsically contrastive character. Guha embeds his critique of liberal historiography in a deeper social and historical argument about the actual course of capitalism in the West and in the East. He has to refer to the bourgeois revolutions because they exemplify the kind of transformation that he feels did not occur in the colonial world, but which liberal ideologues keep insisting did in fact occur. His goal is not a simple refutation of liberal nostrums about colonial rule. He seeks, instead, to develop an analysis of the forces that actually shaped modernization in the colonial and postcolonial worlds, to put that experience in global perspective, and finally, to generate categories more adequate to apprehending that experience. He intends to show, through detailed analysis, that capitalism in India produced a different kind of modernity from that of the West, a very specific form of political rule which he calls dominance without hegemony. Its peculiarity simply cannot be understood without reference to some events which comprise the norm, or the standard, against which the peculiarities of colonialism can be understood. Guha makes this abundantly clear in the opening pages of his book, before he even commences with the substance of his argument.[16] Why Chatterjee thinks he can dupe readers into ignoring this is something of a mystery.

What does Guha mean by the Indian bourgeoisie?

Chatterjee's second, and equally absurd, line of defense is that I misconstrue what Guha means by the term "bourgeoisie" in the Indian context. I take him to mean "capitalists," whereas he in fact uses it to refer to middle-class leaders of the nationalist movement. His critique of the Indian bourgeoisie is untouched by any facts about Indian capitalists, since, Chatterjee avers, he is actually writing about urban professionals and the like.

Is there any reason to believe Chatterjee? Let us begin with the observation that Guha's entire analysis rests on the proposition that the peculiarities of colonial modernization flowed from *capital* having abandoned its universalizing drive. It is *capital* that is the protagonist on both sides of the world, and it is *capital* whose performance is judged against its competence.[17] Now, against this fact, what should be the natural interpretation of "bourgeoisie" as used by Guha—that he is referring to capital, which is the linchpin of his analysis, or that he has reverted to its eighteenth-century usage, without ever informing the reader that he has done so?

For Guha, the evidence for capital's turn away from a universalizing project was its refusal to base its leadership of the nationalist movement on the consent of the masses. The two central essays of *DH* enumerate the myriad ways in which the Indian National Congress marginalized the needs and aspirations of the poor and minority communities, promoting obedience over rebellion, stability and order over revolution. There is no dispute over Guha's healthy contempt for the intellectuals and professionals who were at the helm of the Congress. But none of this changes the fact that for Guha, the Congress and its leaders matter because they were organizing around the interests of another class—the domestic industrialists, who were supposed to be the carriers of capital's universalizing mission but refused.

Midway through the first essay in *DH*, Guha summarizes a series of articles in which Gandhi implored the Indian ruling classes—agrarian landlords and capitalists—to be more accommodating to the laboring classes, so it could garner their consent. Guha observes that Gandhi "hoped that the capitalist class would 'read the signs of the times' and voluntarily surrender its wealth" before mass radicalization overtook the movement. That article, Guha observes, triggered a response from G. D. Birla, who he describes as belonging to "*the most advanced section of the Indian bourgeoisie*" and who urged his fellow capitalists to heed Gandhi's advice.[18] Guha is describing Birla, one of the biggest industrialists in India, as a leading representative of the Indian bourgeoisie. And on that very page, he uses "bourgeoisie" and "capitalist" to refer to the same group of people—something that Chatterjee insists never happens.

Later in the book, Guha offers an explanation for why Indian capitalists refused to follow Gandhi and Birla's advice. He starts by drawing a parallel between the drama unfolding in India and the baseline experience against which he always compares it: Western Europe. The Indian bourgeoisie was trying to present its own interests as universal, much as the European bourgeoisie had done in its own rise to power. But while the latter managed to present its own interests as the common interest, the Indian bourgeoisie could not.[19] At the heart of the Congress's failure was its "failure to assimilate the class interests of peasants and workers into a bourgeois hegemony."[20] The fact that it could not was an expression of "the predicament of a bourgeoisie nurtured under colonial conditions and its difference from its opposite numbers in Western Europe."[21]

In the West, the bourgeoisie was able to gather the resources—both material and spiritual—to bring the working class into a coalition with itself. But in India, by contrast, the contrived character of industrialization under the raj . . . left no choice for the Indian bourgeoisie to develop its interest as anything other than the particular interest of a particular class. Trapped in conditions which did little to encourage any organic growth and expansion, it hardened quickly into a parasitic and precocious outcrop on the surface of colonial society and defined itself sharply by its antagonism with *its Other—the working class*, an antagonism which, from the very beginning, it sought to resolve by discipline rather than by persuasion.[22]

This is a crucial passage, in that Guha makes it clear what he means by "bourgeoisie"—an exploiting class, whose Other is the working class. It is trapped in conditions where it cannot grow and expand as its European counterparts did, and hence it lacks the material basis for incorporating the working class into a hegemonic coalition. So its relation with workers is inescapably antagonistic. Guha draws out the implication: "Thus while the bourgeoisie in the West could speak for all of society . . . even while it was striving for power or had just won it, in India there was always another voice, a subaltern voice, that spoke for a larger part of society, and which it was not for the bourgeoisie to represent." He concludes, "That is why the elite nationalism of the Congress leadership and that party's official platform could never be adequately representative of Indian politics of the colonial period."[23]

For Guha, the Congress represents the hegemonic project of Indian big business. But it can only muster dominance without hegemony, because it cannot break through the limits that are imposed on it by that very class. The class, in turn, cannot offer the same programs and concessions that its counterpart in Europe did during the period of its own ascendancy, because it is locked in antagonistic relations with what Guha describes as "its Other"—the working class. And finally, this latter relation can be traced back to the stunted industrialization of colonialism, which gives the bourgeoisie little room for growth. So, the reader should now ask, what is the most reasonable interpretation of "bourgeoisie" as Guha is using it here? Is it lawyers and civil servants who see the working class as their Other? Or is it Birla and Tata?

There are numerous other such references in the text, but the point should be obvious. *DH* is a book about the universalizing drive of capital and how it failed in colonial conditions. Chatterjee knows this full well. The idea that, in the Indian case, the concept is meant to refer to lawyers and intellectuals is simply absurd.

Is Guha comparing India to 1945 Britain?
Chatterjee's final claim is that Guha's reference point is not Western Europe in the seventeenth or eighteenth century, but England in 1945. I must say, this is Chatterjee's most audacious gambit of all. The fact is that there is no reference at all to Britain at mid-century in the entire book—none that I could find. Virtually all of Guha's discussion, with regard to England, concerns what he calls the "heroic period" of the bourgeoisie's rule—the eighteenth and early nineteenth centuries. Again, readers should listen to Guha himself. At the end of his first essay in *DH*, Guha begins his "autocritique" by observing that "*nothing that has been said above is addressed to the practitioners of colonialist historiography in Britain today*";[24] there is no reference in it to twentieth-century Britain at all. Instead, the essay enjoins Indian historians to ask, inter alia, why it is that Indian colonial institutions cannot be understood "either as a replication of the liberal-bourgeois culture of *nineteenth-century Britain* or as the mere survival of an antecedent pre-capitalist culture."[25]

And so, Guha makes it clear that his frame of reference is Britain of the eighteenth and nineteenth centuries and the historians at work then because it was those historians who established the discourse legitimizing colonialism, presenting the colony as nothing more than an extension of British liberalism as practiced at that time. Hence, Guha's interlocutors are James Mill, Macaulay, Bentham, and others. The insistence that Guha is actually referring to mid-twentieth-century Britain is another sign of Chatterjee's desperation.

ABSTRACT LABOR

Let us now move to the next issue Chatterjee raises, which is my examination of several postcolonial theorists' approach to the concept of abstract labor. The motivation for my intervention was to examine a common charge that postcolonial theory levels at the Enlightenment tradition: that its universalizing categories obliterate all historical difference. They do so, we are told, because they homogenize the diversity of social experience by subsuming it under highly abstract, one-dimensional categories. One example of this is Marx's concept of abstract labor, which either assumes that labor and laborers in capitalism become more homogeneous over time, or is unable to adequately theorize those differences that do exist, since the categories treat labor everywhere as being the same. I show in *PTSC* that this critique is based on a fundamental misunderstanding of the concept, and that the latter can in fact not only appreciate historical difference, but is an essential tool for such an analysis. Hence, while it is certainly true that some universalizing categories might be problematic, it is sheer folly to insist that this is a necessary flaw in all such categories. Postcolonial theory's broadside against Enlightenment universalisms is vastly overdrawn.

Chatterjee accuses me of having misunderstood what abstract labor is. His argument proceeds in two basic steps. First, he has me define capitalism as a system in which there is generalized market dependence; he then objects that such a definition erases the importance of wage labor as an essential component of capitalism, and imputes to me the view that wage labor is unnecessary or irrelevant for the emergence of abstract labor in capitalism. Having described my argument this way, Chatterjee then proceeds to develop an elaborate defense of the connection between wage and abstract labor, showing, he claims, that in denying this connection, I have veered very far from Marx's own conceptualization. Finally, he claims that this gaffe also prevents me from understanding what Dipesh Chakrabarty's critique of the concept tries to accomplish.

The only problem with this criticism is that it is tilting at windmills. My entire argument about abstract labor, and how the category is perfectly adequate for apprehending the social differences with the working class, presumes that for abstract labor to emerge, economic production must be governed by capitalist laws of motion, and labor must work for a wage. There is not even a hint anywhere in my book that wage labor is irrelevant for this process. I do, as Chatterjee says, provide a definition of capitalism as generalized market dependence— but wage labor is simply a form of market dependence, and it never occurred to me that I would have to remind the reader of this elementary fact. Hence, it was never my intention to claim, nor did I imply, that socially necessary labor can be derived from petty commodity production. It is quite extraordinary that Chatterjee would try to wring such a position out of my argument.

Of course, having misrepresented my view in such a fashion, Chatterjee can then proceed to entirely avoid answering my charges in *PTSC*. The central question I addressed was this: do universalizing categories necessarily occlude the study of social difference? And I showed that, in the case of abstract labor, they do not. Chatterjee never even addresses this issue in his response, and indeed, he buries it altogether by going off on a pointless tangent about the importance of wage labor, a fact that I not only affirm, but place at the center of my argument.

It is not surprising that Chatterjee's misrepresentations extend to the work of others as well. He insists that my gross mishandling of the problem of abstract labor bleeds over into my understanding of Dipesh Chakrabarty. Chakrabarty, he argues, approaches the category by asking if capitalism in Bengal jute mills succeeded in "establishing abstract labor as the common measure of labor power."[26] And he finds, we are told, that it did not, because Brahmins insisted on receiving higher than average wages because of their social position. But two points are worth noting here. First, Chakrabarty never links the issue of wage levels to abstract labor in the book that Chatterjee cites. The term "abstract labor" appears on all of two pages in *Rethinking Working-Class History*, and in those pages, Chakrabarty is concerned not with wage determination, but with the cultural changes that capitalism is supposed to bring about—exactly the issue that I do discuss.[27] The real locus of Chakrabarty's arguments regarding abstract labor is not the one that Chatterjee cites at all, but *Provincializing Europe*. And again, there is simply no link in that book between the abstraction of labor and wages.

Even more confusing is Chatterjee's basic premise itself, that some workers demanding higher wages for themselves is evidence that capital in Bengal had failed to "establish abstract labor as the common measure of labor power."[28] This, we are led to believe, is what Chakrabarty tries to show, and what I do not comprehend when I defend the validity of the concept. But how does the mere demand for higher wages amount to evidence against abstract labor? Did these workers actually receive higher wages? If so, how does this undermine the validity of the concept? Chatterjee cannot possible mean that any deviation from a set wage level amounts to a negation of abstract labor, since wage hierarchies are very much a part of Marx's theory. So the question is, how much variation does the concept allow? Chatterjee does not even offer a glimmer of an argument. He merely hints at a fact—workers made wage-related demands based on caste status—and then moves on, as if the answer is so obvious that it does not require discussion. The problem, of course, is that Chatterjee does not give us anything resembling an argument one way or another. All we have is innuendo and chest-thumping.

Chatterjee then proceeds to enumerate a list of arguments that Chakrabarty is supposed to have developed—about workers' rural ties, their consciousness, their religiosity—the implication being that these are also issues that I ignore in my assessment of Chakrabarty.

But these are the very issues that I do take up in great detail, and that I show to be deeply problematic.[29] Where exactly is the weakness in my assessment of Chakrabarty on these issues? Chatterjee never informs us. All he says is that, in the face of all of the various ways in which these aspects of workers' conditions in Calcutta depart from some pure model, "Chibber does not find in Chakrabarty's evidence any reason to doubt the universalizing spread of capital."[30]

In this one instance, Chatterjee is correct—it is very much my view that the persistence of rural ties, the attachment to religious identities, the use of interpersonal coercion by managers, and other problems that Chakrabarty adduces as proof of capital's failed universalization are in fact entirely compatible with the latter. And I spend the better part of three chapters presenting arguments and evidence in support of my view. But Chatterjee does not engage with a single one of them. He never tells us what they have to do with abstract labor at all, and he never tells us exactly what is problematic in my argument about them. He simply continues to argue by innuendo, listing a series of facts about India and implying that their significance is so obvious that merely to state them is to present a case for his view—precisely the view that I challenge with actual arguments in *PTSC*, page after page, chapter after chapter, which he never even tries to counter. What he does, instead, is use a significant part of his paper to argue for a position that I never denied—that wage labor is the precondition for abstract labor. And he ignores every argument I did make about why Chakrabarty and others are deeply mistaken in their criticisms of the concept.

INTERESTS, AGENCY, AND POLITICS

The final issue Chatterjee raises is the problem of peasant consciousness and interests. In *PTSC* I approached this issue by first laying out in great detail what Guha, Chatterjee, and Chakrabarty claim about the nature of subaltern consciousness in India.[31] Chatterjee and Chakrabarty both insist that social explanations based on agential interests are deeply problematic in the Indian context, unlike that of the West, where they are deemed appropriate. Chatterjee in particular claims that Guha's and his own work show that to be true in the case of peasants, and Chakrabarty thinks that he has demonstrated the absence of interest-based action in the case of workers. In *PTSC*, I demonstrate in some detail that the actual facts adduced by Guha, Chatterjee, and Chakrabarty actually show the very opposite—that subaltern groups in India were in fact no less sensitive to their individual material interests than a materialist account would predict. And I then try to provide a positive account of what such interests might be—which are consistent with the empirical historical narratives of Chatterjee and his colleagues—and how a commitment to the existence of such interests need not lead to an imperviousness to culture in social life. This discussion spans Chapters 7 through 9 in *PTSC*.

Chatterjee does not fare well in those chapters, and one might have expected him to respond in some detail to my criticisms, since they are quite detailed. But he responds only by more obfuscation and outright fabrication. First, referring to his own work, he claims that he never denied the importance of peasants' interests in all domains, but only in the dynamics of political mobilization. Peasants were perfectly capable of recognizing their economic interests, he avers; it was in political movements that community tended to trump individual interests.[32] So

I am charged with distorting Chatterjee's argument. He never presented community consciousness as an obstacle to the perception of individual interests.

Chatterjee suppresses the fact that in *PTSC* I produced quotation after quotation in which he claims precisely what he is now denying. Instead of trying to address the evidence in any meaningful way, Chatterjee flatly denies that it exists. Readers who wish to examine it more thoroughly should refer to Chapter 7, Section 2 and Section 4. There we find Chatterjee referring to interest-based judgments as "bourgeois consciousness," which he claims Indian rural agents do not possess, and which he counterposes to their "peasant consciousness."[33] Chatterjee castigates the entire tradition of social science—sociology, Chayanovian rural anthropology, "moral economy" arguments, and Marxism for assuming that peasants act on their material interests.[34] In his more empirical work, Chatterjee repeats these claims, but goes a step further. He now describes the effect of "peasant-communal ideology" to be such that peasants cannot even distinguish exploiters from exploited. They have to be taught this ability by agents from outside the rural community.[35]

Now it is of course true, as I observe in *PTSC*, that peasants feel powerful bonds of commonality with members of their community because they are bound together in various material interdependencies. Hence, there is no denying the importance of community consciousness. But two points are relevant here. First, the sense of community so typical in rural communities is built upon a real commonality of interests. Peasants' sense of mutuality, duty, obligation, and so forth derives from this real interdependence; it is not reproduced apart from it. Second, the issue is not whether a consciousness of this sort exists, but whether it is so powerful as to erase any awareness of individual interests. Chatterjee denies both of these possibilities in the works that I criticize, and does so quite explicitly. Instead of understanding community consciousness as being consistent with individual interests, he counterposes duty to interest, community identity to individual identity, rationality to obligation.[36] Not only is this characterization of peasants bizarre, but Chatterjee's own evidence shows that individual interests were in fact central to peasant consciousness throughout the period he is studying.[37]

Chatterjee seems to realize the bind he is in. In his response, he weakens his arguments, and now retreats to the claim that peasants were capable of identifying their interests in the economic sphere, but continued to have a distinctive community consciousness in their political mobilizations. He now is willing to allow that peasants were aware of their economic interests. But this awareness, he argues, did not guide them in their political struggles. Their political consciousness continued to be governed by community, which retained its autonomous dynamic.

But this position is even more absurd than his earlier one. There are two possibilities that might explain the process Chatterjee has described, in which peasants are aware of their individual economic interests but draw on their community ideology in political struggles. The first is that they continue to rely on community ties in political struggles because it is in their interest to do so. So, for example, they might join hands with jotedars in rural struggles because, even though the latter are exploiters, they are able to contribute resources that smallholders lack. I actually raise this possibility and address it as an explanation in *PTSC*.[38] I pointed out there what I will repeat now: that if this is what Chatterjee has in mind, then it supports the very premise that he wishes to reject—that peasants' political calculations were based on a consideration of their interests. But this would be a "bourgeois consciousness," whose existence Chatterjee denies.

The other possibility is that community bonds persist in politics because even while peasants can discern a clash of interests in the economic sphere, they are incapable of doing so in the political sphere. But if this is so, how does Chatterjee explain such a pervasive cognitive failure on the part of the Indian peasantry? If they can make a certain kind of cognitive operation in their economic relations, what prevents them from carrying out the same kind of operation in another one? If they are aware of, and act upon, their material interests in their economic reproduction, how are they not able to discern these interests in politics? What makes this especially confusing is that the operation involves the same objects—the local jotedars. If a smallholder knows that a jotedar is charging him an unfairly high rent or is sequestering his property and tries to resist it, are we to believe that all is forgiven when the two groups join in politics? When this same jotedar tries to run for office or calls for a political campaign, do we take it that the peasant simply forgets everything he knows about the rents and property disputes and joins in, singing local folk songs and praising this local notable? The mind boggles—yet it is precisely what Chatterjee would now have us believe. His earlier view at least had the merit of consistency.

As a final ploy, Chatterjee tries to bolster his case with another appeal to authority.[39] My defense of agential regard for well-being is taken by him to fly in the face of recent work in social anthropology. But this too is utterly false. Of course, there is, and has been for some time, a strong strand of culturalism in social anthropology. But the trend in recent years is firmly in the other direction, away from the cultural relativism that postcolonial theory endorses and toward more universalistic theories.[40] In fact, some of the most exciting and influential recent work has centered on two facts about agency that Chatterjee and other Subaltern Studies scholars typically deny—that social actors are motivated by a healthy regard for their well-being, and that this motivational structure appears to be operative across cultures.[41] Two aspects of agents' orientation have particular salience: first, that they view cooperation and some kind of other-orientation as important and desirable, and second, that such an orientation is not allowed to spill over into a consistent altruism. In other words, agents are willing to cooperate as long as they do not feel taken advantage of. This appears to hold true in a wide variety of cultural and social settings. The important point for us is that this orientation includes a healthy regard for individual interests, and it undermines the idea that there is a deep chasm separating East from West in agents' motivational structure. Is it possible that Chatterjee is not aware of this massive body of work, even though he is employed in an anthropology department in the United States? Or is he aware of but choosing to suppress it? I will leave the reader to judge which of the two is more embarrassing.

Finally, let us quickly address Chatterjee's defense of his theory of colonial nationalism, which I take up in Chapter 10 of *PTSC*. Recall his argument in *Nationalist Thought and the Colonial World*—that the chief flaw of nationalist ideology in India was that it internalized the Enlightenment ethos of Reason: rational thought, the admiration of science, and most importantly, the drive to modernize the economy. I argued that this turn to modernization was in fact driven by the constraints of the global capitalist system and the demands made by domestic classes. I demonstrated that Chatterjee's argument not only falls flat, but fails to address even the basic considerations that nationalists themselves adduced in defense of their view. Chatterjee now counters that his denunciation of Reason was meant to be ironic.

We should stand back to admire Chatterjee's audacity here. It is not just that he wishes to modify or clarify what he argued in his book. Chatterjee's defense is that, when he criticized Nehru for internalizing the Enlightenment ethos and adhering to a modernizing discourse, he didn't really mean it. He does not tell us what exactly he did mean, so that we might discern the view that propelled his resort to irony. The reader might be curious as to how an entire book, which purported to offer a theory of nationalism and an explanation for its infirmities, was in fact a long satire. But Chatterjee, in keeping with the rest of his response, simply hurls his retort at the reader and walks away.

He does so, of course, because he cannot possibly substantiate it. In fact, his attitude is a tacit admission that he has no real response to my criticism. And even more unfortunately for him, I anticipated a response of this kind and addressed it preemptively in *PTSC*, which readers who do not grasp his argument's blatant absurdity ought to consult.[42] As I argue there, Chatterjee's denunciation of Reason cannot possibly be ironic. The entire structure of *Nationalist Thought* is built around the attempt to prop up the critique of Reason and of the INC as its agent. If Chatterjee was seeking to make a different argument, the architecture of the book, its evidence, and its protagonists would have had to be entirely different. Chatterjee is once again hiding behind a smoke screen.

Conclusion

It is quite remarkable that, in the course of his essay, Chatterjee fails to address any of the criticisms I make in *PTSC*. His response amounts to nothing more than a series of misdirections and outright falsehoods. Instead of addressing Guha's mistaken assertions about the bourgeois revolutions, Chatterjee simply denies that he ever made them. Rather than answering my charge that the Indian bourgeoisie was little differ-ent than any other, Chatterjee announces that Guha reverted to the eighteenth-century use of the term—without ever informing the reader that he was doing so—and hence never made any claims about Indian capitalists. Instead of dealing with the obvious contradictions in his and Chakrabarty's views about subaltern agency and interests, he denies that he ever held the views that I attribute to him—the same views for which Subaltern Studies is in fact known—without ever addressing the reams of textual evidence I provide. In order to rebut my analysis of abstract labor, Chatterjee steers the discussion away from the questions that have animated the debates—whether abstract categories can apprehend social difference—and invents a debate that has never been relevant for postcolonial theorists. And when faced with the obvious weakness of his critique of Reason in his book on nationalism, he settles upon the novel strategy of saying, essentially, that he was *just kidding* when he placed the concept at the center of his analysis.

All this is carried out without engaging with the facts or the texts. Chatterjee does not give us any clues as to where we might find the textual evidence for his assertions. The essay is remarkably free of cita-tions or references. He relies, instead, on continual appeals to author-ity and on innuendo, implying time and again that an assertion must be true because some authority believes it to be, or even worse, that for anyone to believe otherwise would be sheer folly—even though I expend considerable energy and space in my book showing why the views he believes to be true are in fact mistaken.

The only way to make sense of this bizarre exercise is to recognize that it is not meant to be a response to my book at all. It makes much more sense if viewed, instead, as a performance. Chatterjee's essay is designed to allay any anxieties that his followers might have about the foundations of their project in the wake of *PTSC*. It is a palliative, a balm, to soothe their nerves. Subaltern Studies was not supposed to offer only a rival framework for interpreting colonial modernity; it was also supposed to have internalized whatever was worth retaining from the Marxian tradition, thereby inheriting the mantle of radical critique. For years, the Subalternists have focused just about everything they have written on the irredeemable flaws of Marxism and the Enlightenment—

their reductionism, essentialism, imperialist implications, and so forth. It is startling to find Chatterjee now presenting himself and his colleagues as dedicated followers of the Moor himself, their framework nothing more than an extension of his own. The reason, of course, is that *PTSC* challenges the Subalternists on these very grounds. Chatterjee's "response" is an exercise not in addressing my arguments but in dismissing them as irrelevant and reassuring the reader that all the dross that she has been fed for a quarter century was actually nectar. "No need to even read the book," Chatterjee is saying. "We were right after all." Hence the chest-thumping and braggadocio.

But, of course, this strategy comes with a risk—it might turn out that people do actually read, not only *PTSC*, but the texts that Chatterjee defends. I have tried to point to the relevant sections and pages, both in my book and in the other work to which he refers, but the fact is that even the most perfunctory reading of these texts will show the falsity of his claims. No doubt, many of his followers will take their cues from him and try to prop up his absurd declarations. They will twist and turn the relevant passages to wring the meaning from them that they need. Chatterjee knows that there are more than two generations of academics out there who have invested far too much in postcolonial theory; they will not let its obvious infirmities get in the way of its propagation. He knows this, and it is for them that he has crafted his essay. These are the people he is trying to reassure, with his reliance on authority, his re-found Marxism, his blithe dismissal of worrisome facts, and the like. It is a remarkable performance, but a performance nonetheless. The question now is how many readers will fall for it.

CHAPTER 3

Postcolonial Theory and the Specter of Capital

Gayatri Chakravorty Spivak

Penny for the old guy.[1]

Alexandre Aspel told me that I should always try to see what is best in what I read. Jacques Derrida taught us to say "yes" twice to a text. I have tried to read Vivek Chibber's book in that spirit.[2] He himself participates in that by locating Ranajit Guha as the best of the three authors he reads. If, however, the book wishes to "begin . . . to expose the flaws of [postcolonial theory], even to displace it,"[3] I am obliged to say that Vivek Chibber may not be the person to do that. His definitive example of postcolonial theory is the Subaltern Studies group of historians of South Asia (1983–2005). This choice is perhaps not an entirely convincing one. The thrust of the work of the Subalternists was the colonial history of India and the historiography of anti-colonial resistance. They brought about a significant change within the discipline of history—especially the history of South Asia. This change is perceptible in the Indian subcontinent and in the United Kingdom (UK), South Africa, and Australia, where the study of Indian history is more robust. Chibber's need to misrepresent this field in order to make his point obliges him to disregard two of the most powerful Subalternist historians still working in India: Shahid Amin and Shail Mayaram.

Specifically "postcolonial" theory, arising in the United States (US) and UK with Gayatri Spivak and Homi Bhabha, related back to Edward W. Said's *Orientalism*,[4] and to the phenomenon of cultural studies in Birmingham under the auspices of Richard Hoggart and Stuart Hall.[5]

Subaltern Studies certainly came in contact with the US branch of postcolonial studies through Spivak's visit in 1984. (I believe Guha has known Bhabha's way of thinking since the latter was a student at Oxford.) Chibber refers to this insultingly at the beginning of the book, and assumes this to be sufficient proof of the pernicious effect of "post-structuralism," undocumented as such and presented through the generalizations of received wisdom.

In actual fact, Spivak's intervention, perceived as applying standards of literary criticism to history, was hotly contested by Subalternists as well as general historians from and of South Asia. Guha himself was disappointed by Spivak's performance of her co-editorial obligations to the original volume of *Selected Subaltern Studies*.[6] Although her relationship with the collective remained cordial and intellectually productive, Spivak's "influence" on their work is insignificant, if at all there.

Chibber pays no attention to Pan-Africanism (including Negritude), which was the first example of a postcolonial vision. He refers not at all to the significant phenomenon of Latin American postcolonial theory (Walter Mignolo, Mary-Louise Pratt) and Latin American Subaltern Studies (John Beverley, Alberto Moreiras, Ilyana Rodriguez, this last with the connection to Spivak's work which Chibber incorrectly claims for South Asian Subaltern Studies).

In a 306-page book full of a repeated and generalized account of the British and French revolutions, and repeated clichés about how capitalism works, and repeated boyish moments of "I have disproved arguments 1, 2, 3, therefore Guha [or Chakrabarty, or yet Chatterjee] is wrong, and therefore Subaltern Studies is a plague and a seduction, and must be eradicated, although it will be hard because careers will be ruined, etc.," there could have been some room for these references to describe the range, roots, and ramifications of postcolonial studies, so that the book's focused choice could have taken its place in Verso's protective gestures toward the preservation of "Little Britain Marxism," shared to some degree by the journal *Race and Class*. Aijaz Ahmad's *In Theory*[7] was such an attempt. Postcolonial theory is the blunter instrument, and its attempt to disregard the range of postcolonial studies in order to situate Subaltern Studies—confined to three texts—as its representative can mislead students more effectively.

There is no room in this book for perceiving nuance, as described in the following passage at the very opening of Chatterjee's *Nationalist Thought*:

In an ideological world . . . words rarely have unambiguous mean-
ings, where notions are inexact, and have political value precisely
because they are inexact and hence capable of suggesting a range of
possible interpretations . . . This inexact world . . . of dreams and illu-
sions . . . rules established, values asserted, revolutions accomplished
and states founded . . . Critical viewpoint reveals that [a political
revolution] . . . at the same time, and in fundamental ways, is not a
revolution.[8]

Writing as a member of the Subaltern Studies collective, I should say
that we could no doubt profit from a robust constructive criticism of
Chibber's sort. In order, however, to be successful at such a critique,
the critic must not only give the reader an idea of the scope and range
of postcolonial studies, but also be able to enter the actual project of
Subaltern Studies and notice that the two are not the same. Vivek
Chibber is stumped by his desire to "correct" everybody—the examples are altogether too many to quote. Here is a typical sample: "Guha's
mistaken view of the European experience does not simply undermine
his analysis of the postcolonial polity. It also has grave implications for
his more ambitious project of political critique."[9]

There is no hint here of the sense where Chibber might himself be
corrected—with a careful auto-critique, a strong sense of being folded
together in a complicity with the very people whom he wants to demolish in an embarrassingly arm-wrestling way. (If he thinks they ignore
class, they think rigid class analysis ignores subaltern social groups.)
The harder they come, the harder they fall. Interpretation is a responsible task, a risky business.

And so Chibber carries on, merrily mistaking a primary text for a
secondary text as he proceeds to "correct" Ranajit Guha because he is
"wrong" about the British and French revolutions. Guha's "understanding of the European experience is fatally flawed."[10]

In order to prove someone completely mistaken, you have to read
all of what they have written. It is embarrassing to be told that, "judged
in terms of space or of word count, Guha does not devote much attention to the fortunes of the landed classes,"[11] when the entire deep background of Guha's work lies there. The thing to do is to read A Rule of
Property for Bengal[12] side by side with The Small Voice of History[13] to

get a grasp of what is at stake in the work of this counterintuitive historian.

Guha, a seasoned communist who paid the price of his political convictions during a brilliantly maverick career as a historian, created a revolution within the discipline. For Chibber to prove him "wrong"— especially as an orientalist misreader of Europe who believes that the "non-West" has a different psychology—is somewhat like proving W. E. B. Du Bois "wrong" when he calls the exodus of the newly emancipated slaves a "general strike," like the repeated attempts by folks like Bernard Lewis to prove Edward Said "wrong," even, and I do not want to be mischievous, a well-meaning smart sophomore's attempt to show that in the *Poetics* Aristotle is. "illogical."[14]

I will look at the way in which Guha establishes his premises and alliances in *Dominance without Hegemony*.[15] I will begin with a longish quotation from Hayden White, cited by Guha:

> There does, in fact, appear to be an irreducible ideological component in every historical account of reality. The very claim to have discerned some kind of formal coherence in the historical record brings with it theories of the nature of the historical world and of historical knowledge itself which have ideological implications for attempts to understand the "present," however this "present" is defined . . . The ideological dimensions of a historical account reflect the ethical element in the historian's assumption of a particular position on the question of the nature of historical knowledge and the implications that can be drawn from the study of past events for the understanding of the present.[16]

To read this citation correctly, Chibber has to be able to understand the difference between "ideology" and "psychology." (This is also true in the case of his unproductive misreading of Chakrabarty and Chatterjee.) He uses "ideology" in the uncritical colloquial US sense of "ideas held by a particular group." The Subalternists, including, of course, Guha, use it in the Marxian tradition, beginning with *The German Ideology*[17] and continuing through a long critical tradition of debate, which Chibber simply dismisses without discussion because it does not square with his presuppositions, his method being to trivialize the opposition and show, point by point, that every principle emphasized by them—as he understands without his being prepared to read them with the sympathy required to produce constructive, or even destructive, criticism—is just "wrong," as proved by him, QED. This is an embarrassing method. Guha and the Subalternists certainly use the word "consciousness," in the Hegelian tradition, with the lightest touch of psychoanalysis (to which they were never seriously committed), certainly not to be confused with "psychology," the accessible workings of a rational choice/behaviorist model of mind that is presupposed by analytic/US ideology and all thinking influenced by it (an extended discussion would have to make an exception in the case of Noam Chomsky).

Chibber cannot distinguish between "capital" and "capitalism." Here are some examples. "What does capitalism universalize?" he asks. And, in the next sentence, answers: "To assess whether capital abandoned its universalizing mission in its colonial venture, we must first ask, what it is supposed to universalize?"[18] The answers to the two questions are different. Capital is the abstract concept; capitalism and/or socialism are two opposed means of human control of capital, requiring coercive/persuasive ideology and policy. This is where an understanding of "ideology" in the sense used by the Subalternist historians (and many others, of course) would lead to a possibly serious criticism, if needed.

Capital "universalizes," then as now, because it seeks to establish the same standard of exchange, whatever the level of "development." This is, in different ways, colonialism and imperialism. This is how capital's behavior becomes different. Capitalism finesses this by talking of a "civilizing mission," then as now. At the same time, capital produces difference in order to be capital (produce and use surplus). That is called "class." To suggest that "subalternist theorists mistakenly urge that the forms of domination that obtain in postcolonial formation are not capitalist"[19] is itself mistaken because Chibber is focused on a "correct" reading of the French and English revolutions.

Chakrabarty gets it in the rear because Chibber is unable to grasp the difference. History 2 is "the category charged with the function of constantly interrupting the totalizing thrust of History 1," writes Chakrabarty. (Is he thinking of the permanent parabasis whereby, in the old Attic comedy, the chorus interrupts the main action repeatedly, as Fichte noted? No matter.) "To interrupt the totalizing thrust of capitalism"—how did "History 1" become "capitalism"?—"is to undermine its universalization," writes Chibber.[20] Chakrabarty is consistently talking about "capital," and then, in an intriguing move, invokes "translation" into "capitalism" and suggests that that move does not just happen in one way. Chibber cannot read this. The same problem crops up on page 227 before we finally get this narrative:

> Hence, if there is any genuine source of opposition to capital's universalizing drive, it is the equally universal struggle by subaltern classes to defend their basic humanity. That is the core motivation in all those thousands of campaigns for wages, land rights, basic health, and security, dignity, self-determination, autonomy, and so forth— all those Enlightenment concepts against which post-colonial theorists inveigh.[21]

Investigating the absence of internationalism in the rank and file of the labor movement and its relationship to colonialism has to be forgone in a brief review, as must the pre-critical notion that capital's universalization is "market dependence."[22] Any effort with labor worldwide immediately brings up the issue of outsourcing. There is also the gender politics within established organized labor which encourages the cynical concept of "permanent casuals."

The main problem, however, is not labor idealism. The main point is that subaltern social groups are not the international proletariat. That is the basic message of Gramsci's essay on the historiography of the subaltern classes. That he does not know this is clear in Chibber's dismissal of Chatterjee's reading of Gramsci as "references to Gramsci more prominently on display."[23] In order for the South Asian subaltern to find an objective concept for collectivity, it is often the discourse of religion that is mobilized. This is no mere liberation theology, as I will explain below.

Indeed, because Chibber is eager to prove that nothing that the Subalternists acknowledged was more than "trend"-y, he dismisses Gramsci's influence as a trend.[24] When on page 27 he discloses, "I do not analyze the nature of [the Subalternists'] connection [to Gramsci] . . . primarily because of my desire that the reader not be distracted by whether Subalternists have correctly interpreted a given theorist," this reader is obliged to conclude—and not only because of this "correct"-fetishist gurumahashay's demonstrated inability to be auto-critical—that he is not "familiar with the relevant literature."

For then he would have known that Gramsci's main contribution was not "popular history and matters of consciousness."[25] (Gramsci's concern anyway is not consciousness raising but epistemology, education.) Gramsci's main contribution was to notice that, precisely because Italy, with its tail tucked into Africa, is not France, Britain, Russia, or the US, the Risorgimento did not sufficiently assimilate "class" differences created outside of capital logic (basically the incentive to establish the same system of exchange everywhere). This is why the Subalternists chose the word "subaltern." The existence of the subaltern is also evident in the Pan-Africanist W. E. B. Du Bois's writings, in such essays as "The Negro Mind Reaches Out," although, being a distant yea-sayer to Stalin (of whose purge techniques he was unaware, as opposed to the lynching techniques of the Southern bourgeoisie), Gramsci's "enemy," he did not know the word "subaltern."[26] So, not not capitalist, but separated from full capital logic. The distinct difference is that, whereas a Southern Benedetto Croce could become fully "Northern," in a colony, full P (power) could not be acquired by the "improved" (in French, the word is évolué) bourgeoisie. Chibber should have known a bit more about colonialism "correctly" or perhaps remembered that Guha had the lived experience of full colonialism and complicity with the "improved" class. If you are repeatedly going to "prove" a respected senior scholar "mistaken," it is your obligation to research him well. It is in that spirit that I have recommended the introduction to *The Small Voice of History* as required reading. One of the chief insights in Spivak's generation, in India and North and continental Africa, was the inability to use the Enlightenment when the colonial difference was no longer at work in postcoloniality. She "parachuted" across the street in Calcutta,[27] turning left by an open garbage dump, because the Subalternists were theorizing this.

Chibber takes his model of postcolonialism from upwardly class-mobile or professional second-generation immigrants in the US, who do speak of the "East" and the "Non-West," and may sometimes imply culture equals psychology, legitimizing by reversal. By contrast, Subalternists everywhere name countries and colonies.

Here I would like to mention Kathleen Collins, author of the excellent book *Clan Politics and Regime Transition in Central Asia.*[28] Because she wanted to avoid, like the Subalternists, the (racialized) idea that there is some peculiar psychology in Central Asia, she made it her business, although not a trained Europeanist, to include a short narrative "history of Europe" and empirically established a possible relationship between clan/goon politics in the historical gap between the absolutist state and democracy. She does not consult Gramsci. But her intellectual curiosity and disciplinary acumen permit her to rediscover that southern Italy has a conjuncture comparable (of course not identical) to Central Asia—a mixture of capitalist and pre-capitalist ideological formations (not psychological essentialism, as per Chibber)—separating proletarian and subaltern. Chibber, ignoring this type of possibility, takes "subaltern" as a synonym for "proletarian" and offers the usual mechanical Marxist utopian pronouncement.

It is on this level of generality that Chibber insists that what produces a connection between all the "subaltern classes" (according to his definition) all over the world is "physical well-being."[29] There is no grand narrative on the level of "physical well-being," or it is so grand that it is inaccessible to the subject (Lévinas's argument in *Otherwise than Being*[30]). The moment you go from body to mind, from physical well-being to fighting for physical well-being, there is language, history, and "permissible narratives."[31] For example, the mother thinks honor, the daughter thinks reproductive rights. What history happened in between? A change in localized permissible narratives that still cannot touch pharmaceutical dumping. If physical well-being were a race-free, class-free, gender-free grand narrative, there would be no point in having any theories of justice, politics, human rights, and gender compromise. (Ellen Bostrup and Amartya Sen's work on women's notion of preserving physical well-being is by now honorably dated.[32]) Indeed, there is no point in Marx's[33] exhortation to his implied readership in *Capital*, volume 1, to change their self-concept from "victim of the capitalist" to "agent of production." (The "subaltern" is not an agent of capitalist production.) If we go back to "whose physical well-being, by what permissible narrative," we are back in the division within organized labor in terms of outsourcing, of the sub-proletariat, its complete ignorance of the non-generalizable subaltern populations of the world, its usual lack of sympathy for women and homeworkers and its connections with management. The required reading, at two ends of the spectrum, is the entire vanguardism–social democracy debate, of which Rosa Luxemburg's *The Mass Strike*[34] is a part, and the new thinking started by D. D. Kosambi, whom Guha cites at the very beginning of *Dominance without Hegemony*.[35] This is like justifying war or peace through the Christ story (a different permissible narrative). No psychological essentialism here, especially since polymath Kosambi, whose polymath father became a Buddhist under B. R. Ambedkar's influence, is speaking of how the converted Buddhist Emperor Asoka's new imperial-universal notion of dhamma, not to be found in the classic Arthasastra, was in its turn miscast into dharma, both instruments of class reconciliation between sovereign and subject. Historical change, class accommodation, not psychological essence. Just dhamma, dharma, "Improvement," "civilizing mission" in general theory, today "development": allowing invented "tradition" to work at reconciling established class/caste convictions in the lower social strata, related to, but certainly not identical with, building temples and churches.[36] To say that "Guha does not consider that the shift to capitalist social structures might actually fit quite well with the idiom of traditional politics,"[37] or that "postcolonial theory … portray[s] the East as an unchanging miasma of tradition,"[38] is astonishing.

Would Professor Chibber correct Rosa Luxemburg and D. D. Kosambi? No, because he knows they are primary texts. He misses out on Guha because Guha has been placed within an academic battle between what I keep calling Little Britain Marxism and located postcolonial historiographies, here confused with the metropolitan second-generation version, particularly in the US. Chibber's knowledge of the detail of Marx is shaky, but his convictions, coming as they do from a disciplinarization in sociology, notoriously quantitative in the US, with some notable exceptions, such as his alma mater Wisconsin, especially if the degree comes through their spectacular Center for South Asia, are remarkable in their qualitative vigor. I therefore guess that, if I remind Chibber of the famous first paragraph of Kosambi's *An Introduction to the Study of Indian History*,[39] he will perhaps say that, although this is acceptable in a dated classic, his own general idea is that Indian colonial and postcolonial history "are subject to *the same basic forces* and are therefore part of *the same basic history.*"[40] He does not have enough auto-critical skills to know that his own position is also dated and spaced within a turf battle slightly more than academic, that the same basic history is a site of conflictual differences.

Here is Kosambi:

> The light-hearted sneer "India has had some episodes, but no history" is used to justify lack of study, grasp, intelligence on the part of foreign writers about India's past. The considerations that follow will prove that it is precisely the episodes—lists of dynasties and kings, tales of war and battle spiced with anecdote, which fill school texts— that are missing from Indian records. Here, for the first time, we have to reconstruct a history without episodes, which means that it cannot be the same type of history as in the European tradition.[41]

I have indicated that Kathleen Collins found, in accounting for clan/goon politics in some places and not in others, that such politics was determined by the gap between the establishment of the absolutist state and democracy. Into this argument we can also place the colonial state, without direct access to the agency of P at the top and, of course, the totalitarian state.

Let us now consider Chibber's remark about the Subalternists' assumption about democracy: "*Subalternists attribute to the bourgeoisie a democratic mission that it in fact rejected and fought against. The idea that modern democratic culture derives from the beneficence of capitalists is central to Ranajit Guha's work.*"[42]

To begin with, the passage is problematic because "bourgeoisie" and "capitalists" are used as synonyms. (As for the passage on page 147, where Chibber does grant that there is a "link between capitalism and democratization," there he again thinks the Subalternists mean "capitalists" when they say "bourgeoisie"; the bourgeoisie are actually the politico/ideological, the juridico/legal, the intellectual/rentier; a section of the bourgeoisie may be capitalists.) But let us lay that aside. It is not capitalist beneficence that calls forth something that looks like

democracy. Marx abundantly acknowledged capital's social productivity. Capitalism manages it for sustainable underdevelopment. Capital
needs to establish uniformity in order to function well. (I prefer that to
"universalization," but it is not a serious objection, simply a prefer-
ence.) Capitalism, and its organic intellectuals, who are probably
members of the bourgeoisie, finesse this in various ways so that capitalist social relations of production can be preserved. This is not a
romantic belief. It continues to our own time. I am sure Professor
Chibber has read the work of Jack Snyder, Fareed Zakaria, Nicholas
Doyle, and many others, arguing that the enforceability of democracy
depends upon per capita income and a good working capitalist system.
"Exporting democracy" and "liberating women" have also led to some
tremendous wars, beginning at the turn of the twenty-first century, in
the oil circuit of the Middle East; Syria will not be the last domino to
fall. To get a detailed argument about the connection between the
establishment of democracy in the American South and the play of
Northern capital, controlled by Northern capitalists, to undermine
labor's agency of capital, once again I would recommend consulting
W. E. B. Du Bois's *Black Reconstruction in America*.[43]

Chibber's confusion of the bourgeois and the capitalist is a serious
problem if one wishes to understand what people like Guha—and
there were not too many like him when he began—are talking about
when they compare the colonizing and the colonized bourgeoisie.
These are people who are steeped in the long debate between vanguardism and social democracy, within which the critique of imperialism
and the possibility of socialism are launched—even with deep background in inconvenient people like Bakunin, and that is where the
argument is coming from. This is why, if I may leap forward a bit,
Chibber is unable to understand, when Chatterjee is criticizing Nehru
and Gandhi, that Chatterjee may be thinking of the possibility of
socialism, not of giving up on reason; that he may be questioning the
version of reason that grounds Chibber's own conviction that economic
growth is human development—a position opposed by millions of
people in the world outside the academy as well: "In the era of decolonization parts of the Global South have dramatically improved their
material conditions."[44] Kosambi could have told him that many on the
Left thought Nehru was selling capitalism in the name of democratic

socialism. And Ranajit Guha actually quotes a cluster of passages from Gandhi, in *Domination without Hegemony*, claiming that his theories of corporate social responsibility were there to fight socialism. I give one example here: "'I enunciated this theory,' he [Gandhi] said, 'when, the socialist theory was placed before the country in respect to the possessions held by zamindars [landowners] and ruling chiefs.'"[45] Professor Chibber may not agree, but he cannot accuse Chatterjee of illogic if he suggests that, in different ways, Gandhi and Nehru are continuing the old "improvement" logic. Professor Chibber, in spite of the good motive to clean the house of poor theorizing, cannot, to quote my old friend Teodor Shanin, understand that "socialism is about justice, not development"[46] (here our generation understood "development" as "exploitation").

It is also clear that Chibber has not read the Subaltern Studies material clearly. One of their research undertakings was to point at Gandhi's separation from peasant movements.[47] If Chibber wants to get a sense of this, he may also want to look at the exchange between Sumanta Banerjee[48] and David Hardiman[49] in the pages of *Economic and Political Weekly*.

Is it only the Subalternist historians who believe that liberals supported modernization as capitalist development in order to keep socialism at bay? Professor Chibber comes out with a centrist common-sense bit of criticism: "[Chatterjee] simply denies what so many nationalist leaders saw as self-evident—that whatever else the postcolonial state did, it would have to find a way to develop the local productive forces."[50] Is this what Verso wants to propose as a socialist solution, mindful of classes, in globality?

To continue with the things that one must be familiar with in order to point out that Subaltern Studies have not been useful, I cite "abstract average labor," or labor-power. It is not "a *dimension* of *concrete* labors," nor does it "refer to properties that the latter have in common, properties which can be compared with one another and which are rewarded by the market." "The most important such property is" not "labor's productive efficiency, which can be measured in its throughput."[51] It is the product of what today we call "quantification." In order for the capitalist to progress, labor must be put in the form of value ("contentless," says Marx[52] in *Capital*, volume 1), so that calculations can be made. It is as simple as that. Chibber seems not to have grasped this at all, and ignores the ins and outs of the so-called "reification" debates—which are now going completely in the direction of liberal humanism in the work of Axel Honneth and others.[53] Honneth's recent Tanner lecture simply put the critique of reification in the classless identitarian area of "recognition"—which reflects a tendency much more insidious than anything the efforts of the Subalternists might signal. But Chibber is located in the tendency among Little Britain Marxists patronized by the now defunct British New Left, which produces, periodically, peculiar texts demolishing any attempt at expanding the scope of a general Marxist discourse—by which I mean something like the "broad Left" now innovated in Greece, facing the depredations of the eurozone, internal colonialism, if you like—into the interplay of capital and colony.

Again and again, Chibber shows us that capitalism does indeed create social difference. But of course. This is the double bind of capital that Marx pointed out in a spectacular passage quoted by Guha toward the beginning of his book. Capital creates tremendous social productivity and to manage this capitalism must proletarianize; and, after Gramsci, we have also learned to say "subalternize."

Chibber accuses the Subalternists of romantic Orientalism. Because he cannot acknowledge the difference between the conduct of the Industrial Revolution using so-called Enlightenment practices at home and coercion at best in the colonial field within which these practices needed to be played out as the markets expanded, he has a romantic notion of how the entire world has changed, which shows very clearly that he has no idea at all of Gramsci's attempt to distinguish the subaltern from the proletarian. To bring together the subaltern and the proletarian, both seen as riddled with prejudices—and Gramsci was after all in the thick of things, not just writing books—was the last piece of writing Gramsci was engaged in when he was nabbed by the fascists. This piece was already distinctly different from the kind of positive reinforcements that, as a leader of the communists, he had wisely produced for the Turin proletariat hitherto. Acknowledging that the General Strike of 1920 had not worked, he was now looking at the possibility of making long-term change. Once incarcerated, Gramsci[54] expands this concern into the period of self-study leading to a book (which he did not have the time to write) that would take all of this into consideration. And in that period he distinguished the subaltern very carefully as follows:

> The subaltern social groups [gruppi sociali], by definition, are not unified and cannot unite until they are able to become a "State": their history, therefore, is intertwined with that of civil society [an extended discussion would have to consider Gramsci's special understanding of "civil society"] . . . and thereby with the history of States and groups of States. Hence it is necessary to study: 1. the objective formation of the subaltern social groups, by the developments and transformations occurring in the sphere of economic production; their quantitative diffusion and their origins in pre-existing social groups, whose mentality, ideology and aims they conserve for a time; 2. their active or passive adherence to the dominant political forma-tions, their attempts to influence the programmes of these forma-tions in order to press claims of their own, and the consequences of these attempts in determining processes of decomposition, renova-tion or neo-formation; 3. the birth of new parties of the dominant groups, intended to conserve the assent of the subaltern groups and to maintain control over them; 4. the formations which the subaltern groups themselves produce, in order to press claims of a restricted and "partial" character; 5. those new formations which assert the autonomy of the subaltern groups, but within the old framework; 6. those formations which assert the integral autonomy . . . etc.[55]

How Gramsci would have developed these thoughts and his many meditations on the relationship between the intellectual and the subaltern classes can only be surmised. This, however, remains one of his most important themes, precisely because of the fact that the subal-tern is not the proletariat. Politics did not permit him to write his books. Many of his notes end in "etc." The Subalternists must take into account, however tacitly, the difference between the Italian state and the colonial state. They use Gramsci and transform him some. Chibber, ready to tilt at the Subalternists, and unaware of Gramsci's distinction between subaltern and proletariat (although he does comment upon the Risorgimento), produced the universalist romantic utopian leftist narrateme that I have cited above. The sentence "there was simply no way to accommodate subaltern demands for improvement in their living standard, while keeping domestic capitalists on board, except through a modernizing agenda"[56] shows no awareness of the subaltern social groups' distance from the state.

This is a disciplinary problem, an inability to read philosophical writing that is also political, and diagnosing it as nonsense. After all of the attempts by people who are not necessarily less intelligent than Chibber to establish how "discourse" works at the social construction of reality—not necessarily my position, but I can certainly read this work in order to learn from it—Chibber produces a sentence that shows an ignorance of the entire field of discourse studies. I refer him to *Discourse and Power* by Teun A. van Dijk.[57] Structuralism and post-structuralism, never discussed, are similarly dismissed as irrational—this is a book, not a rant! These are fields that, again, the Subalternists assume to be part of the familiar background of all kinds of actors attempting to rethink a Left that was moving more and more toward totalitarianism. I remember clearly that just after 1989, at a Radical Philosophy conference in London, nearly all of the papers presented were still involved with the Jerusalem built on England's green and pleasant land—therefore to call Ranajit Guha useless because he did not understand the British and French revolutions is not surprising from Verso, but it's somewhat shocking nevertheless that this kind of thing still continues. It may indeed be true that in these small countries, which by then had national languages more or less understood by everyone, "the peasants . . . had to reach out to the dignitaries in order to get the reform coalition to turn into a revolutionary one."[58] If, on the other hand, instead of "examin[ing] the British and French experience in far greater depth than does Guha,"[59] Chibber had tried to look at India in deep focus, he would have seen how absurd it is not to acknowledge the obvious differences between Britain and France, taken as "Europe," and the huge multilingual, multicultural, multi-ethnic, multi-religious reality of the Indian subcontinent in the nineteenth and twentieth centuries. It is derisive to say that in "the broad sweep of modern political history in the Global South, there is ample evidence that"—a nice compendious footnote would have persuaded me against my common sense—"in nationalist movements during the colonial era, and continuing into the postcolonial era—organizations of the popular classes have pushed in much the same direction as did their counterparts in Europe."[60] What "counterparts"? In Peru, Guatemala? In Egypt? Bangladesh? Sri Lanka?

This is not a "critique of Eurocentrism." In the elementary schools for the rural landless where Spivak has trained students and teachers to learn and teach the state curriculum for nearly three decades now she tries to make her groups friendly with the wretched map of the world on the back cover of the geography book. She points at the northwestern corner of the huge Eurasian continent and tells them that that is Europe and that, though so small, they still won. She discusses with them how they won and even uses such mid-Victorian examples as James Watt watching the lid dance on the pot of boiling water. She reminds herself not to be an "improver," and discusses with her increasingly more aware co-workers (male and female teachers and supervisors) from the community the fact that she is not drawing profits from the work for and with them. Although they are not well acquainted with the world map and know nothing about colonialism, and have not seen any factories of any significant size, they do understand what profit, or munafa, is. They are subaltern, they have no special psychological essence, they are not "the East," or "the Non-West," they can be examples of a general argument that notices that they vote in a postcolonial nation that they do not know as such. A limiting concept of "Europe" must come to terms with the fact that Europe is part of a much larger world now. Europe's moment was historically important but not all-consumingly determining. Not everyone has to have a correct interpretation of the English and French revolutions. It is enough to think of the relationship between the Chartists and the Reform Bills, even Labour and New Labour; of the *Eighteenth Brumaire*; even Aimé Césaire and Frantz Fanon versus Valéry Giscard d'Estaing. The sun rises at different times upon the globe today. Paying good attention to England and France is not going to "plac[e] Indian modernity in a global context."[61] When the stock exchange closes in London, it must wait for Tokyo and then Mumbai, and in between opens the turbulent and wildly unstable speculative "marriage of socialism and capitalism," where the "turnover rates are ten times higher,"[62] where the rules are much different from Professor Chibber's boutades about capital/capitalism equated, yet uniformization/universalization is raring to break through (like the steam in the steam engines that we traveled by in my childhood and adolescence): Shanghai and Shenzen.

This inability to read any other kind of writing is shown in an embarrassing footnote where, I must say, Chakrabarty would have done well to acknowledge the source. Citing a passage where Chakrabarty is clearly paraphrasing Walter Benjamin's notion of "now time," Chibber asks the rhetorical question, "Is this passage meant to explain anything at all?"[63] It would be more convenient for him simply to dismiss Walter Benjamin as a fool and a knave, and "correct" the "Theses on the Philosophy of History,"[64] but unfortunately the inability to hold on to the present as present is a bit of the mundane experience of life that has been considered philosophically by too many people, including Hegel—another fool to be corrected—for Chibber simply and blithely to dismiss. I am a literary critic, so let me cite an example from poetry, which also should perhaps be dismissed because it does not accede to the Enlightenment as understood by Chibber—a rational choice as defined by academic infighting:

The last line of William Butler Yeats's poem "Sailing to Byzantium," "Of what is past, or passing, or to come," spells a non-accessibility to the stability of the present, a gesture, protecting from claims to influence. The present is a vanishing relationship, constituted by its vanishing. Let us look at Benjamin's powerful articulation, which I will cite again at the end. "The past can be seized only as an image which flashes up at the instant of its recognizability, never to be seen again . . . History is the object of a construction, whose site forms not with homogeneous empty time, but time filled with the now time." Yeats's time, the time for literary action, for literary activism, now time, not a present of the sort that you can catch as something that actually exists.[65]

Here too I comment on Little Britain Marxism, as follows:

Many people think that "homogeneous empty time" was a phrase coined by Benedict Anderson in *Imagined Communities*, a book which does not grant us the ability to understand what we are about, or to understand and use the great economic and political narratives of liberation that come from Europe. Many people think that Benedict Anderson wrote "homogeneous empty time" and that Homi Bhabha opposed it, but in fact, it comes from this extraordinary passage in Benjamin where he talks about the time of action.[66]

When Chakrabarty suggests that there should not be a "simple application of the analytics of capital and nationalism available to Western Marxism,"[67] he is appealing for complexity and not the top-down approach that mere application implies. Chibber is fixated on "political psychology." It is not a question of being "disdainful"[68] (no documentation for this nice psychological term) of subaltern agency; it is a question of, given what the "subaltern" is—as defined by Gramsci, "on the fringes of history" and not yet generalizable—that entire social group falling through the cracks of the theory applied. French theories of "relative autonomy" would not help here, as Chibber suggests in a footnote. The "metanarrative" Chakrabarty is speaking of contains the relatively autonomous fields of politics, ideology, and the economic in a structural fit. In his earlier work as well, he is speaking of the strong hold of an older ideology ("residual" on the Raymond Williams model) rather than a "unique psychological disposition of Indians"[69]—all Indians? Incidentally, Chibber's dismissal of the History 1/ History 2 distinction would also dismiss the entire rethinking of historiography introduced by Fernand Braudel.

As a result of this problem of reading, Chibber does not understand what Guha is doing in the defining sections of *Dominance without Hegemony*. I have given enough examples of this to say here, simply, that, far from asserting that there is an immutable difference in the Eastern psyche, Guha is suggesting that, if "Indian history [is] assimilated to the history of Great Britain"—as Chibber suggests—it would be "used as comprehensive measure of difference between the two countries."[70] Already in the first paragraphs of the book, Guha makes it quite clear that he is not claiming that the European liberals did everything they promised. I think the only difference that he is arguing is that in the context of an imposition of a stage of capital not yet arrived at in the colonized space—here the work of Ritu Birla[71] is essential—the nationalist historians did not recognize that the peasants found in so-called religion a way out of simply individual interests into a more world-historical perception. The description of religion as the insurrectionists' way beyond mere personal suffering toward "the world-historical" matters a great deal today, as does the construction of an "ideal consciousness" for the deserving and undeserving other by the human rights lobby and the self-selected moral entrepreneurs of the so-called international civil society as well as by the proliferation of "empty abstractions [in] tertiary discourse."[72] This use of religion can then be contrasted to the ideological script of dharma as urging patriotism to the Indian nation.

Since Chibber can only see this as an Orientalist statement about the East being psychologically different, he cannot see how bold it is. In the context of the Arab Spring that he brings in at the end of his book, this particular opposition, between liberalism and religion as access to the world-historical, the clash of discursive fields tangling with irregular class and gender formation, becomes crucial. I cannot go there in a review, but this needs to be considered more carefully.

Professor Chibber takes Ranajit Guha to task for "never tak[ing] up the question of why popular forces failed to gather enough strength to push the INC [Indian National Congress] in a more radical direction."[73] Our point would be that the entire work of Guha, Chakrabarty, and Chatterjee is about how this was prevented by both leadership and historiography. But if we are wrong, we ask Chibber why? Is it because they were psychologically "different" from the French and British "popular forces" so many centuries ago?

I want to close with a reference to feminism, of which there is no mention here at all. Some of us have argued for rather a long time that feminist movements had an oblique relationship with the tradition of imperialism. When the nature of this relationship is not recognized, it is precisely the subaltern woman who is ignored. I was visited two days ago by a young Indian American woman wanting to make a film about the rape of Jyoti Singh, by consulting "experts" like Noam Chomsky, Sudhir Kakar, and Gayatri Spivak. I was not able to rise to her request, because I felt that this was not a productive enterprise. In the process, since she was also using the fact that this idea came to her through her son's sex education class in the Midwest of America, I tried to tell her about the use made by men on the Left, so-called, of women who believe in the Enlightenment, just exactly as use is made of women who believe in anti-feminist traditions. I told her that the general sympathy for a mother–son discourse, family values (my son's sex education class), and women who still make use of it would be diagnosed by the most relentlessly honest philosopher of the Enlightenment as keeping women enclosed within an absence of "civil personality," with "tradesmen, servants . . . minors."[74] I told her we must learn to disprove this. I must repeat this at the end of my review because there must be a feminist consideration of Chibber's emphasis on the heroism of the subaltern classes misunderstood as simply part of the world's disenfranchised existing within "the same history as Europe," supporting his desire to dismiss Subaltern Studies as a part of postcolonial studies. That desire I should have liked to contest in terms of my own conflictual but instructive experience with this group. But since I have no foothold in this book except as an object of mockery, I think that would be, to quote the language understood by Chibber and his cohorts, bad form.

CHAPTER 4

Making Sense of Postcolonial Theory

A Response to Gayatri Chakravorty Spivak

Vivek Chibber

I will respond as best I can to Gayatri Spivak's criticisms of *Postcolonial Theory and the Specter of Capital*[1] (hereafter *PTSC*), though, as I will suggest below, the task is not an easy one, owing to Spivak's peculiar style of engagement.[2]

Spivak begins by castigating me for focusing narrowly on Subaltern Studies, even while I claim to critique postcolonial theory. Why do I leave out so much of what has been produced in the field? In reality, I offered an explanation in the book's opening chapter, but, since Spivak does not address my reasons, please allow me to repeat them. The decision to focus on Subaltern Studies was not arbitrary. I was fully aware that postcolonial studies has generated a wide and varied universe of scholarship, expanding across many disciplines. My goal was to assess its contributions in the more empirically oriented fields such as history and anthropology, where it has exercised considerable influence. Hence, right at the outset, I signaled that the focus of the book was a somewhat delimited portion of what the field has to offer. I chose to focus on these areas because my interest was in what postcolonial scholarship has to say about the social structure, politics, and historical evolution of the Global South, since its claims about these phenomena are of considerable interest, and they have been extremely influential across the academic universe.

To examine postcolonial studies in the empirical disciplines, the next challenge was to locate a central cluster of arguments that are associated with it and could be taken to embody a theory, or a research program. In other words, I had to see if postcolonial studies has generated a theory that explains the specific dynamics and evolution of colonial societies, or of the Global South more generally. The arguments I would focus upon not only had to have some theoretical and empirical content, but also had to have two other characteristics, if the project was to succeed—they would have to resonate with the claims being made in the wider field, even in cultural studies, and they would have to be arguments that wielded actual influence in scholarly work. Hence, focusing on arguments that had little influence, or which could not prove their bona fides as genuinely "postcolonial," would undermine the project right at the outset. On these criteria, there can be little doubt that Subaltern Studies was not only a legitimate target for my project, but the most natural one.

First, it is recognized as a legitimate, even central, current of scholarship within postcolonial studies. Works by its founding members are included or discussed in the most widely used textbooks on postcolonial studies, and, just as importantly, its members routinely describe their work as belonging to the field.

Secondly, Subaltern Studies has remained committed to a stable and remarkably coherent set of propositions about the dynamics of the (post-)colonial world, its evolution over time, and the ways in which that part of the globe differs in its structure and culture from the West. In other words, it has generated a core set of arguments that can be taken as a theory and a research program. While it is conventional to mark a break of sorts between the "early" volumes in the series and the later ones, this distinction is misleading in some ways. The real core of the program—the idea of the bourgeoisie's failure to speak for the nation and hence of the subaltern sphere remaining a domain separate from elite culture—was announced famously in the very first volume, and has continued to serve as the foundation for the rest of the project. Much of the subsequent evolution of Subaltern Studies can be understood as a very ambitious project to tease out the consequences of this momentous fact about colonial history.

Thirdly, the arguments associated with the Subalterns do in fact resonate with much of the larger field. Some of these are:

- An insistence on locating the specificity of the East and on examining how and why its evolution differs from that of the West.

- A focus on culture and forms of consciousness as objects of study and a source of historical difference.
- The insistence that subaltern groups in the East operate with their own political calculus and forms of consciousness, different from that of elite groups and from what is projected onto them by Western theory.
- The insistence on purging social theory of its Eurocentric bias and the claim that Western theories are heavily imbued with this bias, Marxism included.
- A boilerplate skepticism toward universalizing discourse, and hence toward many of the theories emanating from the Enlightenment tradition.
- Skepticism toward modernizing discourses, and their defense of rationality, science, objectivity, etc.

These are all absolutely central themes for Subaltern Studies, and they are also at the very heart of postcolonial studies more generally. Indeed, the Subalternists have probably done the most of any group to give real historical and sociological ballast to postcolonial studies. Rather than just asserting that there is an ontological divide of some kind dividing East from West, they try to provide real historical arguments for its plausibility. And the arguments they have developed have been enormously influential, especially since the late 1990s. By the turn of this century, the Subalternists were widely recognized as being the most influential of all the empirically oriented streams within the field—to the point that many of their arguments achieved the status of being encapsulated in new buzzwords, instantly recognizable—nationalism as a "derivative discourse," rescuing "the fragment," the task of "provincializing Europe." One could even hazard a guess that certain key concepts, which they borrowed from others, like "subaltern" or "dominance without hegemony," are as much associated with them as with the terms' originators.[3] In sum, while Subaltern Studies does not itself comprise postcolonial theory, it is one of the best exemplars of the latter's core arguments. In other words, while it does not exhaust the field, it is very much representative of it. Indeed, it is more than that. I did not randomly select Subaltern Studies as but one of many exemplars of postcolonial theory. I settled on it because it is actually better argued, more coherent, and more consistent than much of the rest. Thus, it is hard to find more careful arguments in postcolonial studies explicating why capitalism, and hence modernity, in the East is taken to be fundamentally different from the West, or for why the claims of universalizing theories ought to be resisted.

All this was in the introductory chapter of *PTSC*. Spivak may object to my reasoning, but the decision was not arbitrary, as Spivak seems to suggest. If she feels that it lacked warrant, then she is obliged to at least offer some reason for this judgment, which she does not. The reader is left with a sense that I closed my eyes and plucked a random assortment of theorists out of the basket.

RANAJIT GUHA AND THE STATUS OF PRIMARY TEXTS

A most significant contribution of Subaltern Studies to the development of postcolonial theory is its historical argument for why the political culture of the East is fundamentally different from that of the West. I argue that Ranajit Guha's work is the pivot on which this argument turns, and Spivak seems to agree with my placement of him. Guha argues, famously, that the source of East–West divergence can be found in the divergent characters of the bourgeoisie in the two settings. In the paradigmatic Western experience of England and France, the bourgeoisie led a successful project to capture state power and then create an encompassing, inclusive political culture based on the consent of the dominated classes—it strove, in his words, to "speak on behalf of all the nation." In the East, however, it abandoned any such ambitions and chose to sustain its rule by political coercion, perpetuating the division between the elite and subaltern spheres. This historic failure on the part of the bourgeoisie signalled a structural mutation in capitalism as it left Western shores—a stalling of its universalizing drive. Capitalism in the colonial world failed to properly universalize, evidenced in its failure to create a consensual, liberal political order. Other Subalternists derive from this their famous conclusion that this break in capital's universalizing drive is why theories built on the assumption of that universalization—liberalism and Marxism— cannot find purchase in the (post-)colonial world.

The argument for capital's failed universalization is the foundation on which much of the Subalternist project rests. I show in some detail in *PTSC*—over the course of five chapters—that it is deeply flawed and cannot be sustained in any form. Partha Chatterjee[4] has responded to my arguments with a quite brazen falsehood—that Guha simply does not say what I attribute to him, even though Guha makes it clear in the first twenty-five pages of his book that this is exactly what he is arguing, and then confirms it throughout the course of his text.[5] Spivak now joins the fray with an even more novel stratagem, one that I could never have anticipated—she censures my criticism of Guha not because it is mistaken but because Guha's work has the status of a "primary text," and one does not criticize primary texts.

I read and carefully re-read Spivak's argument here, because it seems impossible to imagine that anyone could believe what she so cavalierly announces. But there is no other way to interpret her—Spivak thinks that there is a class of scholarship, which she calls "primary texts," whose members are to be memorialized and interpreted, but never *assessed*. The task of criticism is to be reserved for something called "secondary texts." What the difference is between them we are never told. But, whatever it is, Guha falls on the protected side of it. To drive the point home, Spivak asks us rhetorically, "Would Chibber correct Rosa Luxemburg and D. D. Kosambi? No, because he knows they are primary texts."[6] I am not sure what to say here. Not only would I feel *free* to criticize Luxemburg and Kosambi, but I would be *obligated* to do so if their theories or their scholarship were flawed. And not only would I respect this obligation, but so have generations of scholars and activists the world over. The distinction that Spivak urges upon us, and the attitude to it endorsed by her, would shut down most of the academy. It is an essentially theological mindset, properly belonging in a church or temple, not a university.

Spivak does propose one other justification for why my criticisms of Guha are misplaced, which needs to be taken seriously. She suggests that my criticism rests on a category mistake. I criticize Guha's argument for being empirically and theoretically flawed—his historical account of the bourgeois revolutions is unsustainable, and his understanding of capital's universalizing mission is mistaken. Because of this, his explanation for the colonial world's political dynamics also largely fails. Spivak offers that this is like criticizing Du Bois for calling the exodus of slaves a "general strike," or criticizing Aristotle's *Poetics* as "illogical."[7] The Aristotle example suggests that certain kinds of criticisms are misplaced because they misunderstand the very nature of the text they interrogate. The text is not vulnerable to the criticism being leveled at it because of the nature of its project. Spivak is right that criticism of this kind is jejune. But it should be self-evident that such is not the case in my treatment of Guha. Guha's arguments are eminently subject to both empirical and theoretical assessment, because they are claims about how the world works, and about the character of historical events. Hence, this defense is no more successful than the call for deference to primary texts.

CAPITAL AND CAPITALISM, BOURGEOISIE AND CAPITALISTS

Spivak further contends that my criticism of Guha elides the difference between capital and capitalism, and erroneously equates capitalists with the bourgeoisie. Let me start with the claim that capitalists cannot be identified with "the bourgeoisie." This is the same argument that Partha Chatterjee used in his riposte, and I will respond to it only briefly, referring the interested reader to my fuller treatment of his argument elsewhere.

Here is what is at stake. Guha castigates the Indian bourgeoisie for failing to integrate the subaltern domain with that of the elites, and, in this, falling short of the historic achievements of the bourgeoisie in Western Europe. I show that the bourgeoisie in England and France never aspired to, or strove for, the goals that Guha ascribes to them, and that, in fact, they were as contemptuous of subaltern interests as their later Indian counterparts. The question here is: what does Guha mean by "bourgeoisie"? I show in *PTSC* that he means "capitalists," and I offer more evidence for this in subsequent work. Spivak now claims that "bourgeoisie" means lawyers and intellectuals, not capitalists. But, however Spivak may wish to define the concept, it is abundantly clear that when Guha uses it he simply refers to capitalists. Spivak is creating an entirely fictitious Guha here, one who only exists in her imagination.

As to my elision of the difference between capital and capitalism, let me start by cautioning the reader that, *pace* Spivak, there is no established convention regarding the distinction. Usually, "capital" is taken to mean "capitalists," people whose actions propel the accumulation process, whereas "capitalism" is used to denote the properties of the social structure in which these actors are located. But there is plenty of room for theorists to take some license with how they use these terms. So when scholars intend to deploy the two as distinct concepts, they usually alert the reader to what each one is supposed to convey. Otherwise, one usually has to glean the intention of the writer by more indirect means, attending to the context, the apparent intention, the place of the argument, and so forth. It is not uncommon for the two to be used interchangeably.

Guha nowhere introduces the distinction in a systematic way and hence never tells us what he means by the two terms. The reader has to infer their meaning by attending to the context. What we do know is that the entity that is supposed to have had its universalizing mission derailed is "capital." But, depending on the context, this expression can mean either capitalists or capitalism. So, for example, it can mean, "When capitalists came to India they did not pursue the same goals as they did in England"; or it can mean, "The capitalism that took root in India did not expand in the same way that it had in England." Guha usually has in mind the first claim when he makes his argument—he is usually referring to political or economic aspirations of the capitalist class. But sometimes he means the second. More importantly, since the two are closely related, the gap between them is not that large. None of this is either very deep or mysterious.

If Spivak feels that I have misunderstood Guha because I elide the distinction, she needs to show that such is the case. In normal academic discourse, when such an accusation is made, the critic offers some evidence to substantiate it by adducing key passages that have been misunderstood, showing how the argument has been distorted through the elision. Spivak clearly acknowledges that I am aware of the distinction between capital and capitalism, so she cannot think that I am blind to it.[8] Which of its subtleties, then, do I miss? I confess that her argument here is almost impossible to understand. The only clear instance she adduces of an apparent elision is when she quotes me as asking: what does capitalism universalize? She then quotes me answering it with reference to capital, not capitalism.[9] So apparently I have substituted one for the other. But I am not doing any such thing. What I say is: capitalism imposes a certain logic upon capital, and by "capital" I mean capitalists. Hence, the structural location of certain actors forces a particular strategy of economic reproduction upon them. I am not ignoring a distinction here; I am in fact utilizing it. The only confusion here is on Spivak's part.

"Little Britain Marxism"

Spivak's only other significant accusation is that my book is a defense of a narrow, boxed-set kind of Marxism which refuses to budge from its orthodoxies. This has become a quite common refrain from postcolonial critics of the book. It is not unusual to see my case against the Subalternists rephrased as they "are not Marxist enough," or that they are wrong because they have the "wrong kind of Marxism." The idea is that I simply hold up their arguments to a fixed set of orthodoxies, and in instances where they deviate from the latter I reject them out of hand. So the battle is apparently between open-ended, creative Subalternists, trying to expand received theory to make sense of a complex reality, and the stolid, unyielding Marxists who cast out anyone who dares to question Holy Writ.

But the accusation is nonsense. In *PTSC*, I do not make a single criticism of the Subalternists on the grounds that their work is a deviation from Marxist orthodoxy. Nor do I defend any of my own by proving its closer fidelity to Marx. Each and every argument I make—whether against the Subalternists or in defense of my own views—is defended on independent grounds, whether empirical or conceptual. There is only one chapter that takes up Marx directly, Chapter 6, where I take up the question of abstract labor. Even in this case, I apologize for having to descend into Marxology,[10] and then try to show that it is worthwhile, not because it was developed by Marx, but because it captures some interesting facts about capitalism. The only other instance in which I bring up Marxology is in Chapter 4, where I criticize Marx for his credulousness toward liberal historiography. Every other argument I make is developed by reference to facts about the world, or conceptual clarification. And every criticism of the Subalternists issues from the same criteria. The arguments offered by Subaltern Studies are to be rejected because they are wrong, not because they stray from orthodoxy.

Spivak knows this, and it is why she is worried enough to write her long attack. If the book had just been a Marxist screed against the heretics, it would have died a quiet death. The reason it has attracted attention is precisely because it is not the "Little Britain Marxism" that Spivak accuses it of being, but an examination of Subalternist arguments on their own terms—by attending to the empirical and theoretical strength of their claims. As for Marxism, there is in fact plenty in the received orthodoxy that is either mistaken or questionable. To give some examples:

- The orthodox theory of historical materialism is almost certainly wrong.[11]
- The labor theory of value may very well be wrong, and if it is not, it can only be defended in modified form.
- The traditional theory of bourgeois revolutions is definitely wrong, as I explain in great detail in *PTSC*.
- Marxism still has a poorly developed moral theory, though that situation is now greatly remedied.

There is quite an extensive literature on these subjects, and I have contributed to some of it, all of which acknowledges and seeks to remedy deep flaws in orthodox formulation. There are plenty of other weaknesses in the theory, but I have listed these only because they are considered to be at the very heart of Marxist orthodoxy. So it is not that Marxist theory is not in need of serious modification, or that it does not have severe weaknesses. It is just that, whatever weaknesses it has, they are not the ones targeted by postcolonial theorists. The biggest problem with postcolonial theory is that it seeks to undermine the very areas of Marxist theory that ought to be retained, that are in fact its strengths—the reality of capitalist constraints, regardless of culture; the reality of human nature; the centrality of certain universal aspirations on the part of the oppressed, which issue from this human nature; the need for abstract, universal concepts that are valid across cultures; the necessity of rational, reasoned discourse, and so forth. And the reason these propositions need to be defended is not that they comprise a doctrine that Marxists seek to uphold, but because they are defensible on their own merits. It has long been a tactic of postcolonial theorists to offer their framework as not only a direct lineal descendant of Marxist theory—which it is not—but also as the only sustainable version of Marxism—which it is emphatically not. Any criticism of their arguments is thereby impugned as an unthinking adherence to orthodoxy, or a search for doctrinal purity. Spivak's characterization of *PTSC* as "Little Britain Marxism" is but the latest incarnation of this, and readers should not be misled by it.

Conclusion

The sad fact is that, apart from the few points that I have taken up above, there is very little in Spivak's essay to which one can respond. To be sure, there is no shortage of accusations, some pertaining to exegesis, others to logic or theory. Spivak certainly seems to feel strongly that *PTSC* is guilty of many sins. But this makes it all the more curious that she expends little or no effort doing what any honest critic would do—taking the time to read the text carefully, locate its flaws, demonstrate to the reader that the argument is indeed guilty of the mistakes of which it is accused.

Indeed, what stands out most about the essay is how it eschews the normal protocols of scholarship in favor of other, less savory tactics. And I would be remiss to say nothing about it, since it is so egregious. There is a very powerful authoritarian thrust in Spivak's essay. It is not just the deferential attitude that one is supposed to display toward certain texts and authorities. It is not just the exalted status of "primary texts." A required genuflection to authority pervades the text. It is surprising to find repeated references to someone's age—the fact that Guha is ninety years old—or to their storied past, or to their fame in the intellectual world, or to their social work during the summer. These are not random facts that Spivak offers the reader; they are bits of information doled out to contrast the worthiness of some people—Guha and Spivak in this case—with the brash, "boyish" critic who is obsessed with "correcting everybody," a "correct-fetishist," as she refers to me. Spivak seems genuinely perturbed, not by the substance of my criticism, but by the very act of it. I am upbraided for not being sufficiently awestruck by the distinction of those whom I have targeted for criticism. The imperious tone, the constant reminder of status, whether based on age or on academic and social standing, is quite shocking to witness in an academic paper. The only place I have ever seen it before was while growing up in India, where it was used with servants and children to remind them of their place in the order of things.

Perhaps this may explain why Spivak does not bother to base her arguments on evidence or logic. Evidence matters if you are trying to persuade someone through argument, not appeals to authority. Spivak, however, writes in the manner of someone long accustomed to treating those around her as supplicants, not colleagues. One would not be much concerned with this, were it not for the fact that at least two generations of students have been socialized into this kind of practice. I doubt that Spivak's style of engagement would be tolerated in any other discipline. So much the worse for postcolonial studies.

CHAPTER 5

Subaltern-Speak

Bruce Robbins

How do you tell the history of the world? Not long ago this question would have seemed naive. The only people enthusiastic about universal history were complacent idiots who thought that history had ended with the Cold War and the twin triumphs of democracy and globalization, or that it was moving toward an ever fuller manifestation of the glory of the Western way of life. Raining on their parade felt like a civic duty.

Those days are gone. Even the idiots are no longer complacent. Now they worry about the decline of American power and the rise of China; they scramble for a techno-fix for global warming and other looming resource-related catastrophes. Few Whig interpretations of history are left afloat. Sinking them no longer seems the most productive way to spend your time. Meanwhile, urgent reasons have made themselves felt (see above) for trying to make sense of history on a planetary scale. And it seems quite possible to do so without being Whiggish about it.

This planet is home to a large number of nations, societies, regions, cultures, communities, and other variably sized human collectivities. Each is, of course, unique. Each has a legitimate claim to a history of its own. Do these claims mean that no single overarching history is possible? The somewhat obscure impulse behind Vivek Chibber's polemical and much-debated book is to establish that such a history is both possible and desirable. His motive, stated somewhere in the middle of his book, is "to tie together the political struggles of laboring classes in East and West as part of one—dare I say it—universal history." Whatever doubts I have about the peculiar version of universal history he comes up with, and I have several, I'm glad he dared.

The target of Chibber's polemic is not postcolonial theory as a whole, about which he says almost nothing. (Verso should have asked him to drop the portentously inaccurate title.) His target is Subaltern Studies, the field created by a group of left-wing historians of South Asia who began publishing in the early 1980s. The Subalterns—represented in Chibber's book by Ranajit Guha, Dipesh Chakrabarty, and Partha Chatterjee, and who also include David Arnold, Gyanendra Pandey, and Shahid Amin, among others (Gayatri Spivak is a sort of fellow traveler)—wrote from within Marxism but against what Chakrabarty called the "deep-seated, crude materialism of the 'matter over mind' variety" implicitly attributed to orthodox Marxism. Crude materialism, these historians argued, did not give enough credit to the culture, consciousness, or experience of India's poorest. There was also an immediate political context that spurred the historiographic question. In the late 1960s and 70s, India's most oppressed had risen up in what came to be known as the Naxalite insurgency, and received less than full-throated support from the established Marxist parties. When Guha and Chatterjee researched peasant revolts against colonial officials and landlords or strikes in Calcutta's jute mills, they were calling attention to a resistant agency for which even the anti-colonial Left seemed unable or unwilling to find a proper place.

The problem, the Subalterns said, was that this agency was articulated in an "archaic" vocabulary—religious, superstitious, hierarchical, premodern—that did not translate into the modern, autonomous, egalitarian subjectivity that Marxism predicted would emerge under capitalism. Capitalism, though very much present in India, showed no sign of dispelling the older social formations that had stalled over India like permanent bad weather. The Subalterns argued the reason lay with the undeveloped colonial "comprador" bourgeoisie, who were completely unlike their structural counterparts in Europe and had failed, during the Indian independence movement, to assume a similarly revolutionary role, leaving the poorer and less powerful classes—the "subaltern" strata—unintegrated into the nation. India, in other words, hadn't followed the path established by liberal or Marxist theories of development, which were outlined from European models and therefore ill-fitted to the postcolonial situation. In Europe, "history from below," which flourished in the creatively revisionist hands of

Marxist historians like E. P. Thompson and Eric Hobsbawm, had been inspired in part by the actual disappearance of Europe's peasantry. In India, the peasantry was not disappearing. On the contrary, an expanding capitalism was somehow reproducing it with all its feudal quirks intact. Archaism remained culturally dominant across the board. Chatterjee made a point of mentioning "industrial capitalists delaying the closing of a deal because they hadn't yet had word from their respective astrologers."

The historians were split on the relationship between the expansion of capitalism and the stubborn persistence of the peasantry. On the one hand, it meant that capitalism was not as powerful as some people thought. At the same time, it meant that the Indian peasantry was more powerful; precisely those qualities (handcraft, superstition, and so on) that did not neatly fit the Western narrative of historical progress were unassimilable by capitalism and therefore a bulwark against it, a potential rallying site for resistance. Guha's interpretation—summed up in *Dominance without Hegemony* (1998)—placed its emphasis elsewhere, on the frustrated role of the bourgeoisie, but his premise was the same: in order to flourish, capitalism needed to subsume nearly everything under its implacable logic, something that manifestly hadn't happened in India.

Generalized, this defense of the cultural specificities of the downtrodden became a polemic against universalizing materialist history as such. To "provincialize Europe," in Chakrabarty's phrase, for the Subalterns did not mean giving up a European vocabulary—far from it—but it did seem to entail rejecting all meta- or master narratives. This not only meant that Eurocentric theories were inadequate to the postcolony, but that the experience of the latter should drastically revise our opinion of the former, and throw in doubt any attempt to universalize based on a single model. Heavily implicated was the particular meta-narrative supposedly established by Marxism, which saw a universalizing, homogenizing capitalism expanding at the expense of cultural difference. "In Defense of the Fragment," an essay by Gyanendra Pandey, strikes the characteristic note. Those who "reduce the lives of men and women to the play of material interests, or at other times to large impersonal movements in economy and society over which human beings have no control," Pandey says, are leaving out human agency. In effect, they leave out India itself. Fragments are the prescribed therapy.

Why was this scholarship such a huge international hit? How did a small group of mainly South Asian historians suddenly get to be world famous? How did they become the symbol of an intellectual paradigm so powerful that Chibber (and others) would come to feel they must be publicly humbled and even humiliated? For one thing, their timing was good. Along with the term "subaltern," they borrowed from the Italian Communist Antonio Gramsci an analysis of how the Italian movement of national independence had failed to integrate significant portions of the population. The Subalterns diagnosed a parallel failure. As in Italy, so in postcolonial India: anti-colonial leaders had cared more about shoring up their own niche in post-Independence society than about representing the whole of the nation, and the new nation-state had left much of the nation unrepresented. The Subalterns' analysis also arrived at a moment when the nationalisms of the decolonizing nations were coming to be perceived—by their own people and international observers alike—as exhausted. Kenya, Uganda, and Indonesia, stars of the Bandung Conference in 1955, in subsequent years had succumbed to dictatorships; India nearly did the same during the Emergency, and the years that followed were ones of persistent economic malaise. To the question *Why did Third World nationalism fail?* many answers could be given. But the Subalterns' answer—that it was wrong from the start, because it had not integrated the poorest of the poor into its project—proved, at least in the academy, to be persuasive.

In the US, Subaltern Studies caught the postcolonial wave (Edward Said's field-creating *Orientalism* had been published in 1978). It also got a great deal of momentum from American-style multiculturalism. If Subaltern Studies was to unseat other, political-economy–based accounts of the unhappy trajectory of the Third World, including Immanuel Wallerstein's world-systems theory and Latin American dependency theory (anticipated, Vinay Bahl has noted, by India's own drain theory), it would need some powerful endorsements. American academia's hypersensitivity to the culture of the Other gave it the needed political oomph. It did not hurt that, like postcolonialism, the Subaltern project of retrieving backward or traditional worldviews had recourse to the most sophisticated, cutting-edge theories of post-structuralist interpretation. Necessarily so, one might say, given that these worldviews had not recorded themselves directly in written transcripts; continental theory offered ways of seeing and productively interpreting silences and gaps in a text. It was certainly a transnational and interdisciplinary selling point for the Subalterns: their content was local and piously traditional while their methodology was global and glossily modern.

Later scholarship in Subaltern Studies followed currents elsewhere in the humanities and social sciences. Influenced by Foucault, the Subalterns questioned the power relations that created the archival sources they were unearthing (*Who produced them? And for what?*). Partha Chatterjee's *Nationalist Thought and the Colonial World* (1986) refined the categories of orientalism for examining power and culture under nationalism. Gayatri Spivak's 1988 essay "Can the Subaltern Speak?" questioned whether it was possible to recover the voices of the truly disadvantaged, and introduced deconstruction into the discourse of Subaltern Studies. In an otherwise sympathetic introduction to a selection of their work in 1992, Spivak criticized their lack of attention to questions of gender. It was a criticism the Subalterns took seriously: subsequent writing by Susie Tharu, as well as Guha and Chatterjee, has tried to remedy the gap. Chakrabarty's own *Provincializing Europe* (2000) assimilated these strands while also attempting to advance them, trying to tease out a notion of modernity that did not rely on Europe as its model and everything else as mimicry.

Early critiques of the Subalterns were sometimes factional (*Do I detect vestigial Maoism?*) and sometimes regional (*Why should South Asia provide the paradigm rather than, say, China? Does all this apply to Africa?*). Much has been made of their skepticism about Western rationality and their corresponding taste for postmodern critics of that rationality, like Foucault and Derrida. Others have questioned their habit of using "elitist" as a killing put-down, which the influence of Foucault and Derrida has ironically served to moderate. Anti-elitism is a dangerous position if (as is often the case) the person making the charge is himself a member of an elite. The fact that Guha comes from the class of absentee landlords he analyzed in *A Rule of Property for Bengal* was first mentioned, it should be said, by Guha himself.

Chibber's polemic represents an emerging and much more profound debate. Taking Subaltern Studies as symbolic of a wider intellectual failure, he asserts in its place the validity and explanatory power of a renewed and unapologetic Marxism, and with it the Enlightenment universals that it relied on. In the view of thinkers like Chibber, the charge that Marxist theory suffers from "Eurocentrism"— represented by decades of thinking, entire libraries of books, and hundreds of academic departments—is sterile and empty. Drawing a line in the sand naturally makes both sides upset, and the debate over Chibber's book has been heated. The field was sowed when his less guarded, even more polemical thoughts about the bankruptcy of Subaltern Studies came out in an interview with *Jacobin*: "When Subalternist theorists put up this gigantic wall separating East from West, and when they insist that Western agents are not driven by the same kinds of concerns as Eastern agents, what they're doing is endorsing the kind of essentialism that colonial authorities used to justify their depredations in the 19th century," he said. "It's the same kind of essentialism that American military apologists used when they were bombing Vietnam or when they were going into the Middle East. Nobody on the left can be at ease with these sorts of arguments." The interview seems at times almost unhinged. A widely read critique by Chris Taylor, an English professor at the University of Chicago, published under the title, "Not Even Marxist," argued that Chibber mistakenly forced readers to "choose sides" between Subaltern Studies and Marxism; moreover, Chibber's brand of Marxism, Taylor suggested, was a bad one. This received a riposte at Verso's blog ("Not Even Marxist?"), which got fought over in turn. The closing session of the Historical Materialism conference at NYU in April 2013 was a debate between Partha Chatterjee and Chibber, and was advertised like it was the return of Ali vs. Frazier.

The heatedness of the debates that flared up around Chibber's book has to do with the place of honor it gives to the showdown between universalism and culture. Chibber's impatience with culturalist interpretation—that is, interpretation that doesn't merely deal with culture but wants to demonstrate how unnecessary and misleading it is to talk about the economic at all—is now widely shared. In an era when purely cultural explanations are no longer as persuasive, "economic determinism" loses its force as a smear. It would be surprising if Chibber's book had not benefited from this development. *Postcolonial Theory and the Specter of Capital* comes bearing endorsements from a political philosopher (Joshua Cohen), an economic historian (Robert Brenner), Noam Chomsky, and, well, Zizek.

According to Chibber, the fact that the world contains many cultures does not get in the way of the project of a universal history. The reason is simple: cultural particularity does not get in the way of capitalism. Guha, according to Chibber, "never considers the possibility that the expansion of capital's economic logic simply did not require the kind of deep cultural transformations that he thinks it does. He does not consider that capital might be able to meet its basic needs by relying on the very cultural forms he thinks are inimical to it—those typical of traditional political economies, suffused with outdated forms of social hierarchy and subordination." It should be no surprise, then, that kinship and religious affiliations have not been swept away by the capitalist tide. It was rational that they be retained both from the viewpoint of labor—they helped rural workers get jobs and survive in the city—and from the viewpoint of capital: employers could use these feudal remnants to weaken their workforces by fomenting splits along caste and other lines. To maintain your cultural identity may make you feel good, but it does nothing to withstand capitalism, which (Chibber repeats) "does not have to obliterate social differences in order to universalize itself."

This point has enormous implications. In a critique of Chakrabarty that also departs from common opinion in the cultural disciplines (by which Chibber as a sociologist is clearly irritated), he insists that the famous line from the *Communist Manifesto* ("all that is solid melts into air") does not after all describe what capitalism characteristically does to the world. It can collaborate with local cultures perfectly well. If it is frustrated, it's no doubt for reasons that have nothing to do with culture—for example, because of pushback by labor unions. In Chibber's eyes, the bar for significant resistance must be set higher than mere persistence in one's identity.

Chibber's position has an immediate payoff. It reminds us that there are things to which capitalism is basically indifferent—things that neither help nor hinder it, and that it in turn does not do much to help or hinder. So the particular cultural forces that would seem to be resistant to capitalism turn out not to be. This has a common-sense verifiability to it. The conspicuous success of capitalism (with all its variations) in places as distinct as China and the UAE suggests, on the face of it anyway, that culture is not always a barrier to capitalism.

In pressing his claim against the significance of the cultural particularity of the Indian peasant, Chibber can be a little nasty. At one point, anticipating his public remarks about the book and Vietnam, he makes the claim that the Subalterns are guilty of orientalism. This is too much, and yet, in fairness, the premise that the Indian peasantry can be defined in such a way that no one who is not an Indian peasant can understand it, as the Subalterns sometimes seem to assume, is almost irritating enough to justify Chibber's rhetorical overkill. No doubt there are aspects of a peasant's experience (as of anyone's) that won't compute as simple self-interest. But for purposes like labor organization and political mobilization, it cannot be taken for granted that those perhaps impenetrable mysteries will determine anyone's behavior. In a discussion of Partha Chatterjee's research on peasant uprisings in 1920s and 1930s Bengal, Chibber credits the valuable empirical description but disputes Chatterjee's explanatory emphasis on a distinctive (and religious) peasant consciousness. To my untrained eye, Chibber makes satisfactory sense of the political behavior of the Bengali peasants in terms of their material interests and without reference to a supposedly unique peasant psychology or sense of community.

Chibber's book makes it clear (once again) that the real problem with respect for the particular is infinite regress. Is it the peasant as such who is the Other of the bourgeois? Or just the Indian peasant? Why are generalizations about the Indian peasant not guilty of ignoring the specificity of the Bihari peasant, or of peasants from the Bihari town of Bhagalpur, or of the Bhagalpuris last Tuesday? Once the anti-generalization machine gets going, there is no stopping it. Better to bite the bullet: understanding entails generalizing. If you don't like it, you can take a time-out in the corner. But don't complain that you feel misunderstood.

Any history from below naturally provokes the charge of essentializing and/or idealizing the worldview of the lowly, and the related objection that it rejects any perspective on the lowly from above,

whether that of the West or that of native bourgeois leaders and intellectuals, including Marxist ones. These charges were leveled against
Subaltern Studies from the outset, and they will always have a certain
amount of truth to them.

Chibber himself does not seem to object to history from below. He
accuses the Subalterns of being anti-Western, but not of being antibourgeois. On the contrary, for him they are not antibourgeois enough.
Maneuvering to outflank Guha on the left, he argues that to accuse the
Indian middle classes of failing in their historic mission to bring rights
and democracy to the subaltern strata, as Guha does, is to be all too
admiring of the bourgeoisie. Chibber's own thinking is more good
guy/bad guy. Piously but implausibly, Chibber gives all the historical
credit for so-called bourgeois democracy to the efforts of the working
class. He does not ask why, if the laboring classes have an elective affinity with democratic rights and liberties, things turned out as they did
in post-1917 Russia or Maoist China. He chooses not to recognize
political complications, past or present, that have given pause to fellow
Marxists and that might compromise the unspotted virtue of his
collective protagonist. If the Subalterns idealize the *culture* of the peasant laborers, Chibber idealizes them just as much, but he idealizes
their *political rationality.*

Whatever else has changed in their thinking, the Subalterns have
always kept a watchful eye out for lazy Eurocentrism. Chibber rather
artfully turns the tables by trying to catch Guha in the act of slavishly
applying to India a European paradigm that doesn't even work in
Europe, let alone India. Guha's extremely influential reading of Indian
independence drew on an extended contrast with the English
Revolution of the 1640s and the French Revolution of 1789. According
to Guha, both the English and the French revolutions managed to
achieve what Gramsci called "hegemony"—a mode of rule involving
to an appreciable degree the consent of the governed. The Indian bourgeoisie on the other hand failed to integrate the lower orders, and the
outcome was "domination" (rule involving less consent and more
physical coercion). This set the stage for the catastrophic exclusion of
the lower orders from national life after independence, the pervasive-
ness of feudal habits of mind, and the lack of a modernizing "bourgeois revolution" across Indian society, as mentioned above.

Trying to undermine Guha's standard of comparison, Chibber disputes the sociology behind this account of both European revolutions. He argues (here I abbreviate radically) that the English Civil War was not anti-feudal (because feudalism in England was already dead) but only a contest within the landed classes over absolute monarchy. And he argues that the French Revolution was not pro-capitalist (because no actual capitalists were present on the scene). He concedes that some seemingly progressive things happened, but they happened only thanks to uprisings from below. Chibber sees these political accomplishments as grudgingly supported by the supposed revolutionaries and in any case quickly and violently rolled back by the forces of counterrevolution. Coercion has always been a large part of the capitalist order. Consent has not been. Dominance without hegemony is the norm in both India and in Europe.

This sounds attractively universal, but it is also wrong, and what is wrong with it gets to the heart of what is wrong with Chibber's book, and with the state of thinking about universal history. If feudalism in England had already been overthrown by 1640, when and how did that happen? Could something as large as feudalism simply disappear without causing any political commotion, without anyone noticing? Is that how the most momentous social changes tend to occur, without any revolutionary tumult, without any changes from deep within society? If so, then politics would seem to be trivial—and economics, now decoupled from it, would also find its duties as an explanatory agent much reduced. In sacrificing the causal connection between politics and economics, Chibber is selling off Marxism's most valued asset: the power to make sense of what happens. If capitalism's rise was not a significant cause of political events in the past, like the French Revolution, then so much the worse for Marxism as a guide to history, whether in the past or in the future.

Chibber's understanding of European history seems to take place in a vacuum; his account of the contemporary world suffers from a similar blind spot. He does not even try to account for the Great Divergence between capitalism in the style of IKEA and capitalism in the style of Rana Plaza. The question of what is specific about capitalism in the East is not posed until page 290 of a 296-page book. As for the West, Chibber's sole point (not an uninteresting one) is that it is less different from the East than it thinks. The West has its political liberties, he says, but even there "capitalists mobilize all available means to increase their power in the organization of work." This is true, but those means are not universally available, and their local unavailability is a fact of some importance. The United Automobile Workers are no longer the force in society they once were, and yet they remain strong enough to ensure that flogging does not happen on the shop floor. If, like Chibber, you insinuate that flogging on the shop floor is the universal norm, readers will suspect that you are not inspecting the premises very seriously.

Chibber is reluctant to march under the banner of "rational choice," to which he allots one brief footnote, but "rational choice Marxism" is probably the best category for him. He is a materialist, but not a dialectical one. His is the pre-dialectical, individualist materialism of self-interest and basic needs. Chibber says he wants a universal history, but his rational choice premises make such a history impossible, or at least dangerously impoverished. His idea of the universal is, well, particular: for him there are only two universals, capital's drive to universalize itself and the attempts of the poor to defend their well-being. Gender and race don't count as universals. What is universal is the self-interested individual. If that were the case, what could history be but an eternal repetition of the same? The rich and powerful will try again and again to maintain and increase their power and riches. Those most injured by their efforts will do what they can to defend themselves. Presumably the dominant class always has, and presumably the oppressed always will. This model unifies East and West under a single principle, but it's an unenlightening principle. The terms of the merger that generates this universal history ensure that it will remain empty and unproductive—not really a history at all.

Here I am somewhat overstating the case. Chibber knows that change has happened, just as he knows that East and West, while sharing a single modern capitalism, have had significantly different experiences of it. He is right to resist explanations of this difference that appeal exclusively or even primarily to culture, which is permanent, rather than to situation, which changes. But he cannot have the universal history that he wants, and makes us want, unless he is willing to give up on the timeless monster he describes as the "asocial individual, hovering above his culture, ranking his preferences and remorselessly disposing of social relations as they lose value on his utility meter."

Where, then, is universal history to be found? In a talk in Shanghai in 2010 about "the West" and what it has meant to modern India, Chakrabarty ended on a surprising note. He conceded that while holding India in "the vise grip of power," Europe had also "created a room for dialogical maneuvers" by exhibiting "enough contradictions within herself to provide the colonized with terms with which to criticize her doings." Then he wondered aloud whether "the prospect of China and India taking their place among the dominant nations of the world," which he welcomed, would "help create new visions of humanity and help humans achieve justice and fairness in a world racked by problems of planetary proportions." His Chinese hosts would have been correct, I think, in perceiving in this a diplomatic hint: that their coming hegemony, while good news in a sense, would not be good news in every sense and thus would require tools of self-critique, as European hegemony had.

Here Chakrabarty hits the true dialectical tonality. Trying to see the big picture at the scale of the Anthropocene, as he demands of his listeners, is a far cry from treasuring every fragment, the tinier and more chipped the better. It's got to feel uncomfortable for all concerned. Your moral and political categories are suddenly less certain, more relative. Chakrabarty looks further into the political future but also further into the past, where the atrocities committed by European colonialism blur together with the conquest and slaughter, plunder and rapine, perpetrated by centuries of non-Europeans. Until recently this larger scale has been the preserve of undialectical materialists like Steven Pinker, who saw history as one continuous process of moral evolution, centered in the European Enlightenment, thereby letting Europe off the hook. A new universal history will not want to do that, but it will want to reclaim this scary scale for itself, this time in a dialectical mode: one that is never quite sure where the struggle for equality is located, only that it's there.

CHAPTER 6

Reply to Bruce Robbins

Vivek Chibber

Since its release in March, the response to *Postcolonial Theory and the Specter of Capital* has, in many ways, been as I expected. From the followers and practitioners of postcolonial theory itself, there has been the predicted hysteria and vitriol. But what has been gratifying, what I did not expect at all, is the steady stream of positive responses, even from within cultural studies and even from some quarters of postcolonial theory. Bruce Robbins's review falls somewhere in between. His tone for most of it is respectful, sometimes positive. He quite ably sets the context for the book's arguments and tries to lay out what is at stake. In this, he rises above the mudslinging that has been the resort of some of his colleagues. But once he sets out his own criticisms, the essay degenerates into a series of distortions and misconceptions. What makes them interesting, and worth responding to, is that they converge with misgivings that even sympathetic readers have expressed. Hence, although Robbins presents them in a very telescoped form, with the predictable helping of snides and cheap shots, they are worth responding to, mainly because of their resonance with other criticisms. I can only give a flavor of the arguments I need to make, since this is a short essay. A longer response will have to wait for another occasion.

The crux of Robbins's criticism comes at the end of his review, and it comes down to three issues: whether my views of the English Revolution of 1640 and/or 1688 are defensible; whether my framework can apprehend the difference between East and West; and whether my materialism is really a restatement of rational choice theory. Robbins quite summarily dismisses my arguments on all three counts. I wish to show here that all of his criticisms are mistaken.

Let us start with the English Revolution. In *PTSC* I examined whether Ranajit Guha's view about the events of 1640 were correct.

Guha, in essence, understands 1640 to be an instance of a "bourgeois-democratic revolution," in which the emergent capitalist class undertakes and accomplishes two goals—the eradication of feudal landed relations, and the establishment of a liberal, consensual political order. I showed that this view is irredeemably flawed, and that it sets up an illusory contrast between the history of the bourgeoisie in the East as against the West. First, the English Revolution was not a war between a rising bourgeoisie and the *ancien régime*, for the economy was already largely capitalist. Second, and most importantly, the victorious post-revolutionary regime had no interest in, and did not establish, the liberal, encompassing, consensual order that Guha attributes to it. In fact it strove mightily to squelch what democratic rights there were. What the revolution bequeathed was a narrow bourgeois oligarchy.

Robbins dismisses this argument out of hand as being wrong. He seems to think that an economic transformation of this magnitude had to have occurred through something like a political revolution. How, he asks, could feudalism have disappeared without anyone noticing, without a "political commotion"? I seem to make politics recede into irrelevance. Two points are worth mentioning here. First, I do not say that feudalism was replaced without any political commotion, or transformation of polical relations more generally. In fact, as I argue in some detail in the book, there was a very important political transformation that accompanied the change in agrarian relations in the Tudor era—the landed classes acquired greater and greater political power for themselves throughout the country by capturing local juridical institutions and in parliament by controlling regional elections. Over the course of a century, they bent the structure of the state toward their own interests, thereby constraining the monarchy in its unilateral power. This was a transformation of epochal significance, in that they slowly turned the state into an organ of their own power—albeit with a monarchical form. The strife in 1640 was the final act in a decades-long effort by Charles to wrest control away from the landed classes, centralizing it again in the person of the monarch. The revolution itself was a war over what kind of state an already bourgeois England would have. My argument doesn't consign politics to irrelevance—it simply corrects an erroneous story about what the battle was fought over.

But even more importantly, Robbins fails to understand the real issue. Even if the traditional story about the revolution were true—that it was a political revolution led by the bourgeoisie against a feudal state—it wouldn't be enough to save the Subalternists' case. For them the central issue isn't whether or not England was already capitalist by 1640. It is, rather, whether or not the capitalists who came to power were committed to a liberal, consensual, inclusive political order—their commitment to "speak for all the nation." This is where they set themselves apart from the postcolonial and colonial capitalists. And on this score, there is simply no debate among historians. What the English bourgeoisie wanted, and what it erected after 1688, was a narrow bourgeois oligarchy, geared centrally toward the exclusion of popular classes from the political arena. The heroic bourgeoisie against which Guha compares that of the East is a historic myth.

I point out the centrality of this issue at some length in Chapter Four, but Robbins seems not to have noticed. Indeed, his entire line of criticism is not based on any empirical grounds at all. He rejects my argument, not because he has any facts to marshal against it, or any historical literature he can cite, but from first principle. He announces from on high what events *must* look like in the advent of capitalism. If a particular narrative fails to conform to his model, well then, so much the worse for the narrative. This is certainly an interesting approach to historical inquiry, but one more properly belonging in a church or synagogue.

Turning now to the second issue, the chasm putatively separating East from West, Robbins fares no better. Now, I have to tread lightly here, since his argument gets very murky. But he seems to think that a focus on the universal properties of capitalism, which he takes me to be recommending, can only end up papering over the real differences between regions. So even though it might be that capitalism has swept the globe, surely we want to explain the difference between "capitalism in the style of IKEA and capitalism in the style of Rana Plaza." Apparently I am not interested in such mundane matters, being slavishly bound to capitalism as a Grand Narrative. As proof, Robbins adduces numbers—it is not till page 290 that I even broach how Eastern capitalism actually diverges from its Western counterpart.

Robbins has to know that he is being disingenuous. My entire book is wedded to showing that taking cognizance of certain universal forces is no impediment to also explaining diversity. The issue of social and historical difference is at the very heart of my argument. The clearest discussion of this is in Chapter 9, on Dipesh Chakrabarty's confused and rather tortured analysis of abstraction. I explain there that the very universalizing forces of capitalism also generate very diverse forms of capitalism, because even though the pressure to accumulate is common across economies, local response to it can be quite varied. This is in part due to the unevenness of the accumulation process itself, but also because of the contingencies of class conflict and local institutional influences. Capitalism thus universalizes its dynamics, but exists in variable forms. Just so readers know how bizarre Robbins's accusation is, my discussion of this issue is in a section labeled "Capitalism and Diversity Revisited" (Chapter 9, Section 6), in which I summarize the argument in its subsection titled "Three Sources of Diversity in Capitalism" (pp. 244–6). So I literally spell out what I am arguing—and Robbins still manages to miss it.

It is true that I do not produce an actual theory, a historical account, of why this or that country—say, a Sweden—turned out differently in its capitalism than another one—perhaps an Argentina. But that is because I have to set the argument at the same level of generality as the theories that I criticize, those of the Subalternists. The argument coming from their camp is not that some particular theory is falling short; it is that any theory built on certain premises is incapable of ever recognizing difference. I try to show that the kinds of theories they impugn are in fact quite capable of appreciating historical diversity, and I show what it is about their logic that enables them to explain both universal processes and divergent social formations. I then point, on page 290, to the veritable mountain of literature that does just that—explain how Sweden and Argentina are both capitalist but still very diverse. I do not offer such an explanation myself because I do not have to, since it has been at the core of several theories' research programs for more than one hundred years, which postcolonial theorists either pretend doesn't exist, or are ignorant of.

Finally, the question of rationality. Robbins seems of two minds here. He accuses me of offering a model of action derived from rational choice theory, on top of which he heaps further opprobrium—not the least of which is the dreaded verdict of being "pre-dialectical." But he also quickly draws back and admits that he might be exaggerating (even my being weak on the dialectic?). Since it isn't clear which of his accusations he actually believes, let me address the question squarely. Do I rely on a rational choice model of action? I have to admit being puzzled by this question, since I go to some lengths in the book—not just in a footnote, as Robbins wrongly asserts—to show how and why my argument is not a version of rational choice theory. Robbins is again a little dishonest here. He uses a quotation from me about the "asocial individual, hovering above his culture, ranking his preferences," and so on, implying that that is the view that I wish to endorse— when he notes perfectly well that, in that passage, I am lampooning that view as one that I reject.

So what is the view that I endorse? Do I reduce agents to asocial automatons? What I actually say in the book—and it is hard to see how Robbins could miss this—is three things. First, that people are largely shaped by their cultures, but culture is not constitutive of human psychology. There are some needs that exist and endure independently of culture, and chief among these is the need to attend to one's physical well-being. Second, that people are typically cognizant of this need and it therefore generates interests that influence political and social interaction. And third, that it is the universality of this need that explains the universality of resistance to exploitation—since the latter typically undermines the former. Note that I don't simply assert this argument—I show that the actual historiography of the Subalterns themselves validates this proposition, even though they deny it (with the exception of Guha, who never denies it).

None of this entails a commitment to rational choice theory. All I am offering is one route to what was once called materialism, and those are two very different animals. I do not imply, indeed I explicitly deny, that people are welfare-maximizers. Nor do I suggest that people are selfish or competitive individualists—the two implications most commonly associated with rational choice, and rightly rejected. What I do say is that people have a healthy appreciation for situations in which they are being oppressed or exploited, that this appreciation holds steady across cultures, and that it generates reasons for action. This is why what we typically see is what James Scott called "everyday forms of resistance." If anyone has an alternative foundation for non-reductionist materialism, I'd be happy to entertain it. I don't know of any.

Furthermore, my argument does not in any way imply that a concern for one's well-being is all there is to human nature. In the book, I offer that people are probably also hardwired for a desire for autonomy or self-determination. But I also say, and I will repeat, that human nature is in fact much richer than either of these—there is the innate creativity, the desire for love, for social ties, for meaning, and so forth. All those needs and capacities that Marx describes in the *1844 Manuscripts* are ones that I accept. The reason I focused on one particular property is that this is the one that is at the core of Subalternist arguments, and it is the aspect of human nature they deny, especially to people with darker skin—and I have to go where my quarry goes. It is worth repeating that Marx, the Enlightenment thinker with the richest conception of human nature, never doubted the existence of basic human needs, nor the importance of material interests as the fount of politics and political struggles. What made capitalism unjust was that it turned—and in so many parts of the world, continues to turn—workers' lives into a struggle around their bare material well-being, suppressing the development of their other manifold capacities. We should of course object to any theory that reduces peoples' motivations to those focused on this one goal—but we should be equally suspicious of a theory that denies or impugns its salience outright. The most deplorable consequence of the "cultural turn" is that it does just this, and Robbins's response is just another example of it.

The sad fact is that every accusation Robbins throws at me was anticipated in *PTSC* and addressed to a greater or lesser extent. Now he is of course free to disagree with the defenses I offer in the book. But in pretending that I don't address the issues he raises, and in simply ignoring what I explain quite clearly and at great length, Robbins only confirms what I predicted at the end of *PTSC*—that the most likely response from the defenders of postcolonial theory would be to dismiss and calumniate outside criticism, rather than addressing it squarely. As I said at the outset of my response, he is not as hysterical or shrill as some others. But he also doesn't manage to rise above the dismal level of debate that the field has established.

Part II.
Review Symposium

CHAPTER 7

Review Symposium on Vivek Chibber's
Postcolonial Theory and the Specter of Capital[1]

Ho-fung Hung

Without any doubt, Vivek Chibber's *Postcolonial Theory and the Specter of Capital* is a bomb. Through the critique of the foundational works of the Indian Subaltern Studies group, Chibber's questioning pierces right into the anti-universalism core of Subaltern Studies and the post-colonial enterprise. Focusing on the historically and empirically grounded works of Ranajit Guha and Dipesh Chakrabarty, Chibber juxtaposes their interpretation of European and Indian histories with his own interpretation, claiming that their case against Enlightenment universalism was premised on erroneous historiography.

In this symposium, I put together five commentaries on *Postcolonial Theory and the Specter of Capital* from diverse disciplinary and geographical perspectives, together with Chibber's response. The debate between Chibber and the defenders of postcolonialism is too important to be confined to scholars concerned about the future of postcolonialism as a fashionable paradigm in certain humanities and social science disciplines. This debate is, in fact, a continuation of the long-drawn debate between the Marxists and post-structuralists, or the modernists and the postmodernists. It is also closely connected to the future of progressive politics in the global North and South.

While Foucault and many post-structuralists accused the universal rationalism of Enlightenment in Europe of fostering many disasters and massacres in the twentieth century, Habermas[2] asserts that the post-structuralist forfeit of universal rationalism, as well as the post-structuralist prioritization of the aesthetics and the particular, is conducive to fascist politics. It is noteworthy that Foucault, in the last years of his life, had become an admirer of Khomeini's Iranian

Revolution.[3] It is equally unsurprising that many statist and ultra-nationalist intellectuals in today's China can comfortably combine the views of Foucault, Edward Said, and Carl Schmidt (as the Nazi legal theorist and the "crown jurist of the Third Reich") in their defense of Third World authoritarianism against the "Western hegemonic ideology" of bourgeois democracy.

The discussion in this symposium focuses on the historiography and theoretical issues raised by *Postcolonial Theory and the Specter of Capital*. The epistemological and ontological clarification in this symposium will help build a foundation for our deliberation on the political—how should public intellectuals choose between uncompromising universalism and uncompromising particularism, and if so, what kinds of universalism and particularism? Is there any virtue and possibility in looking for a middle ground? These questions are of utmost importance for those of us who see theory as not only a tool for understanding the world, but also one for changing it.

CHAPTER 8

On Vivek Chibber's *Postcolonial Theory and the Specter of Capital*

William H. Sewell, Jr.

Vivek Chibber's *Postcolonial Theory and the Specter of Capital* is a critique not of postcolonial theory in general, but specifically of the Subaltern Studies school, as represented by Ranajit Guha, Partha Chatterjee, and Dipesh Chakrabarty. The Subalternists, of course, have focused specifically on Indian history, a subject with which I have only a passing acquaintance. This means that my comments should surely be taken with a healthy grain of salt.

I suppose I must have been asked to contribute to this symposium to say something about the famous entity called "Europe" that Dipesh Chakrabarty[1] and other postcolonial theorists have striven to deprovincialize. After all, Europe is the unavoidable "other" against which the Subalternists have evaluated Indian history—unavoidable because India was conquered and ruled by Britain for nearly two centuries and because Europe, and more recently an expanded "West" that notably includes the United States, have dominated the world militarily, economically, culturally, and intellectually for the past 300 years. Chibber, it should be said, doesn't dispute the necessity of thinking about the history of India in comparison with the West; what he disputes is the way the Subalternists think about it and the conclusions they draw.

Chibber is not a sympathetic critic: indeed, he's basically hostile to culturalist theories, to postmodern literary and philosophical tropes, and to the murky Hegelian and Heideggerian language that appears in the later work of Dipesh Chakrabarty. Chibber attempts to puncture what he regards as the vague and exaggerated claims of postcolonial theorists and to defend a Marxist version of universal Enlightenment values against what he calls the Subalternists' "orientalism." But Chibber doesn't waste time declaiming against the Subalternists. Rather, he seriously and painstakingly subjects their arguments to a dissection that is unforgivingly rationalist. In the end, Chibber convinces me that the Subalternists' major claims are pretty shaky.

The Subalternists' arguments of course evolved over time. Thus Ranajit Guha's *Dominance without Hegemony*,[2] a collection of essays composed in the late 1980s and early 1990s, was written from within a basically Marxist framework, whereas Dipesh Chakrabarty's *Provincializing Europe* insists on Marxism's essential Eurocentrism and its consequent inability to grasp Indian historical developments. But it is remarkable that from beginning to end the "Europe" that the Subalternists grapple with is represented above all by Marxism and by particular Marxist imaginings of European history. This suggests that Subaltern Studies must be understood in part as an ambivalent emanation of a disappointed Marxism, an aftermath, one supposes, of the failed Naxalite movement of the 1970s.

Chibber thinks this disappointment is misplaced, that Marxist analysis retains its utility for understanding economic, social, and political developments both in the "West" and in the developing world. The Subalternists' discontents, he argues, arise from both empirical and theoretical errors.

Ranajit Guha, in *Dominance without Hegemony*, argued that much of India's postcolonial misfortune can be traced to the weakness of the Indian bourgeoisie. In Guha's telling, the Indian bourgeoisie failed to live up to the heroic legacy of their European counterparts, who, in two great revolutions—in England in the 1640s and in France in 1789—overthrew feudalism and established liberal bourgeois states that fulfilled the universalizing drive of capitalism, both by securing the political dominance of the capitalist class and by fashioning hegemonic political orders that extended political rights to subordinate classes. By contrast, the Indian bourgeoisie, in its would-be revolutionary moment of decolonization, gained political dominance but failed to overthrow feudal relations in the countryside or to establish anything like the genuinely hegemonic political order characteristic of Europe.

I need hardly point out that this portrayal of the English and French revolutions is standard-issue orthodox Marxism—and is by now well past its "sell-by" date. The problem, as Chibber argues, is that this old orthodox Marxist account seriously misunderstands European history. Now, I have to say that Chibber's own grasp of French and English history seems to me a bit shaky. For example, he discusses the English Civil War of the 1640s at some length but doesn't even mention the English Revolution of 1688, which most European historians now alive would regard as having a much better claim to being something like a bourgeois revolution. And he concludes, remarkably, that the contribution of the European revolutions to "the birth of modern liberalism" was "weak"—completely ignoring, for example, such founding liberal moments as the separation of powers instituted in England in 1688 or the French Declaration of the Rights of Man and Citizen of 1789. Nevertheless, Chibber's most important conclusions about the European experience seem to me quite correct: that the regimes put in place in the wake of the so-called bourgeois revolutions actually placed stringent limits on the political participation of popular classes and that democratization in Europe owed far more to struggles from below than to the generosity of the bourgeoisie. This, in turn, implies that the Indian bourgeoisie's failure to embrace an egalitarian order, far from constituting a deviation from the politics of the European bourgeoisie or a failure of capitalism's universalizing dynamic, was instead exactly what the European experience of capitalism and revolution should have led us to expect.

Chibber also strives to refute the essentially parallel argument of Dipesh Chakrabarty's *Rethinking Working-Class History*.[3] Chakrabarty asserts in this book that the nature of relations between jute mill workers and capitalists in Calcutta—which were based more on personal authority, caste, and religious identities than on the anonymous labor market and class identities—demonstrates that European capitalism's universalizing mission had stalled on Eastern shores. Chibber replies by showing that European and American capitalists have repeatedly relied on personal authority and particularist identities whenever these could produce a tractable labor force. Again, there was nothing "Eastern" about labor relations that took this form nor did they represent any failure of capitalism to universalize itself.

Chibber's arguments in these two cases have perfectly good Marxist credentials. What he shows here and elsewhere in his book is that

Marxist empirical and conceptual work on the history of capitalism is perfectly capable of making sense of Indian developments—that there is no fundamental conceptual divide between the history of "Europe" and the history of "the East."

This, of course, puts Chibber strongly at odds with Chakrabarty's arguments in *Provincializing Europe*, probably the most celebrated (and certainly the most difficult) work of the Subaltern school. Chibber remarks that Chakrabarty, near the beginning of this book, claims that the "Europe" used as a point of comparison for Indian history is a "hyperreal" entity—in Chakrabarty's terms a "metanarrative figure of the imagination" that is "constructed by the tales that both imperialism and nationalism have told the colonized."[4] Chibber dismisses this claim as a dodge, asserting, quite correctly, that Chakrabarty in fact constantly makes claims about divergences between the real histories of Europe and India.

However, I think that Chakrabarty's "Europe" actually is hyperreal in a somewhat different sense. It seems to me that Chakrabarty constructs a "Marxism" fused with a hyperreal "Europe" that is very much a "narrative figure of the imagination"—and then proceeds to criticize this construct. (Note that "Europe" for Chakrabarty never connotes such eminently European features as Christian fervor, or royal absolutism, or romanticism, or militarism, or Fascism—only the Enlightenment, democracy, liberalism, rationality, capitalism, and imperialism. Such a one-sided Europe is quite unrecognizable to a Europeanist.) In *Provincializing Europe* Chakrabarty, on the basis of a rather daunting reading of Marx, claims to find, but I would say constructs, a highly idealized, unified, teleological and (it must be said) un-dialectical history of capitalism that he labels "History 1," a capitalist history to which "the Enlightenment universals" adhere or that includes within itself "the categories of Enlightenment thought."[5] Next to this he constructs another history, what he calls "History 2," that contains diverse logics of action and belonging and that is "charged with the function of constantly interrupting the totalizing thrusts of History 1."[6] It is this History 2 that especially comes into prominence in the East, where capitalism has been more recently introduced. Chakrabarty claims that historians, both Eastern and Western, have been too mesmerized by the perfect unity and self-identity of History

1 and have underplayed the disruptions and incompleteness that History 2 introduces into the history of capitalist societies.

Chibber agrees that one can reasonably distinguish a History 1 that refers to the specific and necessary dynamics of capitalist accumulation from a History 2 that is not fully interior to capital's life process. But Chibber's version of History 1 is rather stripped down: it's not identified with Europe or freighted with necessity or equated with the Enlightenment. On the other hand, it is decidedly dialectical—the capitalist core is full of contradictions that constantly threaten to disrupt any orderly process of accumulation. That is to say, it actually resembles the capitalism that we all know and love. Chibber's History 2, like Chakrabarty's, is defined as those historical forces not constituted by the core of capitalism. But Chibber insists that History 2 normally poses no particular threat to History 1. It's either perfectly compatible with capitalism, as when capitalists take advantage of differences of religion, caste, or race to divide or discipline their workforces. Or it's basically indifferent to capitalism, as when cultural practices of one sort or another go on with no noticeable influence one way or the other on capital accumulation. Aspects of History 2 can, of course, on occasion disrupt History 1, but disruptions from within the logic of History 1 are far more common and far more consequential. For Chibber, there is no reason either to shun History 1 or to exalt History 2. As you may have guessed, I prefer Chibber's version of the two histories to Chakrabarty's.

To sum up: *Postcolonial Theory and the Specter of Capital* provides a careful, sustained, intelligent, and salutary critique of Subaltern Studies. Its genius is critique, however, rather than reconstruction. Chibber's rationalism, which sometimes gets very close to rational choice, is basically a solvent or a deflator. Chibber has cleared the ground and has usefully indicated the value of Marxist analytical tools. But in my opinion it will take a Marxism more infused with cultural sensitivities to reconstruct a superior history of the postcolonial world.

Let me close with a few final thoughts on the provincialization of Europe. If postcolonial historians really are serious about provincializing Europe, perhaps they should begin by recognizing that Europe is actually divided into many provinces—usually known as nation-states—that have surprisingly diverse histories. The histories of politics or thought or industrialization of England, Spain, France, Hungary, Germany, Norway, and Greece are by no means the same. Differences between the histories of Portugal and England may be as great as those between the histories of China and France. And the histories of none of these countries are identical to the history of capitalism, or the Enlightenment, or democracy. Perhaps we should try banishing the over-inflated collective noun "Europe" from our vocabularies for a few years and treat that broad peninsula at the western end of Eurasia as what it is: a collection of highly diverse provinces, not some unified totality. Chibber's deflation of postcolonial theory should help to point us in this direction.

CHAPTER 9

Back to Basics? The Recurrence of the Same in Vivek Chibber's *Postcolonial Theory and the Specter of Capital*

Bruce Cumings

> Orient and Occident are chalk-lines drawn before us to fool our timidity.
>
> Nietzsche

I have to begin with a disclaimer: I have never been much interested in postcolonialism. Several reasons explain my inattention, and thus my ignorance: first, even though South Asian studies and East Asian studies are joined in scholarly communion (the Association for Asian Studies) and have in common a flagship journal (the *Journal of Asian Studies*), rarely do we read each other's work—indeed I know much less about South Asia than I do about, say, Latin America, not to mention Europe or the United States. An aggravating element is that so much of "Asian studies" really connotes country studies, given linguistic hurdles that scholars need to jump over to be taken seriously. Second, attempts to reinterpret East Asian history through the lenses of postcolonial theory are few and far between, probably because its most formidable capitalist and imperial power—Japan—has been an avatar of rapid state-planned, architectonic industrialization for well over a century, and both Koreas, Taiwan, and China have followed suit. Third, when I did encounter postcolonial scholarship, it was often in a dense, jargon-ridden, impenetrable form (e.g. Homi Bhabha's work), suggesting to me that I might need a second life to master this literature—or maybe I should just move to a different planet. (The exception would be the clarity and brilliance of Dipesh Chakrabarty's work, which I discovered by becoming friends with him.) Last, nothing they or anyone else has written has dissuaded me from a structural perspective—from what they would call "totalizing" theory—in spite of my admiration for the work of Friedrich Nietzsche, Michel Foucault, and other post-structuralists.

From the perspective of the last point, India never seemed to fit the grand narratives of modernity. A *locus classicus* for this view would be Barrington Moore's *Social Origins of Dictatorship and Democracy*, which spells out three routes to modernity: the liberal, the state-led (or fascist), and the peasant revolution (or communist) route. India conforms to none of these trajectories, and so in his chapter on India, Moore homes in on the idiosyncratic to explain this exception to his rules: religion, ethnicity, caste—that is, precisely the difference that appears in Chakrabarty's work. (A less kind take on this difference would be Immanuel Wallerstein's essay "Does India Exist?") Here was a clear goad to scholars of South Asia somehow to explain this aporia, of appearing to stand aside rather than astride the sweep of modern history. So they girded their loins and produced the Subaltern school and postcolonialism—throwing sand in the eyes of all the great modern theories. Their timing was excellent, because if we identify Barrington Moore with the 60s, Wallerstein with the 70s, and Marxism with the modern world from 1848 to 1989, a sudden opening came in the wake of "a period of massive defeats for the Left, all across the world."[1] Or as Ron Inden put it, "Indians are, for perhaps the first time since colonization, showing sustained signs of reappropriating the capacity to represent themselves."[2]

It follows that there is much for me to like in Vivek Chibber's important book. It rehabilitates a convincing structural perspective, whether in Marxist or liberal form, and unlike Moore, provides much evidence that India is not so idiosyncratic after all. I am not in a position to judge his empirical comments on, say, Indian labor, since I have not read Chakrabarty's study of jute workers and therefore have little basis for assessing Chibber's critique. But his analysis of the English and French revolutions struck me as cogent; indeed an important theme runs through the book, namely that the bourgeoisie can be progressive and even revolutionary in seeking its own political rights, but generally resists popular or mass movements by other classes to gain the same.[3] He cites the important study by Stephens, Rueschemeyer, and Stephens, *Capitalist Development and Democracy*,[4] to argue that the same sequence is visible is Latin American cases of democratization (147n), and I would say the same about recent democratizations in South Korea, Taiwan, and the stark case of China—presumably a communist country where an enormous middle class is a good bit more intent on its own interests and rights than on coalescing with disenfranchised workers lacking unions, let alone with a few hundred million peasants in the countryside. Chibber is right that global capital is entirely compatible with a variety of repressive regimes.

Chibber's critique of Ranajit Guha's *Dominance without Hegemony*[5] strikes me as similarly persuasive, at least at the level of how one defines hegemony. Hegemony for Guha means that a ruling class relies less on coercion than on consent, and thereby is able to speak "for all of society."[6] Derived in part from Gramsci, the definition ignores Gramsci's actual situation: sitting in prison in an Italy overtaken by fascism and heavily reliant on coercion. Gramsci meant by hegemony something like the ether that surrounds us, the air we breathe; we do not so much consent to the way in which we are governed, rather we have imbibed certain social, political, and cultural conventions more or less from birth, so that we do what we are supposed to do without having to be told, let alone coerced. This is the most formidable kind of power, and it was what Gramsci meant by "hegemony." It could be true in Jeffersonian Virginia, or in North Korea. At a more mundane level, it seems clear that a bourgeoisie, whether Western or not, does not need "the active consent of subaltern groups"[7] to maintain its power— although consent is clearly to be preferred.

Chibber is also right that neither Marx nor non-Stalinist Marxists ever assumed that there is a single or universal path toward modernity. He cites Trotsky's theory of uneven and combined development,[8] but he could just as easily have recalled Alexander Gerschenkron's non-Marxist analysis of "late" development—namely, that no two industrializations are ever the same, because of idiosyncratic differences in a given country, the timing of "insertion" into competition with previously arrived industrial powers, the opportunity to copy or apply new technologies in pre-industrial settings, and so on. In other words, Gerschenkron found it appropriate to include a host of idiosyncratic ·

differences within his structural theory of industrialization. It is surprising, however, that alongside various golden oldies like Marx, Trotsky, Gramsci, and Karl Kautsky, we do not find the names of Karl Polanyi or Immanuel Wallerstein anywhere in this book. This seems to be because Chibber is wedded to a Marxist stance that class struggle is the motive force in history, rather than the circulationist theory found in Polanyi and Wallerstein, namely that capitalism is a system of production for profit in a world market, gaining its initial momentum in the long sixteenth century.

Perhaps the nonappearance of Polanyi and Wallerstein has something to do with another absence: Chibber's book has nary a single mention of the country known as China, yet China's recent experience of hell-bent-for-leather capitalist development is our clearest case of the palpable recurrence of the same—a Chinese version if not of the universalities of capitalism, then at minimum a variant of the state-led industrialization operating in Northeast Asia for at least eighty years, migrating from Japan to Korea to Taiwan and thence to China. It would be very hard to transfer postcolonial arguments about culture, difference, and idiosyncrasy to any of these countries, and Chibber's critique of the Subaltern understanding of the historical role of the bourgeoisie seems particularly compelling, because in Northeast Asia this class has been brought into being under state auspices (as has the proletariat). And, of course, it is not at all difficult to imagine Marx grinning broadly as global capitalism "batters down all Chinese walls" (from the *Manifesto*, of course).

The reason for China's absence, I would guess, is that its trajectory since 1980 cannot be explained by a theory of class conflict. Chakrabarty's judgment that "there was no class in South Asia comparable to the European bourgeoisie"[9] is equally true of China. Instead the critical moment came in 1978–9, as China's reform program and its insertion into the world economy (connoted as "opening") coincided with the establishment of Sino-American diplomatic relations; here was the clearest possible example of the hegemonic power welcoming a pariah state back into the fold, on the assumption that the world would shake China for many decades to come, not that China would shake the world; sooner or later it would be captured by the gravity of capitalism.[10]

Without belaboring the point, China's experience over the past three decades is entirely compatible with a circulationist conception. I know from many encounters that Wallerstein's theories are considered entirely passé by many prominent social scientists (not to mention being roundly loathed by postcolonial scholars), but I recall sitting on a panel at the 1984 annual meeting of the American Political Science Association as Wallerstein confidently predicted the demise of Soviet and East European socialism, and a subsequent dependency on unified Germany as the central economic power of Europe. I don't recall that he said anything about China, perhaps because he was also enthralled at the time with the idea that Japan would be the avatar of a twenty-first-century world system centered on the Pacific. He wasn't alone in the latter (failed) prediction, but he was quite alone in his (prescient) projections for central and eastern Europe.

Vivek's book has at its base a rigorous theory, one that I largely agree with, but also a kind of diabolical logic: the Subaltern scholars compare the Indian bourgeoisie to an idealized version of the European bourgeoisie; ergo they are Eurocentric in spite of themselves. If Guha's "heroic bourgeoisie" is a bit hard to swallow, can we also say that Chakrabarty's *Provincializing Europe*[11] is similarly blinkered and uncomprehending about European history while simultaneously "relentlessly promot[ing] Eurocentrism"?[12] It would never have occurred to me to say that; instead Chakrabarty's goal is (in Chibber's own words[13]) to encourage theories that are "attuned to Indian realities and freed of European assumptions," a new set of categories appropriate to Asian settings. Chakrabarty's sensibility is close to Nietzsche's acerbic reference to "ancient Asia and its protruding little peninsula Europe, which wants by all means to signify as against Asia the 'progress of man.'"[14] That is, Asians not only are subjected to centuries of colonialism, they also have to sit by and listen to a "hyperreal" construct—namely endless justifications not only for European progress (and dominance), but also for their own subjugation and inferiority, with their only way out being an imitative approximation of modernity that can never quite match the European example. This dilemma could hardly be greater; one sees it in the world-historical moment of Japan's attempt to strike directly at the West, in wartime debates that H. D. Harootunian[15] confronts in his masterful book *Overcome by Modernity*—what would be the meaning of a modernity that has a Japanese essence, one that could overcome the West in every sense of the word? When all is said and done, this same problem animates the ruling ideology of North Korea (*chuch'e*)—the longest-running antagonist of American hegemony in the world.

Unfortunately, Chibber's critique of postcolonialism partakes of a similar presumption, one like that of the colonizer: "One cannot adequately criticize a social phenomenon if one systematically misunderstands how it works."[16] In other words, the Indian bourgeoisie is not only "mediocre," as Guha says,[17] a pale reflection of the European example, but Guha and Chakrabarty don't understand the European version either, and instead end up not only with an inadvertent Eurocentrism, but even imbibe "the Whig theory of history."[18] (After reading that, somehow I expected to read that Guha and Chakrabarty also supported the invasion of Iraq and were bosom buddies of Dick Cheney.) I don't know Guha's work, but this is a preposterous caricature of Chakrabarty's scholarship.

Through a similar sleight of hand, Chakrabarty's insistence on difference and its inherent antagonism toward European universals leads him into another dead end, according to Chibber, not to mention a paradoxical reversal: he revives orientalism—indeed, along with Partha Chatterjee he even revives "nineteenth-century colonial ideology";[19] the Subalternists "promote some of the most objectionable canards that Orientalism ever produced—all in the guise of 'High Theory.'"[20] So does orientalism connote a set of Western representations of Asia, always with a conscious or subconscious intent to measure its difference and its distance from progressive norms, or is it that orientalism rears its ugly head whenever an Asian insists that his culture, society, history, and so forth do not conform to a Western (liberal or Marxist) model? When Chakrabarty "wants the East to have a history of its own,"[21] can we call that orientalism, or can we see in this a self-conscious determination to write history outside of a dominant Western paradigm? By the same logic, one could label Chibber an orientalist in his insistence that there is only one, true way to understand the development of the modern world.

In the end we return to Nietzsche's aphorism from the essay "Schopenhauer as Educator": "Orient and Occident are chalk-lines drawn before us to fool our timidity."[22] Chibber's own subjectivity is betrayed by his insistence on capitalizing "East and West," as if we might easily draw a chalk-line, straight or crooked, between a department store in Tokyo or Paris, or a movie theater in Shanghai or New York. In this he is hardly alone: actually existing orientalism still occupies the best (Western) minds. Jürgen Habermas, a person whom you might think would know better, privileges the West as the site of the origin of his "public sphere" and its contemporary problematic, as well as its ultimate redemption. He concluded one of his books on "modernity" with this statement: "Who else but Europe could draw from its own traditions the insight, the energy, the courage of vision—everything that would be necessary to strip from the . . . premises of a blind compulsion to system maintenance and system expansion their power to shape our mentality."[23]

This is by no means an unusual emphasis for Habermas, even if it is unusually blunt; his whole work is imbued with "the claim that the modern West—for all its problems—best embodies" the values of rationality and democracy,[24] with a now-evident, now-hidden discourse about modern German history (which I think pushes him toward the privileging of norms of political interaction that emerged in postwar West Germany, but nowhere else in German history), and an apparent utter lack of concern for the non-Western experience, except as a species of occasional counter-hegemonic practice in the "Third World." Thus he shares the same prejudices of his cherished predecessor Max Weber (Habermas is most of all a Weberian), but not Weber's passionate and intelligent comparativist project—and in a time when Weber would certainly recognize his own provincialism, were he still talking about "only in the West . . ." But perhaps we better sample the original Weber, what he said then, since we don't know what he would say now:

> Only the occident knows the state in the modern sense, with a professional administration, specialized officialdom, and law based on the concept of citizenship . . . Only the occident knows rational law . . . Furthermore, only the occident possesses science . . . Finally, western

civilization is further distinguished from every other by the presence of men with a rational ethic for the conduct of life.[25]

When we read this, nothing about the postcolonial turn should be surprising; no wonder they all look for the nearest carpet to gnaw. So should we.

CHAPTER 10

On the Articulation of Marxist and Non-Marxist Theory in Colonial Historiography

George Steinmetz

Postcolonial Theory and the Specter of Capital is an important book on a topic of major importance for all of the human and social sciences. The book's implications reach far beyond Chibber's critique of Subaltern Studies, which is his most obvious focus. Chibber's over-arching argument is twofold: capitalism does universalize itself to the colonial and postcolonial world, but at the same time, capitalism does not permeate or encompass all other aspects of social practice. As it stands, this is already an important argument for social theory gener-ally and not just for analysts working on former colonies like India. The crisis of what used to be called western Marxism led to two main responses among Marxists. While many simply abandoned Marxism, becoming "post-Marxist,"[1] others became "neo-orthodox," refusing to acknowledge the autonomy of any social practices from capitalism.[2] Chibber's position is closer to the more nuanced positions of the "regu-lationist" school;[3] it is also compatible with a neo-historicist critical realism[4] that combines an ontology of emergent causal powers with an anti-essentialist epistemology according to which historically varying conjunctures of causal mechanisms interact in contingent, often unpredictable ways to produce empirical events. The fact that Chibber's book's packaging suggests an all-out assault on anyone who would dare to deviate from Marxist orthodoxy does not square with the actual content of the book.

Chibber's book is also framed as a critique of Subaltern colonial historiography. Here again, the book's framing does not provide an accurate sense of the directions in which Chibber's thinking takes him.

Many of Chibber's specific arguments are broadly consistent with the pathbreaking work of the founder of Subaltern Studies, Ranajit Guha.

CHIBBER'S ARGUMENT RESTATED

Chibber's book is presented as a critique of postcolonial theory. This is very misleading. The leading postcolonial theorists, including Edward Said,[5] Gayatri Spivak,[6] Homi Bhabha,[7] and Leela Gandhi,[8] are barely mentioned here.[9] Also missing are postcolonial theory's adopted predecessors, such W. E. B. Du Bois, Frantz Fanon, Aimé Césaire, and Albert Memmi, or its philosophical antecedents, including Hegel, Nietzsche, Freud, and Heidegger. Postcolonial theory started and remains most firmly embedded in the humanities, not the social sciences or history. The two main strands of postcolonial theory have focused on questions of the colonial presence within ostensibly noncolonial cultural texts and practices, on the ambivalences of colonized subjectivity and colonial forms of rule, and on the ways colonizing ideas have prepared the ground for conquest and foreign rule. None of these themes show up in Chibber's book.[10] Instead the book's exclusive focus is the Subaltern school of history, which has very different origins even if there has been a subsequent rapprochement. A more accurate title for this book would be something like *The Subaltern School of History and the Specter of Capital.*

That said, Chibber does make a highly coherent argument, one that can be restated in four main theses:

- Capitalism universalizes itself both geospatially and within a given social formation.
- Capitalism is entirely compatible with political despotism, labor coercion, and the production and reproduction of cultural difference and diversity.
- Although capital may "spread[] to all corners of the world . . . this does not mean that it manages to subordinate all social relations to its particular rules of reproduction."[11]
- Although "it is surely problematic to see capital lurking behind every social phenomenon," it is no less problematic "to deny its salience when it is in fact a relevant causal agent."[12]

CHIBBER'S ANALYSIS OF THE SUBALTERN SCHOOL

In addition to these general theoretical arguments, Chibber shows that there are three key arenas in which the Subaltern school claims that Indian history differs from Western history: first, they claim that the Indian bourgeoisie failed to become hegemonic; second, they argue for a unique form of "power relations" in India; and third, they argue that India has a unique "political psychology." There are three main historians under discussion here: Ranajit Guha, Partha Chatterjee, and Dipesh Chakrabarty. In this section I will present these three main clusters of ideas and arguments.

I. Capital's mythical universalizing mission

The first argument, associated with R. Guha, is that capital abandoned its putative universalizing hegemonic mission in colonial and postcolonial India. Chibber counters that the bourgeoisie is not inherently liberal or modernizing and that capitalism is not the same thing as political and cultural modernization. Since the two key comparison cases for Guha, Britain and France, did not really have bourgeois revolutions of the idealized sort, there is no reason we should expect India to have had them. Indeed, Chibber continues, cultural and political forms of modernization were in some respects more readily forthcoming after the relevant comparable revolution, decolonization, in India than in Western Europe.

This is a very familiar debate for a German historian. The thesis of the German Sonderweg, or special path to modernity, asked why Nazism came to power in Germany and not in other advanced industrial countries. The basic answer focused on the deviation of Germany's developmental path from its Western neighbors. German history was seen as having been pushed repeatedly in destructive and anti-democratic directions by a clash between economic modernity and political and cultural backwardness, and this structural disjuncture resulted from the fact that German bourgeois liberalism was underdeveloped in comparison with Britain and France. Like the Indian bourgeoisie, the German bourgeoisie was said to have failed repeatedly to take the lead in promoting its supposed class interest in liberal democracy, in leading other classes toward that goal. Like the Indian bourgeoisie it failed to suppress the neo-feudal landed nobility, which continued to wield undue influence in politics and culture well into the twentieth century. Another feature of this condition was the so-called "feudalization of the bourgeoisie," the spread of anti-modern cultural values such as conservative anti-capitalism, anti-urbanism, and "cultural pessimism," and a non-hegemonic tendency to resort to state violence that is extremely reminiscent of Guha's diagnosis of the Indian condition.[13] Guha was relying on a version of Marxist political theory and German history that was demolished by the critics of the Sonderweg thesis. Chibber argues convincingly that real capitalism is compatible with a whole range of nondemocratic political and cultural conditions, and that there is no normal set of accompaniments to the spread of capitalism. No historian of fascist Europe, Assad's Syria, or contemporary China should raise an eyebrow at this claim nowadays.

II. Labor discipline, abstract labor, and cultural homogenization

Chibber argues secondly that capitalism is compatible with physical coercion at the point of production and that it produces and reproduces cultural heterogeneity (or "concrete identities") among its workers rather that necessarily pushing toward their homogenization. "It is rational for capitalists to dominate labor" in ways that reach far beyond the autonomic "dull compulsion of economic relations," as long as violence promises profits.[14] In the West as in the East, capitalism has always relied on physical as well as symbolic domination.[15]

Chibber also criticizes the idea that abstract labor leads to cultural homogenization, showing how some postcolonial theorists have conflated these two ideas. "Abstract labor comes clothed in concrete identities," Chibber concludes.[16] Capitalism therefore does not have to dissolve social difference. Even de-skilling is not inevitable:[17] new technologies continually generate new skills, even as old industries may suffer from de-skilling.

III. History 1 and History 2

My favorite section of the book is the discussion of Chakrabarty's *Provincializing Europe*[18] and its critique of Chakrabarty's concepts of History 1 and History 2. History 1 is the history of modern capital, while History 2 consists of all of the multiple, incommensurable histories that develop according to their own specific logics. Chakrabarty's implication is that Marxism would collapse all of the multiple histories of different practices into Capital, even though this is true of only the most totalizing, reductionist forms of Marxism. As Chibber notes, "it is surely problematic to see capital lurking behind every social phenomenon."[19] Chibber argues that the "continued salience of archaic power relations, the resort to traditional symbols, the resilience of caste and kin-based political relations, and so forth—all this can be shown to be consistent with the universalizing tendency" of capital.[20] When Chibber says a practice is "consistent" this does not mean it is entirely subordinated to or determined by capital.

Chibber summarizes his argument against Chakrabarty in four main points:

- The sheer existence of "History 2" does not mean that capital's universalization (as defined here) is incomplete.[21]
- History 2 is not necessarily the main barrier to History 1, and capitalism may be modified by History 2 in ways that are not "type-transforming."[22]
- Instead, History 1 itself is the main barrier to History 1,[23] or in Marx's words, the "true barrier to capitalist production is capital itself"—due to capitalism's logics of competition and crisis. Workers will always tend to come into conflict with the logic of capital accumulation. This opposition to capitalism within capitalism itself is "the only real source of opposition to capital's universalization."[24]
- There is no necessary antagonism between History 1 and 2.[25] The "ensemble of social relations in any region need not be subsumed under one set of rules," and the various practices that comprise the whole can be governed by very dissimilar logics, even as capital universalizes.[26]

SIX CRITIQUES OF CHIBBER

First, in what is overall an admirably clear and sharply argued book, there is a key ambiguity around the question of social crisis or breakdown. If History 1 does not constitute the whole of the society, as Chibber has allowed, why can't there be instability and breakdown in the rest of society (lumped under History 2)? Some examples of instability and breakdown include the death of states, the breakdown of law and order, warfare, terrorism, dictatorship, fascism, and the demise of entire institutions and fields. Fixated as he is on History 1 and the polemic against Subaltern Studies, Chibber doesn't pursue his criticism of one of the weakest points in Chakrabarty's sociology: his lumping of everything but capitalism into a single residual category. Marxism already had a more sophisticated sociology than this in the early 1960s, when Althusser reframed the social totality as a loose congeries of relatively autonomous levels, or ten years later when Bourdieu reframed social space in terms of the field of power and a multiplicity of relatively autonomous fields, each one irreducible to the others.[27]

Second, contingency is not the opposite of causal determinism. The idea of conjunctural contingent causality is completely compatible with the approach Chibber has sketched out. If Marxism is construed as a set of underlying powers, tendencies, and structures, then these will combine in contingent ways with one another and with additional causal mechanisms not theorized by Marxism in producing empirical events. Indeed, Marx's own theory of economic crisis takes this form. There is nothing "fashionable" about the concept of contingency; it is an ontological fact of life in all open systems, natural and social. Repeated patterns or regularities that persist over time and generalize across space are the truly puzzling anomalies.

Third, Chibber raises the question of the limits of compatibility between History 1 and History 2, but he does not take the next step to ask which cultural and political forms might be incompatible with capitalism. Presumably he thinks this varies historically. But I am not sure. This topic, once a mainstay of Marxist social theory, needs to be revisited.

Fourth, the only weak part of Chibber's book concerns the topic of rationality and "political psychology." Guha claimed that the specific forms of colonial rule led to a bifurcation between cultures and repertoires of peasant mobilization and standard modern forms of politics. Chibber's main discomfort with this line of thought has mainly to do with theories of human culture and subjectivity that take seriously the idea that there are multiple forms of rationality—including irrationality—and that motivations are unconscious as well as conscious. These arguments are by no means limited to Subaltern Studies but are in fact one massive alternative pole to Chibber's rationalism in the human sciences. Indeed, sociology even in the United States has tended to lean in the opposite direction from Chibber. Marxism has made alliances with psychoanalysis for a century. There is no inherent connection between the idea of multiple forms of rationality or subjectivity and postcolonial theory.

I don't want to say more about this because I think this argument about rationality is not a necessary part of Chibber's arguments about the nature of capitalism. All of Chibber's arguments about the universalization of capital and its compatibility with non-modern or non-liberal forms of culture and politics are compatible with a less rigid model of culture and psychology. Chibber accuses Chatterjee of harboring a neo-orientalist vision of the Indian peasant, but the supposed irrationalities of the Indian peasant are easily matched by comparable phenomena in Europe. After all, Freud demonstrated pervasive psychic irrationality at the heart of civilized Europe, and his analysis was proven correct not by the events of the twentieth century but by current evidence in biological and neurological psychology for the existence of unconscious and irrational mental processes.[28]

In a way this argument doesn't even hinge on the existence of irrational motives but on the very existence of meaning and culture. Chibber is fighting a battle on his own terrain of sociology in the guise of a critique of postcolonial theory. But all serious versions of sociology and philosophy of social science agree that causal mechanisms or causal powers in the social sciences are inherently meaningful or invested with cultural meaning. In the social sciences we have theories of unconscious habitual action generated by something like a habitus. If we adopt instead the language of Weber we could say that there is a multiplicity of ultimate value orientations. Chibber is implicitly defending an entirely unrealistic vision of man as a rational machine.

A fifth point relates to what Chibber calls political form. Oddly, the discussion of political form focuses mainly on the labor process. There is no discussion of the political forms proper in colonial societies—states and empires. And this arena of politics in the narrower sense is one where Chatterjee's analysis has been of exemplary importance. Chibber ignores the ways in which colonial states preserved or created political forms such as tribes, Princely States, and other indirect rulers, putting limited power in the hands of colonized leaders. Mamdani[29] argues that the system of Indirect Rule increased levels of coercion in colonial states while limiting the spread of capitalist universalism—not because of the lack of political liberalism but literally by limiting the spread of capitalist economic forms. The "compulsions of market dependence" were sometimes actively suppressed by colonial policies, from British Tanganyika and Cameroon South Africa to German Polynesia.[30] To put it in more concrete terms: by placing local political power in the hands of chosen tribal leaders, weren't colonial governments in fact doing something quite different from what governments were doing inside Europe in the nineteenth and twentieth centuries? It is as if European revolutions actively propped up the most backwards sectors of the non-capitalist feudal classes. In other words, it is not correct that the "continued salience of archaic power relations and so on . . . can be shown to be consistent with the universalizing tendency"[31] of capital in all times and places. Some "archaic" modes of life were preserved in ways that were antithetical to capitalism's expansion. I am not talking about capitalists using traditional ideologies to dominate their workers, but about colonial states withdrawing potential laborers from capitalist labor markets altogether—literally limiting the spread of capitalist economic forms.

Sixth, Chibber sometimes mirrors the postcolonial terminology he is rejecting. For example, for Chibber Marx is an "Enlightenment thinker."[32] But Marx is more than an Enlightenment thinker. He is also a nineteenth-century social theorist writing in the wake of Hegelian idealism and Romanticism and preserving some aspects of that very different formation. Talcott Parsons, who had studied with Alfred Weber, recognized this, writing that "Marx considered capitalism a definite and specific system of economic organization, marked off sharply in principle from its predecessor and successor in the dialectical process."[33] Reducing Marx to an Enlightenment thinker is as much of a distortion as Chakrabarty's definition of historicism as a universalizing teleological social theory, which mirrors Popper's misleading definition. In nineteenth-century Germany, from Savigny to Ranke, and on to Mannheim, Troeltsch, and Meinecke in the twentieth, historicism meant almost precisely the opposite of what Popper said it did, signaling an emphasis on the unique, singular, non-repeated, and unprecedented—on the "historical individual," as Rickert and Weber called it.

CONCLUSION

Postcolonial Theory and the Specter of Capital is a highly stimulating book that not only points out some of the analytic and theoretical deficiencies in Subaltern history but also presents a lucid and refreshing take on some classic Marxist issues. Chibber shows how Marx's model of capitalism's universalization can be combined with recognition of the autonomy of many realms of social life from that relentless process. The articulation of Marxism as a regional theory of capitalism with equally autonomous theories of cultural, political, social, and psychic processes is a promising path for the historical social sciences.

CHAPTER 11

Capitalist Development, Structural Constraint, and Human Agency in the Global South

An Appreciation of Vivek Chibber's *Postcolonial Theory and the Specter of Capital*

Michael Schwartz

Let me start by saying that my biggest fear is that *Postcolonial Theory and the Specter of Capital* will be taken at face value: as a systematic and thorough savaging of Subaltern Studies. Unfortunately, it does fit that description quite perfectly. But for me, it is so much more than that, and not even primarily a critique of the currently hegemonic perspective on postcolonial development. Instead, I see it as a modern analog to Engels's *Anti-Dühring*, which created a kind of negative immortality for Eugen Dühring, now known only through Engels's critique. As Engels said in the introduction to that text, he engaged in such a definitive critique because it "gave me . . . the opportunity to develop in a positive form my views on questions which are today of wide scientific or practical interest."[1]

I view Chibber's work as a parallel sort of enterprise. I think the "positive" analysis in postcolonial theory—that is, Chibber's both original and synthetic portrait of the role of class dynamics and the logic of accumulation in the evolution of the postcolonial world—is so compelling that it will become foundational for a rich vein of new scholarship that supplants Subaltern Studies. And—because Chibber, like Engels, has chosen this dialectical format as the vehicle for developing and expressing his viewpoint—he may well confer upon Subaltern Studies a Dühring-like negative immortality. His critique is so devastating that long after the key texts of Subaltern Studies are out of print and out of mind, their ideas will be learned and even memorized by the legion of readers of postcolonial theory.

I want in this essay to call out some of the key components of this "positive" analysis and argue for its value, while calling for Chibber and the rest of us to utilize its strengths, correct its inadequacies, and fully develop its potential as a tool for understanding and challenging the negative dynamics of postcolonial capitalism.

Before leaving the Anti-Dühring metaphor, I want to congratulate Chibber on emulating Engels, because the brilliance of this text derives, at least to a considerable degree, from the method of exposition. Each analytic sojourn begins with perfecting the analysis contained in key texts of Subaltern Studies, then moves to a definitive criticism of the perfected argument. During this process, the criticism is leavened by a careful appreciation and absorption of the many positive contributions of postcolonial theorists, with the best elements becoming building blocks for Chibber's (finally delivered) alternate analysis.

The method works beautifully because even brief presentations of the final positive syntheses are instantly grasped and appreciated, because we are attuned—by the detailed scrutiny of the Subalternists— to the key markers that an adequate explanation must address. But this indisputably productive approach also has its problems, because it often results in a recessive under-emphasis on the dynamic elements in Chibber's perspective. This is particularly visible in the concluding chapter, where he devotes six long pages to reviewing the critique and only one short (though luminous) page to his positive analysis.[2]

Let me illustrate what I think is the problem by tracing his analysis of the origins of structural conflict within postcolonial society.[3] After deconstructing the Subaltern Studies argument that such conflict resides and emanates from survivals of pre-existing formations, Chibber then accepts their claim that these non-capitalist formations play an important role in societal dynamics writ large, while showing that they have not been the locus of anti-capitalist resistance. In his crowning analysis—based on evidence drawn not only from the Subaltern theorists themselves, but also the rest of the postcolonial world, Chibber shows that the big conflicts—those that yield (and threaten to yield) major shifts in postcolonial trajectories—emanate from the contradictions within the sectors of postcolonial society that are most fully absorbed into the process of capital accumulation. In perfecting this negative argument, Chibber actually offers an integration of political economic theorizing around state development and the extensive literature on Third World revolution, while absorbing the best elements of Subaltern Studies.

I want to focus on one key moment in Chibber's argument to point toward what I think is a major area that needs further attention. One of the most compelling passages in the book responds to Partha Chatterjee's analysis of the dynamics of peasant mobilization. Chibber concludes:

> Chatterjee maintains that the defining element of Indian peasants' agency is their insulation from "bourgeois consciousness," from strategies that prioritize individual interests. Their self-identities issue from their membership in the community, and their basic motivations derive from their sense of obligation to this community. If this is true, however, surely it should also mitigate the internal class differentiation of the peasantry ... The emerging rich peasants acquired the land because their peers fell on hard times ... The wealthier peasants had a choice: they could assist their fellow villagers out of a sense of duty, as members of the community, without seeking personal gain; or they could take advantage of their peers' misfortune and usurp their land, their most precious resource ... For the class of jotedars to have emerged it must be the case that a section of the smallholder community chose the latter course of action. They chose to pursue their individual interests. In other words, these smallholders acted on precisely the "bourgeois consciousness" that Chatterjee insists they lacked.[4]

This precise targeting of a key dynamic in the colonial world—the importation of capital accumulation into peasant society and the class differentiation that follows—allows Chibber to demonstrate that rural conflicts were not "conservative" efforts built on the (already fractured) communal solidarity, but rather expressions of the growing class divisions created by the capitalist invasions.

But, at the same time, Chibber rushes past a crucial point which I think emanates from this insight. As he states in other contexts, the old communalism was not obliterated—but instead transmuted—during this process. Such pre-capitalist formations do not disappear; they adapt into the capitalist structure, creating a kind of mutual evolution in which the outcome structure will be unique in each country, and quite different between and within regions.[5] For many pre-capitalist formations, this adaptation has little consequence for the outcome dynamics, but surely this communalism—and the shape of its altered role in the capitalized structure—is a causal vector in the resulting class dynamics. Put simply: what becomes of the communalistic ethos that Subaltern Studies valorizes? It arrives in the new formation in a variety of forms, and Chibber (and those of us who take up his argument) must offer an understanding of the dynamics that determine the outcome formation. Even more important is to codify and understand the varying structural trajectories characterizing the various outcome formations.

I want to offer one avenue of analysis regarding the afterlife of communalism in postcolonial society. From Chibber's argument, we see one regularity that occurs wherever rural capital accumulation is set in motion: the creation of self-aggrandizing rich peasants who have abandoned (much of) the communalistic ethos. But what of the poor (and soon becoming landless) peasants? It seems to me that there is considerable work to be done to understand the circumstances under which they abandon the communalistic ethos and organize against the rich peasants, and those circumstances when they continue to embrace communalism and ally themselves with the jotedars (despite their growing contradictions of interest). I am particularly taken by the contrast between, say, Vietnam and China, which sustained insurrections of peasants against the rural elites, and the American South, where Southern tenants most often joined movements led by the same rural elites who had taken their land and/or exploited their labor. For me, we are sorely in need of an analysis that will allow us to understand what sorts of absorption processes—and related dynamics—yield one or another of these modalities. In India, it would appear that both modalities have developed in different regions and different times, and careful scrutiny using Chibber's analytic tools could well unravel this critical dynamic.

The various strands in Chibber's argument are woven together, and much is lost when we disentangle them. But we need to do so anyway, because leaving them undifferentiated conceals some of the most promising yet unexplored insights. Consider, for example, Chibber's treatment of what he calls "the real engine of democratization."[6] Here he begins with the Subaltern Studies assertion that parliamentary democracy (including its essential accoutrements, such as free speech, equal protection, and so forth) was an organic expression of the imperatives of capitalism ascending—and that the failure of democracy in the postcolonial world must derive from strong pre-capitalist (and axiomatically anti-democratic) forces. Partly, Chibber rebuts this argument through his savaging of the communalism assertions, but this is only the beginning link in what becomes his broader theory of when and where parliamentary democracy arises.

Herein lies another instance in which Chibber preserves elements of the Subaltern Studies analysis: he endorses the proposition that parliamentary democracy was (and is) a consequence of ascendant capitalism. But he stands their argument on its head. He definitively rebuts their assertion of bourgeois activism, and replaces it with subaltern activism.

To accomplish this inversion, Chibber challenges the Subalternists' core argument that pioneering Western capitalists actively fought for parliamentary democracy and its accompanying rights, as soon as their political power allowed it. He demonstrates instead that the rising bourgeoisie and its political allies in England and France resourcefully opposed democracy, and that the arrival of universal suffrage and the other elements of what we now call democracy was a result of sustained struggle by subaltern classes. But he preserves the connection between capitalism and democratic rights, pointing out that it was only with the rise of industrial production that the working class (in alliance with the other subaltern groupings and in opposition to the capitalists) achieved the leverage it needed to demand and win universal suffrage and the other accoutrements of democracy. He completes this tightly woven argument with a gorgeous little comment: "It was only through subaltern mobilizations that capitalism was civilized."[7]

But as beautiful as this argument is, I feel it is only a start. There is so much more that needs to be done here. First and foremost, Chibber (and those of us who work with his ideas) must explain why capitalism confers the needed leverage on the subaltern classes. He makes a start by invoking Marx's founding insight that the gathering of industrial workers into close proximity, and engaged in a production process characterized by ever-increasing division of labor, was the foundation for class formation and therefore working-class agency. But this is only a beginning.

Second, and perhaps closer to the analysis that Chibber provides, is answering a host of questions around class struggle. As we look from country to country (in the capitalist core or the postcolonial periphery), we find a huge variance in the degree of "democratization." This is especially clear if we shift our attention from contested elections as the sine qua non of "democracy" and focus instead on the full array of political, economic, and human rights that are supposed to be integral to democratic society. Once we do this, we see that there is no facile correlation between the extension of capitalist accumulation into the far corners of society and the further extension of democratic rights. Instead, there are huge and changing differences among countries with comparable levels of capitalist penetration. So we need a much more refined understanding of the dynamics of capitalist development to understand the configurations that create the capacity (and the intention) for subaltern classes to civilize capitalism. Let me point to one set of elements that must surely be a major factor in unraveling this conundrum: racism and its categorical cousins—patriarchy, religious intolerance, ethnic discrimination, and so forth. In tracking the successes and failures in civilizing capitalism, we must acknowledge that racism (or any of its cousins) has been a key factor in determining the degree of leverage either available to, or accessible by, subaltern movements. But we must press beyond this proposition to understand when, where, and how the racism process operates—since here too there is great variance in its role, depending on the national or regional setting. There has been some important work on these questions that can be integrated into the Chibberian analysis. One exemplar is Richard Williams's argument[8] that racism (or any of its cousins) is most impactful in defense of capitalist barbarism when racial categories coincide with occupational stratification, generally yielding meager citizenship rights for the racial minority and degraded rights for the "privileged" "majority."

For me this excursion into the nuts and bolts of elaborating Chibber's analysis leads back to the proposition that capitalism absorbs pre-capitalist formations while preserving and evolving many of the elements. Can we comprehend this absorption process well enough to understand how the distinct dynamics that emerge have an impact on the trajectory of economic development, the vulnerability of the structure to democratic reform, and the agency of subaltern masses?

Let me turn now to a third (also indelibly interconnected) element of Chibber's analysis: the structural constraints that led Global South nationalists to pursue modernization (instead of other alternatives, including socialism). In contrasting his perspective with Partha Chatterjee's argument that these policies were expressions of pro-Western sycophantism, he concludes: "Chatterjee's theory of nationalism fails in large measure because it denies the reality of capitalist constraints. It treats rational decisions as having been ideologically driven and, in so doing, vastly exaggerates the role of ideas and grossly undervalues the effects of actually existing structures."[9]

This is yet another of Chibber's insights that emerge from his dialectical method. His assertion of structural constraint is fully persuasive because he has so meticulously demolished Chatterjee's assertion that nationalist leaders could have pursued many different development strategies, and thus effectively rebutted his conclusion that modernization policy reflected ideological commitment. But this method of exposition has deprived us of a full treatment of nationalism as an ideology and its role in determining economic and political trajectories. While Chibber's structural argument is compelling, he is inattentive to the impact of nationalism within the structural constraints he so forcefully articulates. I am thinking here that in the Indian case (and many, but not all others), nationalism was instrumental in muting the class struggle or misdirecting subaltern classes away from demands that might have brought them greater citizenship rights or a greater share of the rewards of development.

And then there is the larger question about the diversities in the types and impact of nationalism in differing postcolonial settings. Vietnamese and Indian nationalism would appear to have had very different impacts on anti-colonial struggles and postcolonial development. In explaining this difference, we may well, as Jeffrey Paige has argued,[10] look to the differing paths of capitalist development as structural determinants that produce different forms of human agency— including different forms of nationalism—and ultimately have an impact on different development strategies.[11]

I think that Chibber points us toward a comprehensive analysis of these issues in his luminous, but all too short, recapitulation of his "positive account of how capital, power, and agency actually work." Here he lists the first two of the four basic elements of his "alternative argument":

> The first is that the universalization of capital is real, *pace* the claims of the Subalternist collective. The colonies' political dynamics did not attain a fundamentally different kind of modernity than did the Europeans'. More precisely, their modernity may have been different, but not in the ways that postcolonial theory insists. Theirs is a modernity that, over time, became no less reflective of capitalist imperatives than the French or German. The second is that the universalizing drive of capital should not be assumed to homogenize power relations or the social landscape more generally. In fact, capitalism is not only consistent with great heterogeneity and hierarchy, but systematically generates them. Capitalism is perfectly compatible with a highly diverse set of political and cultural formations.[12]

But this also points to what might be the least developed component in Chibber's analysis: human agency. He is so occupied with debunking the cultural determinism of the Subaltern school that he does not pay enough attention to the first part of Marx's famous structural axiom, that people "make history, but not as they choose." While Chibber is right to call out the structural dynamics of capitalism that the

Subalternists attempt to sweep away, we also need a comprehensive analysis of the circumstances under which people are able to collectively choose and implement progressive social change. We need to identify and comprehend the broader nexus of dynamic forces that facilitate or constrain our efforts to construct what Perry Anderson has called "a premeditated future."[13]

CHAPTER 12

Minding Appearances

The Labor of Representation in Vivek Chibber's *Postcolonial Theory and the Specter of Capital*

David Pedersen

> Why is labor represented by the value of its product and labor-time by the magnitude of that value?
>
> Karl Marx

In the preface to his *Postcolonial Theory and the Specter of Capital*, Vivek Chibber[1] thanks Neil Brenner for the book's name, writing that "Brenner gets the lion's share of credit for the book's title . . . the title is basically his." Several scholars have questioned whether the book's primary content, a sustained critique of writings by Ranajit Guha, Partha Chatterjee, and Dipesh Chakrabarty, is a fair proxy for the diverse efforts of people who identify themselves as studying or being a part of the "postcolonial."[2] The second part of the title, "Specter of Capital," orients my comments on the book in this essay. It is an accurate choice of terms, because Chibber's book does offer a significant argument about the critical study of appearances, which is a term directly related to the word "apparition" and its close cousin, "specter."

Readers should recognize the word "specter" as a reference to the opening sentence of Karl Marx and Friederich Engel's "Manifesto of the Communist Party" published in 1848: "A specter is haunting Europe—the specter of Communism." Readers also will discern that a tradition of Marxism gets a lion's share of credit for informing the book's content. One of the book's primary goals is to refute the claim, attributed by Chibber to the three authors affiliated with "Subaltern Studies," that critical study of capitalism informed by Marxism is not applicable to the postcolonial history of India. The way that the book approaches appearances directly echoes Marx's metaphorical use of specters and ghosts in his varied analyses of capitalist relations.[3]

There are two different connotations to "specter" that make their appearance in Chibber's book. The first is the understanding that beyond or behind a surface level of particular human sentiments, practices, and habits, however dominant and durable, lies something more basic and material shared by all individuals in any context. The second perspective on appearances suggested in the book is that particular kinds of representations or mediations may actually become more material, mobile, and capable of making things happen in the world. The first modality is about appearances and something behind them. The second approach is about the agency of appearances and their capacity to hide both the conditions that give rise to them and their manner of contributing to perpetuating these same conditions. This essay focuses on these two understandings of appearances and the way that the book's manner of minding them is integral to its critical analysis. I am less concerned with choosing a side in the academic debate to which the book substantially contributes than with using its appearance as an opportunity to push forward discussion about how better to render fully "explanatory critiques" of capitalist relations anywhere on the planet.[4]

INDIA AND EUROPE

Postcolonial Theory and the Specter of Capital is organized as an analytical critique of the writings of Ranajit Guha, Partha Chatterjee, and Dipesh Chakrabarty, among the most prominent scholars associated with the Subaltern Studies collective. Chibber focuses on their work and identifies a constellation of arguments that stipulate several key divergences between Indian and European modernity. Chibber distills three themes, pointing out that the authors participate in an aggregate project of arguing for a radical Indian difference regarding: 1) the character of its bourgeoisie; 2) the relative role of distinctly capitalist power relations; and 3) what Chibber calls the "political psychology" of Indian subaltern actors. Chibber lays out what he understands as the necessary preconditions required for sustaining all the arguments that buttress the claim of a radical India-Europe divergence along the three thematic axes. He effectively tests to see if these conditions are, in fact, manifest in the evidence and logically plausible. Chapter by chapter, he endeavors to show how the evidentiary premises of the arguments in favor of the three distinctions cannot be sustained.

Chibber also specifies an alternative interpretation and approach meant to overcome the stark India/Europe divide, allowing for variation within what is understood as a unitary capitalism, marked by two fundamental tendencies. The first is that capitalists tend to spread and deepen their activities as a feature of their recognition of the requirements of the system in which they participate. The second is that workers, as they experience forms of exploitation through the actions of capitalists, will be inclined to resist this process, motivated by recognition of direct threats to their material or bodily well-being. Chibber calls these "Enlightenment" universal tendencies and he wishes to defend them against the claim by Subaltern Studies authors that they are not applicable to Indian history. In this defense lies the book's first critical approach to appearances.

GHOSTBUSTER

Postcolonial Theory and the Specter of Capital carries a definition of one domain of social life that is understood as separate and distinct from an underlying and more basic reality. In the author's terms, all of these surface aspects or features fall under the umbrella term of "political psychology." Chibber does not explain this expression, though it has a substantial scholarly pedigree, including its early appearance in the German ethnologist Adolph Bastian's 1860 book, *Man in History*.[5] Bastian's work influenced the famous British anthropologist Edward B. Tylor and also directly shaped the scholarship of Franz Boas, known as the founder of US anthropology.[6] It also is associated with the work of US political scientist Harold Lasswell during the 1930s and 1940s.[7] Chibber deploys political psychology as a general hypernym for what he identifies elsewhere in the text as consciousness, culture, identity, ideology, and religion.[8]

Chibber invokes all five of these concepts especially in Chapters 6 through 8, making this part of the book the most concentrated critical examination of how the Subaltern Studies authors treat the content of what Chibber has called "political psychology." He summarizes his interpretation of the Subaltern Studies position in the fourth paragraph of Chapter 7: "They deny that agents share a common set of needs or interests across cultural boundaries, arguing instead that the peasants and industrial workers in the East have a wholly different psychology from those in the West."[9] In Chapter 6, Chibber focuses on Partha Chatterjee's work, which he summarizes as organized around the central claim that "communal norms, not individual interests, were the fount of rural politics" in India.[10]

Chibber's critique rests on examining Guha's *Elementary Forms*, which Chatterjee had drawn upon, as well as Chatterjee's own research on peasants in Bengal and identifying instances where peasants seemed to act according to individual interests rather than shared cultural norms. He focuses on Chatterjee's identification of internal differentiation between a relatively wealthy smallholding fraction, jotedars, who employed workers, obtained rents from tenant farmers, and earned income from lending operations, and the majority of peasants who were primarily subsistence farmers. Chibber argues that this apparent diversity refutes Chatterjee's claim that a singular peasant communal ideology dominated Bengali peasant life, fully masking the relative exploitation carried out by jotedars.

In Chapter 8, Chibber continues this line of analysis, tracing the relationship between collective norms and individual interests through consideration of Dipesh Chakrabarty's book *Rethinking Working-Class History: Bengal 1890–1940*. According to Chibber, Chakrabarty "purports to have discovered that subordinate groups are not motivated by a defense of their interests; instead, they are driven by their valuation of community, honor, religion, and other normative ends." Chibber argues against Chakrabarty's claim that jute workers "remained prisoners of a precapitalist culture"[11] by pointing out that "when migrants came to the city, they constructed new communities when they became involved in trade unions or forged new social solidarities with migrants from other parts of the country. They showed themselves capable of forming a different cultural sensibility—organized around a more secular and economic axis—than the one into which they had been socialized."[12]

In the second part of the chapter, Chibber defends what he calls "a stripped-down, minimal account of rationality,"[13] which he defines as ultimately founded on the "the need to ward off direct bodily harm by others and the need for a livelihood."[14] These two basic needs may be translated into cultural codes in any context and in turn cognized or reflected upon, but they also remain relatively exterior to any culture as basic material prerequisites for human life. According to Chibber, both the jute mill workers and Bengali peasants "made choices, to be sure, but what all these choices had in common was that they were in defense of their physical security. The concern for basic well-being thus constituted the grounds on which the choices were made."[15] In this, Chibber asserts that "culture does not go 'all the way down'"[16] so as to conceal the real interest of human physical well-being.

For Chibber, political psychology is the particular form in which all that both threatens and contributes to bodily well-being makes its appearance. In contrast to Chatterjee and Chakrabarty, who greatly emphasize the relative sovereignty, agentive capacity, and dominance of such appearances among Indian subaltern classes, Chibber insists that this basic need to survive ultimately will, in his words, "cut through" the apparent blanket of any particular culture as if it were no more than a ghost costume. In this, Chibber decidedly is a ghostbuster.

The Appearance of Labor

There is a second manner of minding appearances that is implicit in Chibber's book and it is the understanding that particular representational patterns or mediations are specific to capitalism and, rather than as the content of a finite and discrete political psychology, are quite real and capable of shaping reality "all the way down," independent of any individual. This understanding of appearances as agentive abstractions is not directly claimed or argued by Chibber, nor is it captured by an overall term like political psychology. However, it can be gleaned from Chibber's discussion of Marx's concept of abstract labor and his critique of how Dipesh Chakrabarty has interpreted the concept.

Consistent with his overarching criticism of the Subaltern Studies project, Chibber focuses on how Chakrabarty's recent work, especially

Provincializing Europe, is predicated on finding radical social difference in India that defies assumptions about capitalism based on its European history. Chibber equates what he identifies as the Subaltern Studies authors' aversion to abstract or general categories that suppress such radical difference with a particular understanding of Marx's notion of abstract labor. Chibber is correct to criticize Lowe and Lloyd[17] for their misunderstanding of the category.[18] However, in Chakrabarty's case, aversion to abstract categories in general is not the same as an aversion to the specific Marxian category of abstract labor. This can be better appreciated by considering a passage written by Chakrabarty that appeared as the second chapter in a book titled *Marxism Beyond Marxism,* edited by Sari Makdisi, Cesare Casarino, and Rebecca Karl. Chakrabarty's essay was titled "Marx after Marxism: History, Subalternity, and Difference." In this essay he reflected on *Rethinking Working-Class History* and admitted that he had misinterpreted the distinction between "real" and "abstract" labor in Marx, assuming that real labor referred to the specific efforts of an actual person:

> My larger failure lay in my inability to see that if one read the "real" as socially/culturally produced . . . other possibilities open up; among them the one of writing "difference" back into Marx. For the "real" then, in this reading would refer to different kinds of "social" and hence to different orders of temporality . . . The transition from "real" to "abstract"

is thus also a question of transition/translation from many and possibly incommensurable temporalities to the homogeneous time of abstract labor, the transition from non-history to history.[19]

Chakrabarty continues, explaining his recognition that "the category of 'real' labor, therefore, has the capacity to refer to that which cannot be enclosed by the sign." This gesture to Saussure's semiology and Derrida's critique of it helps explain why Chakrabarty later used the distinction between History 1 and 2. Because he approached the capitalist commodity as a discrete Saussurian sign, a relationship between idea and utterance or structure and instantiation, Chakrabarty totally abandoned the quality of relational dynamism and interaction inherent in Marx's analysis of capitalist value determination. Chakrabarty's History 1 and 2 is as much about structuralism and its critique by Derrida as it is about Indian subaltern history. Remarkably, the anti-foundationalist critique of Saussure's sign logic has helped provide a foundation for establishing Subaltern Studies as a widespread project of critiquing capitalism and its imperial effects from the solid foundation of a locus assumed to be exterior to it.

In his critique of Chakrabarty, Chibber argues that "abstract" is one quality or dimension of "concrete" labor and that this abstract quality is what matters, or comes to be dominant within capitalism, because of the market demands faced by capitalists. Concrete or "real" as in Chakrabarty's admission above may be understood as the wholeness of labor from which the abstract dimension or quality is accentuated and made to count in capitalism. In this sense, Chibber's critique rests on an implicit recognition that there is a dominant appearance to labor within capitalism and that this form and its maintenance is necessary for capitalism. Chibber explains that this is well understood from Marx's inquiries and as such it provides the foundation for his critique of Chakrabarty's distinction between History 1 and 2.

LABOR OF REPRESENTATION

Chibber's argument is correct as far as it goes, but explaining abstract labor as a result of capitalists' profit drive or market logic is only part of the story. It also requires all that yields the regular sale of labor power as a commodity, its use as labor and its congealing in the tools and techniques of such labor. And most crucially, it requires the establishment of money as a universal equivalent. All this is an exceedingly complex social and historical configuration that contains a manner of representation that is necessary for its continuation. These appearances are real in the sense that they cannot be reduced to individual actors or orientations.

In volume 1 of Capital, Marx poses a question about capitalism as representational proclivity by asking "why this content has assumed that particular form, that is to say why labor is expressed in value, and why the measurement of labor by its duration is expressed in the magnitude of the value of the product." The statement suggests that what is at stake in capitalism is an ensemble of representational tendencies that have become generalized, even naturalized. This is not Saussure or Derrida, but instead is the more basic recognition that capitalism entails certain systemic processes of abstraction and representation, which are continuous and unfinished processes. To grasp this means to use abstract as a verb as well as its own product, the noun form, abstraction. Determination is the aggregate social process of abstraction in that it happens independently of what any individual thinks about it. Overall, something is pulling out qualities and dimensions of something else so as to convey something else, a quality of meaning. It is the move from the possible to the actual to the general. Why does the human capacity to work upon the world take the form it does in capitalism? Why is an undefined human capacity shaped in a particular way and not others? Following this perspective, capitalism is inherently about appearances, but these do not exist in relation to their content like a dependent variable in relation to an independent one. Value as the objectification of the most abstract aspects of labor-power is the representational tendency that is specific to capitalism. Besides abstract and concrete, Marx also introduced private and social as two other qualities of labor under any historical conditions. Taken together they comprise all that could go into any product of human labor under any conditions, including labor power itself. This is the infinite whole from which, within capitalist relations, the abstract dimension is pulled out and represented or objectified in the commodity through its money price.

As I have intimated, it now is possible to see that the Subaltern Studies project reflected in part an academic debate over structuralism and post-structuralism. Marx's approach to value determination and his understanding of representation defies both the structuralist and post-structuralist traditions. Rather than code and instantiation or infinite instantiations, it is inquiry into the historical establishment of a specific three-way representational tendency involving labor, value, and labor's product and another three-way configuration among labor-time, value, and magnitude or measure. In inquiring into capitalism, Marx asked how and why these arrangements came into being and were sustained.

The current crossroads in the discussion sparked by Subaltern Studies and critiques like Chibber's is that both seem to require a foundation from which to critique capitalism. It is History 2 for Chakrabarty and it is the defense of individual interests based on ensuring human bodily well-being for Chibber. The Subaltern Studies position has been attractive over the past two decades and it joins a classic tradition in anthropology of seeking cultures or cultural formations that provide fully formed alternatives to "Western" modernity.[20] (Subaltern Studies scholars have explicitly remarked on the influence of British and French anthropology on their work.) An individual interest in the protection of bodily well-being may be a limit to culture or political psychology, but it also is what capitalism necessarily draws upon to "universalize." It is the basis of most human medical research and the incredible translation of such science into widely consumed capitalist commodities. Protection of bodily well-being is as much the basis of capitalism as the grounds of its critique. In this, it doesn't offer a limit to any representational system nor the positive content of a horizon beyond it.

The challenge is to occupy a different kind of ground for critique that does not rely on concepts like the non-West or biology. We similarly would do well to dispense with the academic categories of economics, politics, and culture—the different disciplines that substantiate their (false) separation into discrete domains, each with their own equilibrium-seeking logics of supply and demand, checks and balances, and words and ideas.

If we recall Marx's early recognition that what people are anywhere and anywhen is greatly defined by what they produce—"making something more from nothing but"—and also how this is organized and accomplished, then the foundation of critique, including living struggles, is all that is not yet available or possible in the current form and organization of productive life on the planet. This is as much "cultural" or "psychological" as biological and material.

CHAPTER 13

Confronting Postcolonial Theory: A Response to Critics

Vivek Chibber

Postcolonial Theory and the Specter of Capital was written as both an intervention and a contribution to theory. It was intended to offer an assessment of one of the most influential theoretical frameworks in the humanities and social sciences since the 1990s, and a response to their criticisms of received frameworks. George Steinmetz wonders why I chose to focus so strenuously on Subaltern Studies as the stand-in for the larger theoretical corpus. He observes correctly that there are many other prominent theorists associated with postcolonial theory (hereafter PCT), such as Gayatri Spivak, Homi Bhabha, and others. The reason is that it is the historians and anthropologists in the field who have moved beyond a theory of postcolonial culture, and developed something close to a sociology of modern capitalist forms, as well as a theory of why capitalist modernization has proceeded in the way that it has. And among these more sociologically minded theorists, there is no doubt that Subaltern Studies has wielded an influence that is deeper and wider than any other current within the field. Its most prominent members have generated not only an empirically, historically based argument about the course of modern capitalism in the colonial world, but one that is remarkably coherent and consistently developed over time. As I explain in the introduction to the book, it is not my view by any means that Subaltern Studies covers the gamut of arguments or concepts in postcolonial studies. But it is representative of many of the central ideas that are associated with PCT; it is extremely influential; and its internal consistency makes it not just representative, but the most attractive and plausible denizen of this body of work.[1]

PCT claims to show that the theories and categories associated with the most influential frameworks of the twentieth century—liberal political theory and Marxist theory—cannot apprehend the actual course of economic and political development in the colonial world. Both approaches are rejected because of their supposed determinism and teleology, which blind them to the specificity of the colonial and postcolonial world. Postcolonial theorists reject what they take to be an illicit universalism in these frameworks, a prejudice that categories and predictions coming out of the European experience must be equally relevant to the specific experience of the Global South. Because it is flawed, this universalism turns out to generate a pronounced Eurocentric bias in both liberal and Marxist theory. And this, in turn, only perpetuates the political and economic dominance of the West over the East. Or so they claim. This rejection of Eurocentrism forms the basis of their normative critique of Western domination, and in more recent work, of the heavy hand of universalizing theories more generally.

There is a great deal at stake here. If the arguments coming from Subaltern Studies are correct, then we are obligated to overhaul much of what is currently practiced in the social sciences and humanities, roll up our sleeves, and craft entirely new frameworks for understanding the evolution of much of the world. Even more, the foundational basis of our criticism of modern capitalism has to be rejected and new political theories have to be crafted that have no truck with Enlightenment universals. It is therefore a little surprising to see how little effort there has been toward a serious assessment of the actual evidence that PCT adduces in support of its claims about the actual differences between East and West, the shortcomings of the received frameworks, the real drivers of historical trajectories, the fount of social agency, and so forth. So the first challenge I undertook in *Postcolonial Theory and the Specter of Capital* (hereafter *PTSC*) was to assess these arguments on their own grounds. And by this I mean to reconstruct them, to tease out their implications, and then to see if they stood up to empirical and logical scrutiny.

My verdict in the book is that the arguments developed by PCT and Subaltern Studies fail on both theoretical and normative grounds. With regard to theory, PCT fails in its Subalternist version because it cannot adequately explain the patterns of historical development in the advanced and late developing parts of the capitalist world. It insists that the defining characteristic of the Global South is its deep and abiding structural differentiation from the advanced capitalist world, a difference so deep, so fundamental that it requires an entirely different set of categories. I examine these claims and argue that none of the arguments adduced in their favor withstand scrutiny. There are differences between the two parts of the world, of course; but they are not of a kind that resists analysis through the inherited explanatory frameworks. I conclude that the Subaltern critique of Enlightenment theories is baseless. Furthermore, I argue not only that the arguments made by Subalternists for the specificity of the East are questionable on empirical grounds, but that they also cannot provide the basis for political critique. This is because, their rhetoric notwithstanding, they end up reviving and refurbishing some of the most objectionable orientalist canards about the East. So, far from providing a means of overturning Eurocentrism, Subaltern Studies gives it a new lease on life—for Eurocentrism is just the dual of orientalism.

THE UNIVERSALIZATION OF CAPITAL

Well, these are my conclusions. What are the bases on which I defend them? We start with an assessment of the Subalternist argument against the universalizing categories of Enlightenment thought, chief among which are the ones central to Marxist and liberal social theory— categories like capitalism, universal rights, class, citizenship, and so forth. PCT and theorists from Subaltern Studies argue that the relevance of these categories is highly dubious outside the West. The reason for this is that they presume that the social milieu that they are examining has been transformed in some relevant way by capitalism— in other words, their use presupposes a properly universalizing capitalism. But—and this is the key—capitalism failed to universalize once it left European shores. It is not that the transformation that it is supposed to bring about is yet incomplete. It is, rather, that capital mutates in such a way that it cannot universalize. Dipesh Chakrabarty is especially emphatic on this point. Subalternists deny that it is just a matter of waiting until the social transformations associated with capitalism are complete. Their view is that capitalism cannot universalize, and this is why the categories of the Enlightenment are irredeemably flawed when they are put to use in the East.

So what accounts for the necessity of capital's failed universalization? There are two arguments that Subalternists make in this regard, one developed by Ranajit Guha and the other by Dipesh Chakrabarty. For Guha, the key lies in a deep historical failing in the colonial and postcolonial bourgeoisie, namely, that it failed in its duty to "speak for all the nation," to create a liberal political culture in which political rule was based on the consent of the masses. He contrasts this with the experience of the West, in which capital created a culture of rights and liberality, in which rulers treated the ruled as formal equals even while they exploited them. The pivotal events in which capital advanced this agenda were the great bourgeois revolutions of 1640 in England and 1789 in France. But in India, in its "bourgeois revolution"—that is, the Independence movement—Indian capital forswore any such mission. Instead of overthrowing the ancient regime, it accommodated to it and instead of embracing its mission to speak for all the nation, it chose only a pursuit of its narrow economic interests. Hence, capital's rule in the East turned out to be based on outright domination rather than on hegemony, whereas in the West, the poles were reversed—capital ruled hegemonically, and coercion played a subordinate role. The different character of the bourgeoisie in the two instances created radically different political modernities.

Dipesh Chakrabarty accepts Guha's historical sociology, but adds to it another dimension, which provided independent grounds for the denial of capital's universalization. He begins with the observation that capital strives to subordinate all social relations to its own logic. But, he says, this compulsion is not equally successful across the board. There are some practices that do become absorbed by capital. Chakrabarty calls these practices "History 1." But then there are others that, even while they are influenced by capital, still manage to retain their integrity and resist total subordination. These Chakrabarty calls "History 2." Chakrabarty then adds the proviso that for capital to have successfully universalized, it must be the case that History 1 obliterates History 2. But of course, he observes, History 2 can never be extinguished. No social formation loses all traces of its local culture, local institutions, and so on. He then concludes that, since History 2 can never be extinguished, since some social practices resist the "totalizing" drive of capital, we must acknowledge that capital never in fact succeeds in its universalizing drive. And since it does not successfully universalize, the universalizing categories of the Enlightenment, which presume that History 1 has in fact won out, only serve to obscure the real nature of postcolonial societies. They fail to appreciate its heterogeneity, they wipe all traces of social differences, and impose on this rich diversity the homogenizing categories of Western thought.

In assessing these arguments in *PTSC*, I take a conservative approach. I grant to the Subalternists their premise—which is by no means obviously correct—that for Enlightenment categories to have relevance, capital must be shown to retain its universalizing drive. As it happens, I believe that the premise can be easily rejected, but I keep to it in order to make the Subalternist case as strong as possible. So let us assume that it has warrant. Can we agree with the claim that capital cannot universalize once it leaves Western shores? I argue that neither argument for capital's abandonment of its universalizing drive can be defended.

Guha's argument for there being a historic break between the political projects of the bourgeoisie in the West and in the East flows from a highly mythologized story about the great bourgeois revolutions, one that was rejected decades ago by historians. I show this in great detail in Chapters 3 and 4 in *PTSC*. All the critics in this forum accept my reconstruction of Guha as well as my criticism of him. But William Sewell worries that while my basic argument regarding the so-called bourgeois revolutions is convincing, I am not sufficiently attentive to some of the real shifts that they did facilitate, and he brings up, as an example, the importance of 1688 for the separation of powers in the English state and that of 1789 for ideas such as the Rights of Man. But Sewell is reading my argument in an unduly narrow fashion. My argument for the importance of the English and French revolutions is meant to assess whether they performed the functions assigned to them by Guha, and for him, their achievement is very specific—they were instances in which capital fought for, and successfully created, a political culture based on the inclusion of the laboring classes, in which their participation in the political process was not only allowed but welcomed by the new ruling class. My downgrading of the revolutions' achievements should be read against the claims that I am assessing. I do not deny their significance altogether. It is not that I am unaware of the shift toward a constitutional monarchy in England or the promulgation of the Rights of Man in France. My argument is twofold—that the shifts that did occur were nowhere near what is needed to validate Guha's argument, and second, that insofar as there was a movement toward greater inclusiveness, it was not because of the universalizing mission of capital, but because of pressure from the laboring classes. Sewell is correct in his claim about the revolution's legacy for the issues he raises, but his observation is quite consistent with my argument.

I am pleased to see that all of the critics also largely agree with my rejection of Chakrabarty's argument, though they raise some related issues that are quite interesting. Chakrabarty sets up a test for the universalizing process that is absurdly stringent, one that, to my knowledge, no social theorist has ever countenanced. I argue against Chakrabarty that capital's universalization does not at all require that capital absorb History 2 into its logic. For that to be the test, it would require that every social practice, every aspect of culture, ideology, and social institutions become reflections of capitalist imperatives. The mind boggles at the thought. A more reasonable litmus is that capital merely has to ensure the subordination of economic practices to its logic, moving against the autonomy of cultural and social practices only if they interfere with or undermine the economic. Chakrabarty only allows two possibilities in his universe—practices either directly support capitalism or they are a threat to it. But it is entirely possible that practices can be outside the orbit of commodity production and be neutral toward it—a possibility that he does not consider. But if this is so, then there is no necessary conflict between History 1 and History 2, and the non-incorporation of History 2 is not evidence of capital's failure to implant itself. Furthermore, Chakrabarty is mistaken in locating the sources of instability to capitalism in History 2. I argue that the most important sources of instability are in fact exemplars of History 1—centrally, problems within the accumulation process itself, which lead to economic breakdown, and laborers' defense of their material interests, which are universal in scope.

George Steinmetz raises a very pertinent issue when he wonders if my arguments for History 1 as the main source of instability are too hasty in pushing aside the importance of History 2. He observes, correctly, that I put a great deal of weight on my claim that capitalism can subsist in happy coexistence with practices and institutions in History 2, and hence, that an affirmation of its universalizing drive need not blind us to the fact of historical diversity. But, Steinmetz suggests, is it not possible that there might be plenty of instances in which elements of local cultures or practices, in places where capitalism is taking root, might in fact be inimical to its reproduction? If so, should we not take seriously the corrosive powers of History 2 for the universalizing tendency of capitalism? I entirely agree with Steinmetz on this, and in fact, I point out in *PTSC* that History 2 can block or destabilize capitalist reproduction.[2] My argument is not that History 2 can never be a source of disruption; it is that whether or not it is so is a highly contingent matter, whereas there are elements of History 1 that are systematically in tension with the stability of capitalism. I argue for the asymmetry between the two as sources of instability within capitalism, not for the irrelevance of History 2.[3]

Steinmetz also proposes, in a related argument, that I could have tried for a more ramified conception of political forms, presumably in Chapter 5 where I discuss the kinds of power relations that are consistent with capitalism. He regrets that I confine my discussion to the labor process, to the detriment of any consideration of the state or other political institutions. If I had done so, he continues, I might have considered how there have been instances in which colonial states blocked the spread of capitalist relations—not liberalism, but the production relations of capitalism itself. This would be an instance of the actual blockage of the universalizing tendency, even on my definition of the term. Steinmetz is again quite right. In the history of colonialism, there have in fact been plenty of instances in which states impeded the growth of capitalism by giving support to traditional social relations. But my ambition was not to insist that capitalism has taken root in every corner of the globe, or to present colonialism as an engine for capitalism's growth, as Bill Warren[4] did famously in his work a generation ago. As I say in *PTSC*, whether or not capitalism has in fact taken root in a colonial setting is an empirical matter;[5] it did so unevenly, sometimes very slowly, sometimes rapidly, and sometimes it was not until the postcolonial era that it spread. There are even regions where its development continues to be episodic and weak. My argument was that even where such developments occur, they cannot provide support for the Subalternist argument, which is not that capital's universalization might be blocked here and there, but that it either loses its very capacity for universalization (Guha) or never had it in the first place (Chakrabarty), since it is necessarily blocked by History 2. To put it more precisely, Steinmetz suggests the possibility of a causal property's realization being blocked, while the Subalternists argue for that property being shed altogether. *PTSC* is ranged against the latter argument, and happily acknowledges the possibility of the former.

THE OTHER UNIVERSALISM

So, one kind of universalizing process that is defended in *PTSC* is the spread of capitalism around the globe. A second one that occupies a prominent place in the book is the fact of some universal basic needs among human beings, and from that I derive the possibility of real interests that bind together members of a class. In *PTSC*, I show that Partha Chatterjee and Dipesh Chakrabarty deny both the motivational force of basic needs and the salience of individual interests for non-Western actors. They do not reject the very idea of real need and interests—they just think that Eastern minds are not motivated by them. I show that their arguments against the salience of interests are mistaken and, indeed, that the empirical research of Subalternist historians— including and especially Chatterjee and Chakrabarty—itself demonstrates that non-Western actors are every bit as aware of their objective interests as are Western ones. All of the critics seem basically sympathetic to my argument, though Steinmetz and Sewell both express some skepticism toward my positive account of practical reason, Sewell worrying that it amounts to a version of rational choice theory, and Steinmetz seeming to think that my view amounts to a denial, or at least a denigration, of the fact that all action is meaning-oriented.

Does my argument amount to a version of rational choice theory? I proposed in *PTSC* that it does not, in large measure because I reject a maximizing model of rationality. But perhaps Sewell is right that this does not merit casting it out of the family of rational choice. In the end, the label matters less than the plausibility of the core arguments. Steinmetz's concerns are more germane here, since they question the viability of my arguments. But he is mistaken if he thinks that my view calls for meaning-free action. The affirmation of rationality does not require that social agents perform their actions outside the meaning universe that they occupy. I go to some lengths in *PTSC* to make this clear.[6] What it rejects is the idea that the acculturation of social actors can be such as to make them oblivious of their basic needs; I suggest that the pursuit of these needs does not exist outside of culture, but that, because they act as such a powerful motivational force, cultures have to create codes and conventions that respect and acknowledge them. I cannot develop this point here, for lack of space, but I refer readers to the discussion in *PTSC*, Chapter 8, Sections 3 and 4. My point here is that Steinmetz seems to have misunderstood my argument, and imputed to me a view that I explicitly reject. Now, it could be that I am mistaken in believing that it is possible to uphold the reality of interests, while also allowing that all action is meaningful in orientation. So perhaps it is the case that arguing for basic needs and objective interests requires that we take actors to be asocial or outside of culture. But I do not believe that this is so, and in my view, sociological theory, as it is practiced today, is burdened by a quite profound confusion around this issue.

The needs that I affirm in *PTSC* play a central role in any viable social theory. As Doug Pederson correctly observes, it is on their basis that we can explain the ubiquity of resistance to social domination—especially resistance to wage labor; but, Pederson continues, even the very spread of capitalism is hard to explain except by reference to actors' real needs. It is hard to see why laborers in every part of the world, every culture, in every setting where they are expropriated, end up offering their labor power for sale, if it is not because of their desire to uphold their physical well-being. And it is equally hard to see why the wage contract breeds resistance and conflict in every part of the world, if it is not because those same laborers try to defend their autonomy and their well-being against the depredations of their employers.

Now Michael Schwartz is certainly correct in his observation that while I stress the importance of universal needs and interests, it remains insufficiently developed in the book. The main problem is that while I maintain their ubiquity as sources of motivation, I do not give much of an explanation for why their actuation or efficacy is so uneven. My failure on this score is partly because of space limits—there is only so much a book can do. But it is also for two other reasons. The first is that, as a work of critique, the book will tend to operate on the same level of generality as the theories that it interrogates. Since the basic Subalternist argument is for a denial of individual interests, I naturally strive to demonstrate their salience as a basic social fact. I pay less attention to the variations in their realization. But the second reason is that there is a veritable ocean of social science research that does just this, and Schwartz's scholarship is a great example of some of the best work that assumes rationality on the part of actors and then explains the variations that he points to. My goal in the book was to suggest that this enormous body of work is not vulnerable to the criticisms that PCT makes of it—that it gives short shrift to culture and to agency, that it is parochial, that it denigrates social differences, that it homogenizes the social landscape, and so forth. And having shown that these criticisms are unfounded, *PTSC* suggested that we can go back to this work to continue the project of understanding the real sources of social contestation, since PCT does not offer much in this direction.

CONCLUSION

So what *PTSC* argues, in the end, is that Subaltern Studies fails in the case that it makes against the universalizing categories of the Enlightenment, which include liberal and Marxist theory. This is important because, as I suggest early on in this essay, the Subalternists have made the best and most careful of all the arguments in the post-colonial arsenal. It is important to note what the implications are. Bruce Cumings objects to my characterization of their arguments, in particular to those of Chakrabarty, as orientalist. He wonders what is wrong with Chakrabarty's ambition to generate a framework that is "attuned to Indian realities and freed of European assumptions." But my criticism is not directed toward Chakrabarty's ambition, since it is one that I entirely endorse. What makes Chakrabarty's arguments orientalist is not their stated goal, but their content. Insisting that non-Western people do not have a bounded conception of the self, that they are only motivated by obligations to larger groups, that their consciousness is fundamentally religious, while Westerners are basically secular, that the reliance on Reason is a Western convention, that rationality and objectivity are Western—these are the claims that Chakrabarty and his colleagues make, and it is on the basis of these ideas that I characterize them as orientalist.

It is gratifying to see the response that *PTSC* has generated in so short a span, even though much of it has been hysterical, as I predicted in my concluding chapter. The reason is not hard to fathom—as Ho-fung Hung points out in his introduction (Chapter 7 of this volume), there is a great deal at stake in this debate, not just intellectually, but also politically. PCT has emerged and flourished at a time of general retreat for progressive forces, perhaps more so than at any other time in the modern era. For the generation of students and activists just coming of age, the only form of critical or radical theory they have ever encountered is some version of PCT or its cousins. Many of the ideas associated with progressive movements of the past century— of universal emancipation, egalitarianism, class organizing, internationalism—now seem quaint to them, if not odious. These are the ideas I try to defend and revive in *PTSC*. Perhaps Michael Schwartz is right that, in the not-too-distant future, the theories associated with PCT will seem as little more than a bizarre interlude, a temporary descent into self-absorbed tomfoolery by intellectuals. But here today, it is apparent that these currents, however odious their ideas may be, wield tremendous influence in the intellectual landscape. One can only hope that Schwartz is right and that it will soon be behind us.

Part III.
Commentaries

CHAPTER 14

Subaltern Stakes

Timothy Brennan

> With dialectics, the mob comes to the top.[1]
>
> Friedrich Nietzsche

Frantz Fanon, or at least his American translators, famously wrote of a dying colonialism.[2] If today we hear of a dying postcolonialism, it is because no amount of parsing can rid the term of its many ironies. Alongside the "post" of a supposed aftermath lies the metallic reality of a penetrating, if at times indirect, imperialism—still deepening in Puerto Rico and Palestine, and recently expanding into significant new territory in Afghanistan, Iraq, and Ukraine, replete with their pro-Western juntas and complicit local satrapies. Colonialism, it seems, is not altogether dead. The immiseration wrought by capital continues to express itself in broadly cultural, not only military or financial, ways, displaying all the hallmarks of that older system of resettlement and reeducation. Quite apart from the Western dominance of global news, entertainment, and trends in higher education, a massive diaspora of semi-permanent legions of Western tourists, expatriate fun-seekers, missionaries, mercenaries, academic theorists, real estate speculators, and diplomatic ensembles all make the late-nineteenth-century era of the Berlin Treaty look comparatively underdeveloped.

The term "postcolonial" is constitutively troubled, then, since it carries with it the strategic temporizing of its inception—the incongruity of its discursive tones and themes, in contrast with a rather blunter reality of imperial propaganda, foreign torture chambers, and the stealing of others' lands. Against this stark backdrop, the debates prompted by Vivek Chibber's magisterial *Postcolonial Theory and the Specter of Capital* seem a little narrow.[3] To lay bare the inner workings of the influential academic field known as "postcolonial theory," as he sets out to do, would first require clarity about this catachresis at the core of its idea—some account of how the earlier traditions of anti-colonial thought suddenly, and violently, became *post*colonial in a hostile takeover in the metropolitan academy of the mid-1980s.

Postcolonial studies emerged uncertainly, without even a settled name, primarily within academic departments of literature. In retrospect, certain signature events appear now to have helped call it into life: the publication of Edward Said's *Orientalism* in 1978, the "Europe and Its Others" conference at Essex University in 1984, and the special issue "Race, Writing, and Difference" from *Critical Inquiry* (1985), the most prestigious American journal in the humanities. As the postcolonial began to coalesce around a number of related themes, its brief acquired consistency: to expand university curricula in order to include non-Western sources, to uncover and promote historical acts of native resistance, and to challenge the misrepresentations of imperial history, forging a new vocabulary to contest Eurocentrism. On all of these grounds, the initiative proved very successful and its effects—not only in scholarship but in mainstream publishing and the arts—have, over the years, been largely positive.

OTHERING EUROPE

Although the creation of English departments, postcolonial inquiry was far from only literary. Already by the early 1970s, disciplinary revolutions prompted by the unsettlings of Franco-German "theory" had yielded mixed kinds of writing in the literary field itself—works of philosophy, really, that combined the techniques of ethnography and history in a language speckled with Marxist and anarchist terms and attitudes. To most in the humanities at the time, postcolonial studies simply *was* cultural theory in one of its specialized institutional forms—that is, predominantly continental, and largely psychoanalytic, semiotic, and phenomenological. These particular strands of the philosophical past were now wedded, as though they possessed a genetic compatibility, to a critique of Eurocentrism. "Postcolonial theory," then, was the name that came to be affixed to an unlikely marriage—an othering of Europe articulating itself in the concepts of a specialized group of European philosophers and their various late-twentieth-century disciples in an ambiguous rejection of "Western Man." The content of this theoretical amalgam in all of its variants—drawn primarily from Friedrich Nietzsche and Martin Heidegger by way of postwar interpreters such as Jacques Derrida and Michel Foucault—stitched together a number of plausible, but not obviously related, themes: skepticism toward the emancipatory potential of the Enlightenment, the idea of "otherness" as an ontological fact (in the form of being or alterity), and the death of the historical subject as a willed or active self. With unfeigned militancy, theory set about codifying forms of resistance that explicitly precluded Marxist contributions to anti-colonial independence, not simply as the by-product of its search for fresh paradigms, but as a central and self-defining *telos*.

Postcolonial studies gained momentum in an environment marked by the end of the postwar economic boom (1972), the media rhetoric of what Fred Halliday at the time called the "Second Cold War" (1983), and the fall of the Berlin Wall (1989). Under these pressures, the thematic emphasis tended to shift away from wars of maneuver to the mutual complicity of colonizer and colonized, from class antagonisms to migrancy and "sly civility," from a struggle over political sovereignty to a rejection of the so-called oppressiveness of modernity, on the one hand, and the "productivist" bias of political economy, on the other. This volatile ensemble, militant in tone but resonating with more conventional attitudes in the general culture, swept victoriously through the humanities and into the arts, anthropology, history, geography, and political science. As the laboratories of theory, literature departments found themselves in the vanguard. No field was left untouched by their initiatives under the sign of "the subject," "difference," and the "interstices." The irrepressible élan of the larger movement made proclamations of a "Copernican break" seem reasonable. New journals came into being to give the new agenda a voice—*Interventions, Postcolonial Studies, Transition, Public Culture*—and older venerated journals were retooled to fit the new dispensation. A pantheon was born, whose principal figures are now widely known—Edward Said, whose *Orientalism* was supposed to be the field's founding document, but with elaborations later provided—in a very different vein—by scholars like Gayatri Spivak, Peter Hulme, Abdul JanMohamed, Homi Bhabha, and many others.

THE EMERGENCE OF SUBALTERNISM

Subaltern Studies, by contrast, had a very different aetiology. It was developed by mostly Indian social historians rather than cultural critics, and before 1988 remained influential, but only relatively so, and within a small orbit. Launched in 1982 by Ranajit Guha in a three-volume series on colonial India—it would later grow to more than ten volumes—this was above all a rebellion against the elite historiography of the Indian freedom movement. By reading between the lines of official documents, or extrapolating from new archival discoveries, they sought to provide a portrait of the intelligence and improvisational skill of peasant insurgents. If their Marxism was somewhat unorthodox, they nevertheless drew their inspiration from Antonio Gramsci's supple theories of hegemony, the state, "common sense," and, of course, the "subaltern" itself, one of his major coinages in the *Prison Notebooks*.[4] Guha's teacher had been instrumental in bringing Gramsci to the attention of intellectuals in West Bengal, where his writings had been enthusiastically discussed since the 1950s—in the translations of the US edition of 1957. The movement also took some of its impetus from important precedents in the antinomian histories from below produced by veterans of the Communist Party Historians Group in Britain, especially perhaps Eric Hobsbawm's *Primitive Rebels*, Rodney Hilton's *The English Rising of 1381*, and Edward Thompson's *The Making of the English Working Class*.

By 1986, the focus of the subaltern group was beginning to shift away from the spontaneous consciousness of peasant rebellion. In place of anecdotal accounts of local struggles, one was more likely to find a sweeping interrogation of "modernity." As one of the original members Sumit Sarkar himself lamented, the presence of subalterns in their work waned, replaced by a stress on historical ruptures, the dangers of universalism, and the "fragment"—an open-ended, ahistorical datum offering itself up to hermeneutical improvisation while resisting incorporation into a theory of the social whole. Truth came to be defined more as *need*—that is, as what one could make out of the record for one's purposes. History, the suspect progressivism of a narrowly empiricist historical materialism, was held to be inferior to subaltern *memory* and the felt realities of indigenous "culture." Subaltern Studies, in short, had discovered postcolonial theory.

In time the relationship came to be formalized. The official enlistment of Subaltern Studies into postcolonial theory took place when Spivak, along with Guha, edited a collection of the group's essays from the 1980s, with a foreword by Said. *Selected Subaltern Studies* (1988) essentially inducted them into the larger field, although this required a good deal of conceptual translation. In order to welcome Subaltern Studies into the emergent camp of postcolonial theory, Spivak had to get around the problem that its historians were focused on individual and collective subjects whom they had described as sentient, feeling, struggling actors in history, as opposed to representational "traces." Spivak's delicate operation was to allow "subjects" to be both there and not there at the same time, permitting tactical allusions to the (illusory) subject in pursuit of a larger project, which she called the "critical force of anti-humanism." It was by entering this discursive milieu that Subaltern Studies acquired the theoretical credentials that gave it international prominence, in turn rendering it a conduit for postcolonial notions in the social sciences.

CHIBBER'S INTERVENTION

Vivek Chibber's study took shape in the force fields of this history, if not always in full awareness of its details. A professor of sociology at New York University, Chibber had already written a favorably received book, *Locked in Place: State-Building and Late Industrialization in India*.[5] This finely textured study of the post-colonial Indian state explored the dynamic relative power of bourgeois interests in the demobilization of labor. The long chapter on the "myth of the developmental bourgeoisie," in particular, anticipates some of his arguments in the new book, proposing, for example, that the new India—unlike China and Russia—had set out along a capitalist path as though to show that "planning need not presuppose the abolition of property, but could, in fact, be harnessed to the engine of capitalist accumulation."[6] Its development was blocked, however, by "the widespread and organized resistance of the business class."[7]

Still, little in this earlier study would prepare anyone for the event that *Postcolonial Theory* became, not least because Chibber had never traveled in postcolonial circles and was entirely unknown there. Accused by some of caricaturing the Subaltern project, of being inauthentically postcolonial, too Europe-focused, or hyperbolic, the book has risen above much of this criticism to be respectfully discussed in specialist sociology journals, highbrow French Maoist reviews, Indonesian newspapers, American crossover magazines, and the blogosphere.[8] Featured at Historical Materialism conferences in New Delhi, New York, and London in 2013, and debated in academic conferences and roundtables, it triggered revealing exchanges between Chibber and his detractors. His ripostes have been vigorous, enlightening, and, for the most part, persuasive.

The arguments laid out in the book, after all, are nothing if not well-supported, at least on the grounds that he chooses. Chibber's procedure is to restate the claims of Subaltern Studies—his paradigm case for postcolonial theory generally—letting it speak for itself in lengthy quotations, and then submitting these claims to a series of tests. This is very thoroughly done, and it is among the most distinctive features of the book. His conclusion is that the Subaltern Studies understanding of capitalism is flawed, its portrait of Marxism distorted and tendentious, and its insistence on the cultural difference of subaltern consciousness uncomfortably essentialist. In fact, it is a new, if concealed and self-alienating, return to the orientalist claim that rationalism, secularism, and realism are disqualified from being of the "East," that only the absolutely peripheral has found a space outside the hold of the ideologically polluted West, and then only so long as it is fixed in its otherness, impervious to any other otherness.

Building his case on a close reading of three of the principals affiliated with the Subaltern Studies collective—Guha, Partha Chatterjee, and Dipesh Chakrabarty—Chibber fixes his attention on what he considers the cornerstones of their supposed revision. These involve postulating the failure of capital to universalize itself in India and the consequent inability of the Indian elites, in contrast with their European predecessors, to achieve hegemony by way of democratic institutions: the Indian bourgeoisie was not heroic but timid, and Indian subalterns were marked by an obdurate cultural difference resistant to Western norms—religious modes of thought primarily, but also practices of kinship and loyalty that made Western modernity a closed book.

Chibber refutes these assertions effectively, with a great deal of evidence and counter-argument, amplifying contentions found in others before him.[9] He explains, reasonably, that the Subalternists confuse universality with homogeneity: that, contrary to their flattened portrait of capital's logic, its own history even in Europe was as uneven, non-linear, and complex as in the global periphery. Moreover, it is undeniable that the material needs of life—food, housing, and shelter—motivate subaltern classes everywhere. Struggle over them is, in fact, the *universal* condition of conflict between elites and the poor. For its part, the bourgeoisie of Europe displayed the same timidity and treachery as its Eastern counterparts, and, like the latter, had to be pushed from below in order to make possible the establishment of basic democratic institutions.

A HISTORY MISPERCEIVED

Here, however, despite the argument's firm ground, we begin to see *Postcolonial Theory*'s lack of contact with the ideological universe it set out to diagnose. To claim, as Chibber does, that Subaltern Studies is postcolonial theory's "most illustrious representative" is not only to reverse the order of influence, but to fail to see that internalizing the already entrenched positions of postcoloniality allowed the Subalternists to acquire a more general reach.[10] So it is not that postcolonial theory "became influential"—as he writes—when it allied itself with Subaltern Studies, but the other way around.

The book's reception has to this degree been frustrating. It is as though on one side we find in boldface a renewed emphasis on class, revolution, and capital; on the other, "subaltern thought"; but in neither, any attention to how structural adjustment, World Bank austerity measures, or Natopolis are mediated by living agents, repudiating the claim that capital's imposed limitations are natural laws impervious to the rebels' logic. Between Chibber and his detractors, thought and structure have been kept safely distant from one another. On one side of the agon, materialism appears as a bulwark against the vagaries of the contradictory; on the other, the contingent is home to a sacred principle, a barrier against all determinations. Since the politics of Subaltern Studies took shape in the elevation of signifying or discursive regimes, we might say that the problem of the *literary* reverberates throughout the debates around Chibber's book: in part, as he would have it, in the form of an idealizing, culturalist contamination, but also—in a move he neglects—as the concern of one of the most vital currents of twentieth-century Marxism itself. To this degree, the literary remains the blind spot of an otherwise admirable polemic.

What would it take to challenge fully the claims of postcolonial theory? It would, at the very least, involve questioning the field's self-conception as a Copernican break; and it would take submitting its purportedly anti-Eurocentric theoretical basis to greater scrutiny, in a more intellectual-historical investigation going beyond Chibber's comparative study of capital transition and bourgeois revolution. Both lines of questioning take us, somewhat unexpectedly, back to the interwar era.

Seeing itself as an inaugural leap, postcolonial theory makes an extreme claim: that all scholarship in the West before it should be considered nothing less than "an embarrassment"—as one set of commentators put it—marked by shameful neglect of Third-World emergence and non-Western ways of being.[11] But such a charge elides the insurgent sociologies, oral histories, and black and ethnic studies of the preceding generation; it moves one to write, as postcolonial critics frequently have, as though there had been no early twentieth-century scholarship on the impact of global capitalist expansion, no economic theorizations of the system known—for the first time—as imperialism itself; no critical explorations of the political aesthetics of the Latin American "boom" in the 1970s; and, for that matter, no dependency or world systems theory.

ANTI-COLONIALISM IN EUROPE

Key precursors were left out of the conversation, even as their ideas were often quietly borrowed: Jean-Paul Sartre and *Les Temps modernes*; the Chilean media critique led by Armand Mattelart in the early 1970s;

the writings of Oliver Cromwell Cox on race and class; Basil Davidson on African state-formation; Leo Wiener on the role of Africa in the pre-Columbian New World; the acute imperial histories of James Morris, V. G. Kiernan, and Eric Wolf; C. L. R. James on Lenin and black liberation. All at once these rich contributions—really part of a substantial, interlocking system of writing in the broadly Marxist environs of critical theory, Left philology, and the solidarity movements—were abruptly severed from the present.

Postcolonial theory thus implausibly presented itself as a kind of "year zero" of anti-colonial thought; the prevailing assumption has been that the early twentieth century, prior to postwar decolonization, was "a period of largely uncontested imperialist enthusiasm."[12] But this is to overlook the years between the two world wars, when European consciousness of the colonies abruptly changed. A new culture of anti-colonialism grew up and thrived in the art columns of Left newspapers, cabarets of the political underground, and the cultural groups of the Popular Front. Shock waves from the Russian revolution on Europe's eastern periphery were dramatically and immediately felt throughout Asia and the Middle East. International organizations sprang up, bringing emissaries from throughout the colonies, meeting European intellectuals on a formally equal footing in a single front with a shared anti-imperial agenda.[13] Intellectual ferment on this scale was a rarity in European history. The sponsorship of anti-colonial rhetoric and practice created a massive repertoire of images, tropes, and vocabularies that hovered over everyone's thinking—from Right to Left—throughout the period.

Sensitive engagement with non-Western cultures and thinkers—in the work, among others, of Ilya Ehrenburg, M. N. Roy, Larissa Reissner, Nancy Cunard, and Sergei Tretiakov—a deeply ethical resistance to empire—in Willi Münzenberg, Rosa Luxemburg, César Vallejo, George Padmore, and Ho Chi Minh, all active in Europe during these years—an examination of the aesthetic and epistemological rubrics of colonial rule—in Carl Einstein, Paul Nizan, Diego Rivera, and Alejo Carpentier—these were initiated not by the postcolonial turn of the 1980s and after, but much earlier, between the world wars, and by intellectuals white and black, European and non-European, in the broad ambit of the international communist movement. Chibber mentions in passing Karl Kautsky, Leon Trotsky, and others who explored the dynamics of agrarian economy and uneven development, but the sense of this broader politico-cultural history is missing, and its vexing relationship to theory and method goes undiagnosed.

RACISM IN PHILOSOPHY

As for postcolonial theory, we need a better sense of its own prehistory, above all, with respect to the neo-racialisms of the interwar philosophical *demi-monde* upon which it drew. For what needs to be acknowledged are the ways in which postwar French thought wove together the threads of a German philosophy least compatible with it. The main strands in this fabric were, firstly, the key interwar reception of Nietzsche's earlier *Grosse Politik*, the "great politics" of a new cosmopolitan elite that would beckon resentful proletarians to go to the colonies where they might escape socialist enslavement and rediscover their manhood by bringing colonial subjects into line;[14] secondly, the *Kriegsideologie* of Martin Heidegger and others who sought to save German civilization with a new imperium enriched by German metaphysical depth, fighting the shallow shopkeeper mentality of the twin behemoths, Washington and Moscow; and, finally, Edmund Husserl's phenomenological paeans to the European mind as against the intellectual poverty of its global minions.[15] Leading the postwar enthusiasms—and creating a paradigm for so much of what theory later became—were Georges Bataille, who playfully subverted the ideals of anti-colonial liberation in *The Accursed Share* (1949), and Alexandre Kojève, whose profound influence on postwar French thought is commonly recognized.[16]

Europe, which Kojève called "the vanguard of humanity," faced the specter of its own end, he argued, in the postwar "Sino-Soviet actualization of Robespierrian Bonapartism." Sneering at the "accession of Togoland to independence" and "the self-determination of the Papuans," Kojève considered such movements little more than a communist bid to eliminate "the numerous more or less anachronistic sequels to its pre-revolutionary past."[17] If such pronouncements were idiosyncratic, they are nonetheless signposts along the route that postcolonial theory traveled—in its own mind "subversively"—from the murkier side of that same Europe it wanted to provincialize.

The more immediate theoretical models for postcolonial theory were, of course, Foucault and Derrida, though very few of the disturbing implications of their affiliations with these interwar ideas have been mooted. This has to do in part with the ways in which a theoretical eclecticism confounds the past, generating insights but also blocking, or at least muddying others. To take one example, although *Orientalism* is generally considered Foucauldian, Said explicitly distanced himself from those aspects of Foucault's thought deriving from Heideggerian sources. While known for his study of orientalist "discourse," Said understood by that term a concept derived ultimately from a Marxist theory of ideology.[18] His argument might be said to bear on ideology in a more traditional sense—in that his conception of discourse, unlike Foucault's, does not preclude the idea of guilty agents of power, people with agendas and privileged interests, constituencies of active belief and policy, or the basic *injustice* of the orientalist worldview. It was more than contradictory that these multiple interrogations of the human as agent, as historical subject—deconstruction's insistence on the written over the oral and the vernacular, say, taken to be examples of a suspect "metaphysics of presence"—would be so widely attacked and undermined by the very forces that were seeking, apparently, to promote the emergence of peripheral peoples.[19]

PHILOLOGICAL TRADITIONS

These half-understood collisions of various traditions attain a greater salience when we begin to give a name to the cultural and literary theories of Marxism against which the interwar philosophical right devised its counterattack. Our current renderings of intellectual history downplay severely the extent to which Marxism could be seen as belonging to "philology" in the expanded sense in which Erich Auerbach used the term in his 1924 German translation of Giambattista Vico's *The New Science*. There he defined it as "anything that we now call the humanities: the whole story in the strict sense, sociology, national economy, the history of religion, language, law and art."[20] Both Marxism and philology adhered to historical forms of knowing at a time when they were under intense attack from Saussure's followers—"neo-lalists" in Gramsci's terms—logical positivism, and the emergent formalism of Prague linguistics. Interwar Marxism found a common cause with philology in that both looked to the sedimentary traces of a past, to the creativity of the unnamed, unheralded, subaltern elements of society. Both were skeptical of the philosophical move to evacuate the historical subject and to insert, in its stead, a fetishized subject of writing—what Gramsci sardonically dubbed "calligraphism."

Gramsci himself marks the linkage explicitly: "The experience upon which the philosophy of praxis is based cannot be schematized; it is history in its infinite variety and multiplicity, the study of which can give birth to philology as a method of scholarship for ascertaining particular facts and to the birth of philosophy understood as a general methodology of history."[21] From the rather different tradition of the circles around the Frankfurt School, Walter Benjamin makes this connection even more strongly in *The Arcades Project*, when he expresses his intention as being in part "to prove by example that only Marxism can practice great philology, where the literature of the previous century is concerned."[22] Even in passing, these examples show that a true accounting of Marxism's contributions to reflexive knowledge cannot bypass its humanistic and interpretive dimensions or sources, and much of what Subaltern Studies thought it was correcting in Marxism with its focus on the particular, the fragmentary, and the multiple is found here in philological Marxism—expressed much earlier and without theory's anti-historicist prejudices.

LIMITS OF PLAIN SPEAKING

Such matters are, for all his book's merits, unaddressed—even unimagined—by Chibber, even though they direct us to the central and silent question at the heart of the conflict of traditions into which he inserts himself: what does it mean *to read*? The problem of evidence and truth brings us face-to-face with the substantive issues raised by *Postcolonial*

Theory regarding the transition debates in post-Independence India. Otherwise supportive readers begin to question the book at the point where he announces that he will confront subaltern "theory"—its historiographical practice—but not theory as postcolonial studies has always understood the term. Avoidance of this particular institutional encounter makes it impossible for him to meet his audience where it lives, limiting his ability to grasp the discursive and epistemological art of his interlocutors.

It is reasonable to say that the integrity with which Chibber pursues his object sometimes gets in the way; it is the positive side of a negative trait, a plain-speaking rationalism that treats each argument innocently, as though its pragmatic unpacking might lead to its undoing. For example, he poses a much-needed corrective to the Subalternists' misreadings of Marx, but loses the opportunity to reinforce the accuracy of his sociological arguments by demonstrating Marx's reliance on the truth-contents of his own suasive literary style. Anyone who has closely read Hegel will know that truth has a form, and that form is a substantive aspect of both his arguments and those of Marx. The literary element in Subaltern Studies attends to this dimension, however tendentiously, and for this reason it cannot simply be evaded. Effective resistance to its lures, in fact, demands that it be met head on.

The way in which something is expressed has, for Marxism as well as for postcolonial theory, a great deal to do with its truth in the Hegelian sense that truth is an active exchange, the "making" of a concept adequate to its object. Marx's polemical manner is not only a rhetorical strategy but a particular kind of intelligence that allows for insights not possible only in a dispassionate, social-scientistic dwelling on materialities. The famous use of the image of the "fetish," for instance, or the description of the commodity as a "hieroglyph," are much more than Hegelian residues in Marx's writing. Despite his repeated mockery of Hegelian abstraction in favor of the sensuously material, such figural language enables the philosophical point that the material basis of society is brought into view by the conceptual, in a process of intellectual synthesis that is the work of the writing itself. As Keston Sutherland usefully puts it: "Marx's thinking in *Capital* is philological as well as satirical just as the risks of style in his satire are themselves the work of thinking and not a mere decoration of it."[23]

TWO STYLES OF ARGUMENT

Chibber dismantles the pretences of subaltern historiography with admirable precision. Even when it appears he has gone too far, over-stating his case—some readers have taken his charge of "orientalism" to be such an instance—a comparison with his sources reveals he has been judicious, often in the face of intemperate reactions from certain quarters. On the other hand, the weaknesses he probes are few in number and of similar type, and his arguments for this reason tend to drag. Even more, the structural categories of his argument—class, revolution, liberalism, labor—have a settled definitional character lacking the supple attention to reversals and incongruities that charac-terizes more interpretive approaches. The bad infinity of Subalternist claims to an abiding otherness cannot be displaced by the invocation of capital and class if the terms come off as dead universals. The syllo-gistic ordering of his argument is too reliant on a logic of rebuttal—mere negation—and thus fails to capture dialectically the reliance of his opponents on the very Marxism they appropriate, if only to distort.

Chibber's intervention is likely to strike those involved in postco-lonial theory as borrowing from their realm but without having the hang of it. There are also some fundamental mistakes. He takes the "cultural turn," for instance, to refer only to post-structuralism's unwel-come influence on disciplines outside literature, whereas Left-Hegelian critique from very early on opened the door to a particular investiga-tion into culture as a site of political and economic training, evalua-tion, and understanding—in the work, among others, of Engels, Alexandra Kollontai, Georg Simmel in his poetic, non-Marxist sociol-ogy, or Trotsky on everyday life. One could argue, thinking of Raymond Williams, Henri Lefebvre, and Georg Lukács, that materialist theories of culture are among the core insights of twentieth-century Marxism.

To be fair, Chibber never claims to be comprehensive, and there is throughout his performance an ingenious clarity and calm that is *pedagogically* superior to most before him. And yet, to justify exclud-ing an engagement with cultural theory, he avows that "what matters is not whether [the Subaltern historians] are true to this or that theoreti-cal tradition but whether they have produced sound arguments." The problem is that what is or is not "sound" or "true," or indeed an "argument," has a great deal to do with one's "theoretical tradition." As Nietzsche presents "genealogy" in *On the Genealogy of Morals*, for example, it is not, as it is sometimes taken to be, an aleatory, multi-causal, subaltern history, but a theory of reading. Nietzsche counsels us first to enlist the "perverse" in order to stimulate agreement with the seductions of the antinomian; next, to replace the subject who wills with a textual "will to truth"; and finally, to avoid refutation, never denying the truth of one's antagonists—since critique only empowers rivals by honoring them with engagement. This taste for outmaneuvering rather than arguing with opponents is powerfully connected to the methodological coups represented by a number of the central figures of postwar theory—Althusser's "symptomatic reading," Deleuze's productivity of truth, and Derrida's confidence in semantic plenitude—the illusion of any definitive interpretation. Each of these strategies courses through the postcolonial corpus. Together, they definitively express its outlooks and procedures.

So, to demolish the pretensions of the Subalternists' "infelicitous terminology," in Chibber's words, is at least in part to miss the point. He says he finds the formulations of Chatterjee and Chakrabarty elusive, vague, obscure, and difficult to understand. But this is a little like finding geometry abstract or obituaries brief. The manner is intrinsic to the project. The methods of this kind of cultural theory—and we can by now agree that Subaltern Studies falls within their orbit—are based not on historical accuracy, context, or intention, but on the production of political outcomes by way of a textual occasion. Earnest criticism of opponents, in Chibber's vein, effectively leaves unexposed what Alain Badiou aptly calls "the power of the false."[24] And this is what has to be addressed, among other things, in any fully effective critique of postcolonial theory.

TWO STRAINS IN MARXISM

Reviewers have seen *Postcolonial Theory* as a showdown between Marxism and postcolonial theory, though I would suggest that it also illustrates a more interesting conflict within Marxism itself. Implicit in the exchange is a culture/science divide that neither Chibber nor his reviewers—critical or otherwise—seem to recognize: the internal bifurcation of humanist and social-scientific interpretations of Marxism found in the debates of the late nineteenth and early twentieth centuries. These are still very much with us.

Confrontation was liveliest, perhaps, in the resistance of Georges Sorel and Paul Lafargue to what both took to be the mechanistic Marxism of Rudolf Hilferding and Georgi Plekhanov—indeed, Sorel explicitly enlisted Vico in his book-length study of 1896 in order to re-inject into the idea of social transformation the "poetry" of his forbear's sociological imagination.[25] Traces of that confrontation are legible also in Gramsci's embrace of the Russian "revolution against *Capital*" and his frequently testy dismissals throughout the *Notebooks* of the positivism of Achille Loria and what he called "Lorianism" in favor of the "active"—cultural—element in social strata always struggling over their own political status with uncertain outcomes. A more recent pairing of this sort might be found in Edward Thompson's challenge to Louis Althusser.[26]

Such pairings point to a larger divide over the theoretical regeneration of Marxism in the postwar period: on the one side, the well-known models derived from Spinoza by Althusser and Antonio Negri—Karl Korsch was complaining about Plekhanov's creation of a Spinozist Marx as early as the 1930s; on the other, philological, side, the less well-known, but earlier and arguably more far-reaching presence of Vico in the work of Marx, Lukács, Horkheimer, and others, including, of course, Said.[27] Vico's attractions for Marx and later Marxists are, by this light, not hard to explain. In the early eighteenth century, his defense of historical writing against the scientific Enlightenment's claims that it was pointless and arbitrary—a prejudice articulated most unguardedly by Descartes—rested in *The New Science* on class struggle and the centrality of labor to civilization. Vico, the materialist, was the first to write history combining its objective material conditions and its qualitative, felt textures. The first sociologist, he is also the first to argue that specific ideas, linguistic innovations, and forms of art correspond to a period's conditions of social organization—a view that many have seen as the genesis of Marx's historical materialism.[28] Vichian configurations of Marxism have received very little attention, and yet they are centrally relevant to the debate generated by *l'affaire*

Chibber, not least because in them its apparent antinomies—which are partly exacerbated by the framing of Chibber's argument as a rejection of "culturalism"—are in principle superseded.[29]

MARXISM IN POSTCOLONIAL THEORY

Given these considerations, one can appreciate the otherwise puzzling fact that *Postcolonial Theory* has received so much attention in a milieu where so many critics of postcolonial theory before him were ignored. Conspicuously endorsed by leading figures on the Left as a break-through, the book was actually written very much in the wake of Marxist critics within postcolonial theory who had been skewering the postcolonial "pseudo-radical establishment"—Slavoj Žižek's words—for more than two decades. The "specter of capital" has haunted post-colonial theory for quite some time. Throughout the 1990s and early 2000s, Marxist critics of the postcolonial turn chipped away at the edifice of the problematic idea of the "West" itself, disempowering its hold on a field predicated on civilizational oppositions, mapping a vital Marxist counter-trend within the field, a force that now found itself in a visible constellation that the postcolonial establishment could not ignore.[30] Benita Parry's early broadside in the *Oxford Literary Review* (1987) against the "exorbitation" of colonial discourse set a new tone, reclaiming Fanon from his latter-day postcolonial interpret-ers, such as Bhabha; Fernando Coronil, already in 1992, was urging nothing less than the decolonization of postcolonial theory; and Neil Lazarus's work distilled the Marxist critique of postcolonial theory in a series of influential essays, finally bringing a number of heterodox ideas and thinkers into institutional centrality with his *Cambridge Companion to Postcolonial Literary Studies* (2004). The scope of the work, much of it prominently published and discussed, was by no means limited to the "literary and cultural front," to which Chibber somewhat dismissively refers in an early footnote, even if no one before him had previously examined in so systematic a manner the compo-nent elements of bourgeois revolution in a comparative mode.[31]

This neglect of precursors extends also to Chibber's antagonists. It bears noting that Subaltern Studies encompasses more than three scholars (or three books). Setting aside the narratological focus of Subaltern Studies, its deployment of a Foucauldian *récit de crime*, its moving dramas of the *adivasis* and village widows who speak in "sobs and whispers," Chibber in some ways neglects its best work: Gyanendra Pandey on the construction of communalism; David Arnold on the Indian body, disease, and medicine; Bernard Cohn on language and colonial command; and Shahid Amin on the silences of elite texts.[32] Much of this oeuvre is empathetic, gritty, and intelligent—a world apart from the extreme cases of Chatterjee and Chakrabarty (perhaps especially the latter)—where the caricatures not only of Marxism but of history and the human are no longer incidental but programmatic. Even when Chibber praises Guha's work, he does not convey any sense of the passion of the writing—extending from his influential reading of the *Grundrisse*, and his keen analysis of colonial dominance, to his spirited asides on some of the more outrageous moments of colonialist historiography, a literature Guha describes as "still incarnadine with the glow of imperial 'achievements,' a language that permits racist insults to pass in everyday use as harmless jokes."[33]

Chakrabarty partakes much less of Chibber's focus—labor and the state—than he does of the art of conversation, the "textures" of language, and untranslatability. He quotes Derrida, proclaims Heidegger his "icon," and lingers over Benjamin's Kabbalistic moments and his eschatological forebodings. By counterposing memory to history in order to set up a contrast between the subaltern and the intellectual, he replicates the familiar Heideggerian masquerade of the philosopher presenting himself as a lonely warrior battling the speculative chaos of European metaphysics. Although an intellectual—and not a subaltern—in this way he can assume the guise of a village seer, charting his path through the woods of thought, gnomic, intuitive, revelatory. Heidegger's reactionary peasant sublime is in this way replicated in this postmodern avatar.

But none of the tone of this *contretemps* can enter the frame, since Chibber's professed interest is only in "the empirical work." In Chakrabarty's argument, he complains, "reasons have to be based on beliefs, wants, values, and so on, all of which are culturally constructed," just as Chatterjee assumes "the deep significance of culture and consciousness." But this is to assume that the insistence on "culture" led inexorably to all their errors and elisions: the foggy treatment of capital or the one-sided assumptions about subaltern consciousness. Even when referring to work as critical of Subaltern Studies as his own, the same apparent hierarchy of concerns prevails.

LEGACIES

One might be inclined to overlook Chibber's hostility to culture as an object were it not for the fact that it actually deflects him from his target—for instance, one of Chakrabarty's principal tropes, the affirmation of the present "against itself" in colonial formations. This idea, we should recall, is taken from Ernst Bloch, whose highly original investigations into the cultural domain of religiosity—as a committed Leninist—throughout the 1920s and 1930s are totally elided in Chakrabarty's predictable charge that Marxists have nothing productive to say about religion. He thus embraces what in Bloch was actually a lament: "the plurality that inheres in the 'now,' the lack of totality, the constant fragmentariness, that constitutes one's present."[34] If, that is, the entwinements of culture and objective being were integral to Bloch's way of thinking, they are missed by both Chakrabarty and Chibber. A more supple foray into and against the Subalternist project would have dwelt on these often imitated—and somehow also reviled—interwar Marxist precursors who zeroed in on the very intellectual dissonance between city and country, center and periphery so mulled over in contemporary subaltern work. Bloch wanted to wrest people from the grip of an "ascetic contemplation of the unresolved myth of dark old being or of nature"—a point that could not be more germane to Subaltern Studies' identitarian faith in the airtight otherness of the Indian collective subject.

The advantage of having claimed for oneself sole authority both to evoke and to be the subaltern is that one can refer, without self-consciousness, to a "Western historiography" that supposedly narrates history as a progress of awareness, and do so while being coy about the degree to which one is speaking in and through this so-called West. If Chakrabarty reflects what the historian Vasant Kaiwar aptly calls a "remarkably narrow" historical curiosity—"with rich descriptions on one side (Calcutta) and rather stark, schematic outlines on the other (Europe)"—such reductionism is also evident in Spivak's recent review of Chibber's book.[35] There she dismisses its publisher, Verso, for its "little Britain Marxism" as though it were not Verso that, more than anyone, introduced metropolitan readers (East and West) to the writing of intellectuals and activists from Brazil and China to Italy and India, creating by all accounts the most far-reaching international Left public sphere anywhere since the Second World War.

Clearly, as such reactions indicate, the political differences swirling around the debate over who has the right to speak and in what disciplinary or theoretical language are very real, even irreconcilable; for that very reason it matters a great deal how one expresses differences—both as a matter of hitting the mark and of demonstrating the strengths of one's own position. My bid would be to give more sway to the vital inheritances of a humanist intellectual *generalism* that has, for so long, animated Left-Hegelian thought in the form of a properly philological and interpretive Marxism.

Postcolonial Theory and the Specter of Capital, Review Essay

Stein Sundstøl Eriksen

I

Since its launch in 1983, the book series *Subaltern Studies* has had a profound influence on academic debate in and about India. The series was published by a group of historians and social scientists based in Calcutta, led by Ranajit Guha. From the 1990s, the group and the book series were to become familiar far beyond India, no doubt helped by the publication in 1988 of a selection of articles from the series in the US, with a foreword by Edward Said and an introduction by Gayatri Chakravorty Spivak. The group's influence has perhaps been strongest in the humanities and in the field of postcolonial studies, with which it came to be associated.

The first volume of the series came out in 1982. In the preface to the first volume, Ranajit Guha proclaimed that the aim of the series was to write a "history from below," and to rectify what he described as the "elitist bias" of existing research. In line with this programmatic aim, in subsequent volumes, studies were published about peasants, workers, and other marginalized groups (lower castes, tribals) in colonial and postcolonial India. Taking their inspiration from Western theorists such as Antonio Gramsci (from whom the term "subaltern" was borrowed) and E. P. Thompson, the series had its origin squarely within the Marxist tradition.

The context of the establishment of the series was the situation in India in the 1970s, when the development model chosen by the Nehru-led government after independence appeared to unravel. A number of national strikes broke out, and a violent Maoist rebellion emerged in the late 1960s in a village called Naxalbari in West Bengal. And in 1975,

Prime Minister Indira Gandhi (daughter of Nehru, the first prime minister) declared a state of emergency. When the emergency was lifted two years later, the Congress party was badly beaten in elections. However, two years later, Indira Gandhi returned to power in new elections.

For the founders of Subaltern Studies, these developments showed that Indian modernity was of a fundamentally different nature than Western modernity, and that Western theories of development and modernization could not explain developments in India. Specifically, the Indian bourgeoisie did not have the kind of hegemony enjoyed by the Western bourgeoisie. Hence, in the Gramscian terms employed by the Subalternists, it had to rule by force rather than by consent. The situation was therefore best described as a form of rule with domination without hegemony.

However, over time, the theoretical orientation of the group shifted away from Marxism, and by the mid-1990s, its leading representatives such as Partha Chatterjee and Dipesh Chakrabarty had abandoned Marxism and adopted a postmodern or post-structuralist position, taking their inspiration more from Foucault than from Marx and Gramsci.

II

The theoretical shift from Marxism to post-structuralism in Subaltern Studies has been strongly criticized. Perhaps most significantly, one of the group's own leading members, Sumit Sarkar, publicly left the group for precisely this reason, arguing that the group had abandoned the project of writing history from below, and that "the subaltern" had disappeared from Subaltern Studies.

However, Vivek Chibber's new book *Postcolonial Theory and the Specter of Capital* is the most sustained critique yet of the school. Perhaps surprisingly, Chibber does not mainly focus on the Subalternists' shift from a Marxist toward a postmodernist perspective. Instead, he seeks to show that the foundations of the project were fundamentally flawed from the outset, and that its basic assumptions have been the same throughout the school's evolution.

Chibber summarizes the core arguments of the Subalternists in six theses:

1. The colonial bourgeoisie, unlike that of the West, was never able to establish itself as hegemonic. Crucially, instead of challenging the power of the feudal elite, it incorporated them into the new political order. As a consequence, it was unable to align itself with subordinate classes and create a political alliance which incorporated workers and peasants.

2. By refusing to dismantle feudal power, the bourgeoisie abandoned its "universalizing mission." This has two aspects. First, it meant that the bourgeoisie was not able to successfully claim that its own interests coincided with those of peasants and workers or claim to represent the nation as a whole. Second, it meant that economic hegemony was not accompanied by real democracy and political liberalism. The failure of universalization implies that the evolution of capitalism in the Global South is fundamentally different than in the West, and that theories constructed on the basis of the Western experience cannot be appropriate for understanding the nature and evolution of capitalism elsewhere.

3. As a result of 1) and 2) a different kind of modernity has emerged, in which capitalist/bourgeois power relations coexist with forms of domination associated with pre-capitalist social relations. Hence, there is a disjunction between capital and power, which means that capitalism has not become universalized.

4. Because of the failure of capital's universalizing mission, the bourgeoisie did not integrate subaltern culture into its own modernizing discourse. There is therefore a subaltern domain of politics, related to, but distinct from, that of the ruling classes. This domain is characterized by form of politics associated with pre-modern societies, a form of politics which cannot be grasped through the conceptual categories of Western theory that presuppose the universal applicability of theories based on rationality and bourgeois individualism. These categories only apply to the elite domain, where Western individualism and capitalist forms of thought have been influential. Hence, the bourgeois language of politics cannot explain the nature of politics in the subaltern domain.

5. Because the bourgeoisie failed to integrate the elite and subaltern domains, the bourgeois leadership of the national-ist movement failed to "speak for the nation." The reason for this failure was that while the bourgeoisie had internalized the Western narrative of modernization and progress and the ideology of individualism, these were foreign to the subalterns. Nationalist ideology therefore represented a false universalism, in the sense that it claimed to speak for a nation that in fact did not exist.

6. The theoretical implication of the differences between Western and non-Western capitalism is that the conceptual categories derived from the Western experience cannot be appropriate for analyzing non-Western societies.

According to Chibber, all six theses are wrong. The first thesis, first formulated by Ranajit Guha, is wrong because it is based on a false understanding of the role of the bourgeoisie in the West. It was not the case, Chibber argues, that the bourgeoisie achieved hegemony in Europe. Rather than incorporating subalterns in an anti-feudal coali-tion, the bourgeoisie in Europe, like in India, made compromises with feudal powers and supressed political pressures from below. The Subalternists therefore rely on a false historical sociology of European capitalism to justify their rejection of Western theories. As a basis for this conclusion, Chibber draws on (mainly Marxist) analyses of European history, such as those of Robert Brenner, Ellen Meiksins Wood, and Rueschemeyer, Stephens, and Stephens.

Thesis 2 is wrong mainly for conceptual reasons. The assertion of capital's failed universalization rests on a definition of capitalism in which liberal democracy is seen as a constituent element. This confla-tion of capitalism and liberal democracy is the basis for Guha's claim that capitalism abandoned its universalizing mission in India. According to Chibber, however, capitalism and liberal democracy should be conceptually separated. The universalization of capitalism should instead be understood as the universalization of market dependence and the compulsion of capital accumulation. While this compulsion may take a variety of forms, there is still an underlying common economic logic. This common logic does not depend on liberal democracy, and the universalization of capitalism is therefore, according to Chibber, fully compatible with the persistence of coercive political and interpersonal relations. Capitalism can therefore be universalized even without bourgeois hegemony and social homogenization, and is entirely compatible with the persistence of pre-capitalist forms of domination. The fact of cultural difference is therefore not proof of capital's limited universalization.

It follows from this that the third thesis is also wrong. According to Chibber, "capital does not have to obliterate social difference in order to universalize itself."[1] And if the universalization of capitalism is compatible with the persistence of cultural difference and with the preservation of pre-capitalist forms of coercion and interpersonal domination, the basis for the claim that Western theories are unable to account for the specificity of colonial and postcolonial capitalism disappears.

Chibber's critique of the fourth thesis focuses on the claim that subaltern politics is based on forms of consciousness where notions of rationality and interests are irrelevant. Instead, such politics are based on notions of community and traditional social ties such as caste, ethnicity, and family. Peasant consciousness is inherently traditional and distinct from the rational individualism characteristic of bourgeois consciousness. This "culturalist" view, according to Chibber, amounts to orientalism, because the Orient is seen as inherently irrational and its inhabitants as incapable of mobilization based on the rational pursuit of interests.

The problem with the fifth thesis is not so much its main empirical claim—that nationalist ideology failed to "speak for the nation"—but the basis for making this claim. Subalternists argue that the reason for this failure was the fact that the nationalist elite adopted the aims and ideology of modernization, which were alien to the subalterns. Nationalist ideology therefore appeared irrelevant to subaltern concerns, and "the nation" was nothing but an imposition. According to Chibber, however, this amounts to an extreme form of idealism, in which the policy of modernization appears simply as an ideological choice. In fact, he argues, this choice was a rational response to real capitalist constraints. The analysis of the Subalternists (mainly Chatterjee in this case) therefore "vastly exaggerates the role of ideas and grossly undervalues the effects of actually existing structures."[2]

Finally, at a theoretical level, the claim that Western theories are necessarily Eurocentric and therefore incapable of explaining developments outside the West is wrong because it wrongly assumes that Indians and other non-Western peoples (or at least those that do not belong to the elite groups whose thinking has been influenced by the West) think and act in ways fundamentally different from those in Western societies. This, according to Chibber, amounts to "resurrect[ing] the worst instances of Orientalist mythology . . . by assigning science, rationality, objectivity, and similar attributes to the West, thereby justifying an exoticization of the East."[3]

III

It is clear that Chibber has written an extremely ambitious book. On the face of it, it is simply a thorough critique of postcolonial theory in general and of three members of the school of Subaltern Studies in particular. However, it is far more than this, and raises a number of fundamental issues, including the meaning of universalism, the understanding of capitalism, the relevance of Marxist theory, and the role of ideology in social scientific explanations. Hence, it raises issues of importance for social theory in general, and not just for studies of former colonies.

I cannot discuss all these issues here, and instead will focus on a few of them. First, however, a note on the accuracy of Chibber's textual interpretations. In a response to Chibber's book, Partha Chatterjee has claimed that he (Chibber) completely misunderstands Ranajit Guha's argument. Rather than comparing the evolution of capitalism in the East and the West, Guha's point is to compare Western liberal ideology with Eastern realities. Hence, he does not make any claims about what actually happened in Europe when capitalism emerged, but simply criticizes what liberals assumed would happen in India with the introduction of capitalism.

However, this defense is hardly convincing. First, reading *Dominance without Hegemony*, there can be no doubt that Guha makes a series of empirical claims about European history. One example will suffice here:

the bourgeoisie . . . in Western Europe . . . had led the struggle against
feudalism and established its hegemony over the peasantry, whereas
in India the influence it gained over the rural population in the 1920s
and 1930s did not develop into a full-fledged hegemony because of
its reluctance to break with landlordism.[4]

Second, if it had been the case that Guha only compares liberal
ideology with Indian realities, the basis for rejecting the relevance
of Western theories for understanding developments in India
would disappear, according to Chibber. After all, Guha asserts that
the failure of the Indian bourgeoisie to establish hegemony is what
explains the specificity of Indian capitalism. This argument presupposes that the bourgeoisie succeeded in Europe, since if the bourgeoisie failed in establishing hegemony in Europe as well as in
India, how can its failure in India explain the difference between
Western and Indian capitalism? Chatterjee's defense of Guha is
therefore misplaced.

What about the other arguments made by Chibber? One of his key
aims is to defend social scientific universalism. As we have seen, Guha
argues that capital in India "abandoned its universalizing mission."
This "mission," according to Guha, has two components. First, it refers
to capital's economic logic and its tendency toward self-expansion:
driven by the imperatives of economic competition, capitalists are
compelled to accumulate ever more capital. The second is that as it
expands, capital must also transform traditional societies' cultural and
political forms.

In India, Guha argues, capital failed on the latter dimension, as it
did not transform traditional societies' cultural and political forms
and "replace them with laws, institutions, values and other elements of
culture appropriate to bourgeois rule."[5] The combination of its alignment with feudal landlords and its adoption of a policy of modernization meant that the Indian bourgeoisie failed to acquire hegemony
through consent over subaltern groups.

Chibber argues that this represents a false understanding of what
the universalization of capital implies. Contra Guha, Chibber argues
that the universalization of capital does not require a transformation
of laws and institutional forms at all. Capital is compatible with a

variety of institutional forms, including non-liberal or "traditional" ones. Consequently, it can also be universalized without bourgeois hegemony and a liberal political order. To be universalized, capitalism only needs to transform the institutions required for its reproduction. As long as accumulation of capital is possible, elements of traditional culture can very well coexist with it, and cultural pluralism and difference is not incompatible with its universalization.

According to Chibber, the same misunderstanding underlies Dipesh Chakrabarty's distinction between what he calls History 1 and History 2.[6] History 1 refers to the processes, institutions, and structures that constitute the conditions for capitalism's reproduction. They represent, he says, the "life process" of capitalism. History 2, by contrast, refers to the institutions and social relations that do not contribute to the self-reproduction of capital.[7] They may be absorbed into capitalism, but their reproduction is not subordinated to the logic of capitalism. The existence of History 2, according to Chakrabarty, shows that capital's universalization is incomplete. Moreover, it shows the limits of Marxist theory, since this theory can only account for History 1, and not for the processes, structures, and institutions that fall under History 2. But according to Chibber, if capitalism is compatible with the persistence of traditional culture and existing institutions, the existence of History 2 is no indication of capital's failed universalization. In addition, the argument that the existence of History 2 constitutes a reason for rejecting Marxism is based on the most reductionist interpretation of Marxism. Hence, Chibber concludes, Guha's and Chakrabarty's argument is doubly invalid.

So far, so good. Chibber convincingly shows that Guha's and Chakrabarty's understanding of capital's universalization is invalid, and that the conclusions they draw on the basis of that understanding must be rejected. However, from this, Chibber draws the conclusion that capitalism has in fact been universalized. He comes to this conclusion based on an alternative understanding of universalism, composed of two elements.

The first component is that mentioned by Guha (but quickly discarded), namely the compulsion to accumulate, which is the result of producers becoming market-dependent. Chibber, following Robert Brenner, sees market dependence as the defining feature of capitalism, and argues that if producers are market dependent, capitalism has been universalized.

But showing that capitalism can be universalized without abolishing cultural pluralism is one thing. To be fully convincing on this point, Chibber's argument must specify conceptually what the universalization of capital would require. Chibber does not present any clear criteria for establishing what its universalization entails. While he does not make any claims about the actual universalization of capitalism in India, arguing that this is an empirical question,[8] he argues that capitalism, wherever it exists, universalizes the compulsion to accumulate. This follows from his definition of capitalism, focusing on market dependence and the compulsion to compete. However, this definition is quite vague. Within the Marxist tradition, capitalism is usually conceived as having a horizontal and a vertical dimension. Horizontally, the key feature is competition between actors (firms and individuals). In a capitalist economy, all actors are compelled to compete for market-shares. Vertically, capitalism is characterized by specific class relations, in which the producers are separated from the means of production, and can only reproduce themselves by selling their labor power. The combination of these two features—generalized market dependence and commodification of labor—is what constitutes a fully developed capitalist system. On the basis of this definition, it seems quite clear that capitalism has not, in fact, been universalized in India. In particular, labor has not been fully commodified, as the majority of the population have not become wage earners.

But does a universalization of capitalism require the commodification of land and labor? Based on Chibber's definition, generalized commodification of labor is not a necessary requirement for capitalism to be universalized. This may or may not be a valid view, but it is certainly not uncontroversial. However, since Chibber does not elaborate on the definition of capitalism, it is not entirely clear what its universalization would imply. While this lack of specification does not in any way invalidate Chibber's critique of Guha and Chakrabarty, it leaves his own understanding of capitalism's universalization unclear.

The second component of Chibber's understanding of universalism is "social agents' universal interest in their well-being."[9] Here, Chibber criticizes Chatterjee's (1982) and Chaktrabarty's (1989) analyses of the nature of peasants' and workers' agency, or what he calls their "political psychology." Chatterjee and Chakrabarty, Chibber argues, reject the assumption drawn from Western theory that Indian subalterns act "rationally," on the basis of interests. Rather than acting on the basis of a utilitarian calculus characteristic of bourgeois consciousness, peasants' and workers' actions, according to the Subalternists, are based on community, religion, and honor. Understanding them therefore requires new, indigenous categories, which do not project Western, bourgeois forms of rationality and action onto Indian peasants and workers.

Against this, Chibber defends the notion of universal interests and argues that Chatterjee and Chakrabarty overstate cultural difference. He then goes on to defend the universality and indispensability of the notions of rationality and interests, and attempts to show their incompatibility with the "culturalism" underlying Chatterjee's and Chakrabarty's theoretical claims. Here, he defends a soft version of rational choice theory, where the existence of non-economic preferences and moral motives are acknowledged, and actors are seen as "satisficers" rather than "maximizers."

It can be debated whether Chibber misinterprets Chatterjee and Chakrabarty on this point. In his response to Chibber, Chatterjee[10] says that he never denied that considerations of interest existed among Bengali peasants. Likewise, Chakrabarty, in *Rethinking Working-Class History* (1989), makes a number of references to needs and interests. This is acknowledged by Chibber as well, but he claims that Chatterjee and Chakrabarty draw theoretical conclusions that contradict their own empirical evidence. Thus, he uses Chatterjee's and Chakrabarty's own empirical material to demonstrate that their theoretical conclusions are invalid.

This is convincing enough. Chatterjee and Chakrabarty make a number of claims about the primacy of "community" and the irrelevance of interests, which are at odds with their own empirical evidence. Whether Chibber's interpretation is accepted or not, we can, at the very least, conclude that Chatterjee and Chakrabarty are elusive on this point, with different statements pointing in different directions.

However, at this point, Chibber takes the argument one step further than he needs to in order to refute their arguments. While it is important to insist on the universal relevance of interests, the appeal to rational choice theory is not necessary to substantiate this. Moreover, the soft version of rational choice theory that Chibber endorses can easily slide into tautology. If any action and any end pursued by an actor can be described as "rational," it is not clear what we gain by insisting on the actors' rationality.

But it is quite possible to accept the universality of interests without endorsing rational choice theory. Thus, an actor's interests can be seen as constituted by his or her position in a social structure, while at the same time, it may be seen as an empirical question whether the actor a) is aware of his or her interests and b) acts on the basis of an intention to maximize/satisfice them. In other words, interests exist, but whether actors are aware of them or their actions motivated by them is an empirical question. This is the case both in the East and in the West. Chibber's appeal to the "political psychology" of (soft) rational choice theory is therefore unnecessary. And in light of the fundamental objections that have been raised against this theory, it only weakens an argument that is more than strong enough without it.

IV

All in all, Chibber's book is an impressive achievement. He convincingly shows that Guha, Chakrabarty, and Chatterjee base their analyses on a false understanding of Western modernization and misleading theoretical assumptions regarding the nature of capitalism, the relationship between capitalism and democracy, the role of culture, and the nature of difference between the West and the East. Through his critique, he also demonstrates the continued relevance of Marxist theory.

However, postcolonialism is diverse, and not all varieties are based on these theoretical assumptions. Chibber's critique does not therefore invalidate all forms of postcolonial theorizing, some of which is quite compatible with Marxism. His book is therefore best seen as a critique of Subaltern Studies, rather than of postcolonialism in general.

Also, while the critique is by and large convincing, his alternative account of the same issues is partly unspecified and partly unconvincing.

The lack of specification especially applies to his concept of capitalism. Even if one accepts the emphasis on market dependence as a defining feature of capitalism, there is a need for further elaboration of what this entails. The least convincing part of his argument is the defense of rational choice theory. Fortunately, the core of his critique does not depend on this defense.

CHAPTER 16

Looking for Resistance in All the Wrong Places? Chibber, Chakrabarty, and a Tale of Two Histories[1]

Viren Murthy

Just when it appeared that the debate between postcolonialists and Marxists had ended in something of a stalemate, Vivek Chibber's new book, *Postcolonial Theory and the Specter of Capital*, was published in 2013, in which Chibber attempts to rethink the significance of postcolonialism and Marxism. The book continues some earlier arguments made by Aijaz Ahmad and Arif Dirlik, but Chibber takes the debate to a new level with more detailed analysis and criticisms of the postcolonial and Subaltern Studies theorists' arguments.[2] His book reveals that the conflict between postcolonialists and Marxists is not merely about identity or the problem of Western hegemony but involves fundamental questions about how to understand global capitalism and resistance. Given the larger issues on which the book touches, it is not surprising that scholars have responded to the book from various directions. Exemplifying one prevalent form of critique, Chris Taylor contends that Chibber is unaware of or covers up the similarities between postcolonialism and Marxism and ends up producing "enlightenment jibber-jabber."[3] Despite the polemical nature of his comments, Taylor highlights two points that are at stake in the Chibber–postcolonialism debate, namely, the relationship between postcolonialism and Marxism and the role of Enlightenment universality in contemporary political practice. Behind all of these questions lies a perennial issue for Marxism, namely, how to conceive of the relationship between capitalism, thought, and culture in various regions of the world, especially those countries on the periphery of the global capitalist system.

In the beginning of his book, Chibber tells readers that his central "concern in the book is to examine the framework that postcolonial studies has generated for historical analysis and, in particular, the analysis of what once was called the Third World."[4] Chibber analyzes postcolonial theory not merely as a theoretical exercise, but rather because the object of postcolonial theory overlaps with his own area of research, namely, how to think about capitalist development and politics in a postcolonial world. He is inspired by anti-colonial Marxists and activists, including Mao Zedong, Amílcar Cabral, and Kwame Nkrumah. At stake in this debate is precisely the legacy of anti-colonialist Marxism and Third World movements. How should we understand these forms of resistance in light of their potential to create a postcapitalist future?

The debate between postcolonialists and Marxists is about both the nature of global capitalist modernity and consequently the forms that resistance against global capitalism and imperialism could or should take. The postcolonial theorists claim that Marxist categories and many anti-colonialist concepts are inadequate for understanding colonial difference. They fault anti-colonial movements for framing independence struggles in terms of the Enlightenment, which takes European society as a model. The postcolonialists claim that as capitalism moves from the metropoles to the colonies, it changes in form. Therefore, the categories of Marxism, liberalism, and the Enlightenment, which emerged out of a European context, are inadequate to make sense of the reality of capitalism on the peripheries of the world system. Moreover, postcolonialist theorists assert that because both Marxists and anti-colonialist thinkers have emphasized Western values and the nation-state, they merely replaced foreign colonization with self-colonization. The suppressed premise in postcolonial discourse is that the movement of capitalism from Europe to the peripheries implies not only a change but also possibilities for a different future. Consequently, self-colonization leads to blocking such possibilities and remaining locked in a vicious circle of imitation and inadequacy. Chibber argues that the postcolonialists find a change in capitalism because they have an inflated conception of capitalism and therefore do not know where to look for it or to find resistance to it. In this sense, his argument is primarily theoretical in that he suggests that

if postcolonialists worked with a different understanding of capitalism, they would have come to different conclusions.

These debates often overlook that different understandings of
capitalist modernity often entail diverse ways of coming to terms
with the ghost of Hegel. Initially, postcolonialists discussed the
discrepancy between the European and Indian bourgeoisie and often
appear to be no friends of Hegel. Indeed, like post-structuralists,
Hegelian totality is one of their main objects of attack. On the one
hand, they argue against the totality of capitalism by claiming that
capitalism changes fundamentally when it travels to the peripheries.
On the other hand, however, when postcolonials criticize anti-
colonialist and Marxist intellectuals and activists for reproducing
Eurocentric discourse, they presuppose something like a totality at
the level of discourse. Postcolonials contend that a Eurocentric ideological structure, represented by the Enlightenment and an idealist
representation of capitalism, does not map onto a disjunctive reality.
This ideological structure is the Hegelian totality that postcolonials
love to hate.

Initially, postcolonial theorists placed the blame for the construction of this Eurocentric discursive totality on the influence of
imperialism, local elites, and anti-colonial and Marxist thinkers in
colonized regions. However, Dipesh Chakrabarty's work goes a step
further and tries to ground Eurocentric discourse and the impulse
to repeat this discourse in various parts of the world in capital itself.
It is in this context that we must understand Chakrabarty's theory of
History 1 and History 2. History 1 represents the abstractions associated with capital, including the ideals of the Enlightenment, while
History 2 represents remnants from the past and the affective imme-
diacy of phenomenological life, which can never be completely
subsumed by History 1. As Chakrabarty connects these two histories to the logic of capital, he draws on a number of Hegelian
Marxists, including Moishe Postone. For all their differences,
Chakrabarty and Postone articulate positions that appear to overlap, especially when compared with Chibber. In particular, Postone
would suggest that one totalize capital further and that both History
1 and 2 are two sides of capital, which in many ways completes
Chakrabarty's attempt to ground Eurocentric ideology in capital,

while at the same time seriously circumscribing Chakrabarty's phenomenological alternative.

From this perspective, the debate between postcolonial theorists and Chibber hinges on two extremely significant questions: (1) How should we think about difference in a global capitalist world, especially with respect to the problem of the universality of the human condition? (2) Can one use the concept of capital to ground both the Enlightenment and anti-Enlightenment discourse? These questions are of course huge and crucial to most endeavors in the social sciences and the humanities, not to mention to those who are interested in a theory that aims to transform the global capitalist world. The questions ask whether, how, and to what extent Enlightenment ideals, local traditions, rational interests, the nation-state, or the working class can play a role in resisting capitalism.

Chibber and postcolonials, especially Chakrabarty, differ on how to answer the above questions; however, they both launch their position through immanent critiques. Recently, Neil Larsen defined immanent critique as implying that theory "is not just applied but is immanent to" their objects.[5] Postcolonials see themselves as Marxists and consequently construct their positions from what one could call an immanent critique of Marxism. Chakrabarty derives his categories through reading Marx's *Capital* and also finding what he sees as potential within capitalist society. Chibber's mode of critique attempts to show where the postcolonials' texts themselves point in a different direction. For example, he will argue that Chakrabarty and Partha Chatterjee both actually provide evidence that workers and peasants are motivated by interest rather than communal feeling or religion. Chibber also contends that the postcolonials misrecognize their objects of critique, namely, the Enlightenment and capitalism.

In what follows, I will continue the above trend by attempting an immanent critique of both Chakrabarty and Chibber, showing that both only partially grasp their object of critique, namely, capitalism. However, I would also like to stress another issue with which neither Chibber nor Chakrabarty seriously engages—the immanent critique of capital. In Moishe Postone's words, such an immanent critique must be able to locate the "'ought' as a dimension of its own context, a possibility immanent to the existent society."[6] Assuming that we are discussing capitalist society, this will mean expounding a theory of capitalism that shows how a postcapitalist society is both normative and possible.

I will begin with a general discussion of Chibber's problematic and his own immanent critique of Chatterjee through reading Ranajit Guha, before moving to Dipesh Chakrabarty's engagement with Subaltern Studies and Marx, focusing on his distinction between History 1 and History 2. In this way, I will bring out the immanent Hegelian possibilities in Chakrabarty's text. Then I will briefly treat Chibber's critique of postcolonialism's totalizing readings of capital and touch on his own alternative, which draws on Marxist attempts to save the Enlightenment from capitalism. Finally, drawing on a number of Marxist theorists, I continue the effort to ground History 1 and 2 in a theory of capital that accounts for unevenness and show how capital could point beyond itself, thus suggesting how ought is immanent and possible in capitalist society. In this context, I explore the potential for a politics of History 2 that is oriented not toward the past but toward the future, in particular, a future beyond capitalism.

I. Chibber: culture, interest, and Ranajit Guha

Before Chibber devoted a book to the critique of postcolonial theory, he had been interested in the various responses that countries on the periphery had to the global capitalist world. However, he was already somewhat suspicious of the cultural turn, and this informs much of his critique of postcolonialism as well. In her comments on Chibber's first book, Elizabeth Clemens remarks that "in Chibber's universe of comparative politics, it is as if everything happened except the cultural turn."[7] Chibber agrees with Clemens's remarks, adding that his book emerges from an "alternative universe" not only because he does not take the cultural turn, but because of his focus on class analysis.[8] In light of these remarks, we could consider Chibber's work as subtitled, "How Not to Take the Cultural Turn." In other words, the cultural turn becomes problematic when it obscures the dynamics of class and capital. In these cases, the cultural turn and its close cousin, the linguistic turn, can end up becoming ideologies often connected to false

dichotomies such as those between East and West. Indeed, the concluding chapter of Chibber's *Postcolonial Theory* is called "Subaltern Studies
as Ideology," and he makes the dual claim that postcolonial theory
obscures the dynamic of capital and produces "profoundly Orientalist
constructions of Eastern cultures."[9]

This does not mean that Chibber is insensitive to regional
differences. His problem concerns more the way in which postcolonialists explain difference. For example, in the early chapters of
Postcolonial Theory, he takes issue with the way Guha and those
who follow him contend that the failure of modernization in India
is due to the lack of hegemony of the bourgeoisie. Against this, he
contends that even in Europe, the ideals of modernity and the
Enlightenment were not promoted by capitalists but by labor movements. Indeed, in his first book, he argues that it is precisely the
success of the Indian capitalist class that partially explains why,
after the 1970s, the Korean developmental state succeeded while
the Indian developmental state failed. In a response to a symposium on his first book in *Comparative and Historical Sociology*, he
gives readers the following summary of his work: "Korea exempli-
fies a case where domestic capital supported state-building, hence
allowing for its success; India, in contrast, experienced a massive
campaign against such a state by its business class, hence forcing
state managers to retreat on their agenda, leaving the state with a
relatively feeble planning apparatus."[10]

Chibber's concerns overlap with those of the Subaltern Studies
group and the postcolonialists in that they were all interested in understanding the uneven development of the global capitalist world.
Moreover, like the postcolonials, he underscores the autonomy of politics from capital. However, Chibber does not think of the autonomy of
politics as cultural, but in terms of what we could call the relative
autonomy of the managerial class from the capitalist class.[11] In short,
Chibber and postcolonial theorists differ with respect to how to interpret the cultural turn, and this different analytical framework leads to
different interpretations of Indian history.

In particular, by downplaying the importance of culture to
explain historical difference, Chibber focuses on human agents
following interests, which he believes informs actions in all societies,

including peasant communities. Put simply, Chibber contends that culture does not imply radical incommensurability and that there are some universal traits of human experience that we can use to understand the peasants in India. Partha Chatterjee, on the other hand, contends that peasants' actions, especially when engaged in rebellious action, stem from fundamentally communal motives. Chatterjee writes:

> What the principle of community does as the characteristic unifying feature of peasant consciousness is directly place it at the opposite pole of a bourgeois consciousness. The latter operates from the premise of the individual and a notion of his interests (or, in more fashionable vocabulary, his preferences). Solidarities in bourgeois politics are built up through an aggregative process by which individuals came together into alliances on the basis of common interests (or shared preferences). The process is quite opposite in the consciousness of a rebellious peasantry. Their solidarities do not grow because individuals feel they can come together with others on the basis of their common individual interests: on the contrary, individuals are enjoined to act within a collectivity because, it is believed, bonds of solidarity that tie them together already exist. Collective action does not flow from a contact among individuals; rather, individual identities themselves are derived from membership in a community.[12]

Chatterjee posits an antinomy between bourgeois and peasant consciousness, especially Indian peasant societies, where the former is completely individualistic and the latter is communal. Therefore, in the case of bourgeois societies, solidarity can only emerge *a posteriori*, while in Indian peasant societies there are a priori bonds, which form the condition for action. By opposing individual and community, Chatterjee participates in a larger discourse beyond geographical distinctions such as East and West. Communitarian philosophers, such as Michael Sandel, invoke a similar argument at a more general level when they criticize liberals for focusing on the disembedded individual and hark back to a time when American values were not so tarnished by industrialization.[13]

More problematically, the Japanese conservative thinker Watsuji Tetsurō made a similar statement in the 1930s, in order to criticize the rapid urbanization and commodification that was taking place at the time in Japan.[14] If we turn to China, in the 1930s and 1940s, Mao Zedong and the more conservative Liang Shuming argued precisely about the universality and particularity of the Chinese peasant. Although Mao inspired scholars associated with Subaltern Studies, Mao's own words seem to support Chibber. Mao wrote: "Chinese society has its own particularities, its own cultural tradition, and its own ethics, which is not wrong for you to emphasize. Chinese society also has qualities in common with Western societies, which include class opposition, contradiction and struggle. These are its most fundamental attributes, which determine social progress. You overemphasize its special nature and neglect its universal nature."[15] Although Mao does not stress individual interests in this observation, he clearly sees the rifts in society as crucial to peasant life. His use of Marxist theory and class analysis in China was premised on the universality of such conflicts. Interestingly, both the Indian postcolonialists and some members associated with the Chinese "New Left," such as Wen Tiejun, expound a position similar to Liang Shuming and stress the particularity not only of peasant life but also of Chinese and Indian peasants.[16] Chatterjee sees himself as elaborating a position that Ranajit Guha made in *Elementary Aspects of Peasant Insurgency in Colonial India*, which he claims provides evidence for this view of the Indian peasantry.

However, through rereading Guha, Chibber contends that *Elementary Aspects* actually supports his own and, we could add, Mao's position. This should not be surprising because the book was first published in 1983, when many of the Subalterns were closer to Maoism than they are today. Chibber points out that because Guha describes meetings and deliberation among peasantry, this presupposes that peasants needed convincing that rebelling was in their interests. Moreover, Guha underscores that denial to cooperate would result in denial of cooperation with fellow villagers, which would affect the potential participant both economically and socially.[17]

Chibber provides sufficient evidence for us to conclude that Guha probably takes individual interests more seriously than does Chatterjee, but there are other more pressing issues related to the debate between postcolonials and Marxists that emerge from Guha's texts. Specifically, Guha's text is largely about the problem of politics, temporality, and action in peasant rebellions, rather than about theorizing the problem of peasant interest. These issues require us to move from our brief description of the Chibber–Chatterjee encounter to a confrontation between Chakrabarty and Chibber's respective work.

II. CHIBBER, CHAKRABARTY, AND THE PROBLEM OF MODERN POLITICS

A. Interests, peasant rebellions, and modernity

Chibber finds in Guha support for his claim that peasants are not naturally united with their communities and that they are capable of thinking about their interests. However, Chibber explains that Guha's main claim was to underscore, against Eric Hobsbawm and others, that peasant rebellions were not prepolitical but drew on informal sources to formulate their own inchoate politics.[18] Here we glimpse the complexity of Guha's argument, namely that on the one hand, peasant rebellions involve deliberation while, on the other, there is something collective and spontaneous about them, which nonetheless deserves to be taken seriously as politics. As Guha writes: "For it is the subjection of the rural masses to a common source of exploitation and oppression that makes them rebel even before they learn how to combine in peasant associations."[19] This citation again implies that peasants are aware of interests at some level, but also that Guha emphasizes spontaneity, contingency, and the transience of group activity, which he does not want to relegate to the prepolitical. Indeed, much of Guha's analysis in *Elementary Aspects* touches on how rituals, religion, and other activities charged with affective intensity helped to catalyze rebellious action.

Chakrabarty's reading of Guha begins by bringing together the unorthodox, spontaneous, collective political action of peasants in colonial India and modernity. Chakrabarty contends that Guha saw that the political consciousness of peasants was part of modern capitalism and colonialism; it did not represent something incomplete. In Chakrabarty's words, Guha "insisted that instead of being an anachronism in a modernizing colonial world, the peasant was a real contemporary of colonialism, a fundamental part of the modernity that colonial rule brought to India. Theirs was not a 'backward' consciousness—a mentality left over from the past, a consciousness baffled by modern political and economic institutions and yet resistant to them."[20]

Neither Chakrabarty nor Guha would completely deny the importance of interest in analyzing peasant rebellions; however, they would underscore that there are other, more affective and experiential aspects of these rebellions that cannot be reduced to interest. Indeed, the meaning of interests is conditioned by the various semiotic systems in which they are embedded. Guha goes to great lengths to show how the conflict between traditional semiotic systems in North India and the new set of colonial sign systems also provided the conditions for rebellion. In short, when the colonial regime invented new semiotic apparatuses while making use of existing ones, peasant insurgency by the subaltern classes emerged as a negative consciousness against the colonial and local elites and their semiotic systems.[21]

Chakrabarty wants to understand this ensemble of colonial elites, local elites, and subaltern resistance as modern and not outside the world of global capitalism. He contends that this has significance beyond analyzing peasant rebellions, since even today, in the popular media, India is described in terms of people living in different times. As a foil, he cites a *Wall Street Journal* article that claims that "Indians are capable of living many centuries at once."[22] The above statement implies that remnants of the past remain in India, which is not the case in European modernity. In Chakrabarty's view, the author did not understand that such apparent remnants are actually reconstituted by capitalist modernity.

This is a Hegelian move on Chakrabarty's part, because rather than seeing a conflict between the premodern remnant and the modern capitalism, he moves to a more totalizing concept of capitalist modernity in India that has four aspects: the legal institutions associated with the Enlightenment that emerge with colonialism, direct domination, religious practices, and finally various modes of peasant consciousness and uprisings. From this perspective, one would not merely chastise Enlightenment-oriented intellectuals for seeing the Indian peasants as backward or even explain this position based on their class location. Rather, this is the dominant discourse in a world of global capitalist imperialism, and that which falls out of this discourse, such as the experience of the subalterns, tends to be invisible. In short, the developmental narrative, which is taken up by many Marxists, actually supports capitalism by adopting the standpoint of capital and failing to see the hidden possibilities of rebellions operating on a different logic. Here we glimpse how Chakrabarty wants the subaltern peasants to be both inside and outside capitalist modernity; they are not an anachronism and so inside, and yet they are outside to the extent that their logic escapes capital. This outside-inside will be crucial to Chakrabarty's theory of history and his critique of progress.

In the context of a critique of progressive history, Chakrabarty sets E. P. Thompson up as a type of Marxist variation of the *Wall Street Journal* reporter who claimed that Indians live in many times. Thompson puts this vision into motion by theorizing how peripheral nations could overcome their nonsynchronicity. Chakrabarty cites Thompson, claiming that "without time-discipline we could not have the insistent energies of the industrial man; and whether this discipline comes from Methodism, or of Stalinism, or of nationalism, it will come to the developing world."[23] In Chakrabarty's view this is an excellent example of a historicist narrative that stresses linear historical progress without considering multiple temporalities or possibilities. He further contends that various concepts such as the passage from formal to real subsumption and uneven development are all different versions of the above thesis by Thompson in that they relegate India and other countries on the periphery of the global capitalist system to a type of waiting room of history. They must move from formal to real subsumption or wait until uneven development can become even. At a basic level, Chakrabarty does not deny a basic insight entailed by the above statements: the logic of capitalism is such that it needs to expand beyond its borders, and consequently time management and real subsumption will pervade the world. Anyone who looks at India and China today would not be able to deny this. However, his point concerns the heterogeneity implied in this process. Real subsumption and the spread of time management does not imply a homogeneity of life forms and experiences or the eradication of residues from the past. This is precisely where History 2 begins.

B. Modernity, Abstraction, and Residues: History 1 and History 2

In the previous section, we saw Chakrabarty criticize a position similar to one that Chibber ascribes to Guha and other Subalterns, namely, that India was caught in two times, one premodern and one modern—living many times at once. Against this, Chakrabarty attempts to ground his argument about different histories in capitalism and the outsides it produces. On the one hand, we have capital or History 1, "global in its historical aspiration and universal in its constitution," whose "categorial structure" "is predicated on the Enlightenment ideas of juridical equality and the abstract political rights of citizenship."[24] On the other, Chakrabarty hoped to show that in the translation of capital into that which was outside, something emerged that was beyond both capital and the Enlightenment. This is History 2.

Chakrabarty now has a huge task ahead of him: he must connect both the Enlightenment and that which escapes it in capital. This is what we might call Chakrabarty's immanent critique of capital because History 2, which resists capital, only exists in capitalist society. We can understand Chakrabarty's attempt to link the Enlightenment and capital with reference to what the Marxist scholar Jacques Bidet has more recently referred to as the "meta-structure of capital."[25] From the beginning of Marx's *Capital*, when Marx speaks of commodity exchange, he presupposes a certain legal structure, the equality of human beings, who are free to sell their labor power on the market. This abstract structure is then available to challenge the inequalities that capitalism inevitably reproduces and consequently could produce the desire to realize a world beyond capitalism. By invoking something akin to this metastructure, Chakrabarty connects the logic of capital to certain fundamental ideas of the Enlightenment.[26]

Chakrabarty grounds the Enlightenment in the abstract side of capitalism and the commodity, and this leads to a discussion of abstract labor in which he draws on I. Rubin and Moishe Postone. He notes that although abstract labor has in some sense existed in all societies, it becomes universal in capitalist society and this makes possible the existence of abstract labor as an analytical category: "In a capitalist society . . . the particular work of abstracting would itself become an element of most or all other kinds of concrete labor, and would be thus more visible to an observer."[27] From this perspective, we can understand how abstracting labor could be connected to other abstractions associated with the Enlightenment. Abstract labor, in Chakrabarty's interpretation of Marx, is the "hermeneutical grid through which capital requires us to read the world."[28] This hermeneutical grid has a social basis in the regulation and intensification of labor for the sake of increasing productivity. We will see that this abstraction encounters various forms of resistance.

1. Concrete Life as Resistance to Capitalism

If he stopped here, it would be as if capital does not allow for difference and life. But Chakrabarty attempts to show that within Marx there are various ways of identifying difference and contradiction in capitalism, and he draws on the distinction between abstract and concrete labor to discuss the way in which Marx posits life as constantly resisting capital. Life refers to "the abstract living labor—a sum of muscles, nerves, and consciousness/will—which according to Marx, capital posits as its contradictory starting point."[29] This starting point is contradictory because living labor embodies the possibility of resistance to capital. Chakrabarty cites Marx and then makes the following explanation: "And labor power as 'commodity exists in his [the laborer's] vitality . . . In order to maintain this from one day to the next . . . he has to consume a certain quantity of food, to replace his used-up blood etc . . . Capital has paid him the amount of objectified labour contained in his vital forces.' These vital forces are the ground of constant resistance to capital."[30]

Living labor and life in general, on Chakrabarty's reading of Marx, is that which capital constantly needs to create value but, at the same time, can never domesticate.[31] In other words, despite all the disciplinary mechanisms under capital's control, there is always an excess of life that is necessary for capitalism but cannot be completely consumed by capital.

At this point, Chakrabarty compares Hegel and Marx on the problem of life in the following manner: "Life, to use Hegel's expression, 'is a standing fight' against the problem of dismembering with which death threatens the unity of the living body. Life, in Marx's analysis of capital, is similarly a 'standing fight' against the process of abstraction that is constitutive of the category of 'labor.'"[32] Capital both posits and threatens life and living labor in the process of its reproduction. Chakrabarty understands labor as two-sided, both abstract and concrete, and consequently he understands Marx's project as one of protecting life from the process of abstraction.

2. Beyond Concrete Life: Life as Belonging

It would appear that Chakrabarty has already grounded the abstract and concrete sides of life in the dynamic of capitalism, and thus he would have accounted for particularity and universality, or difference and homogeneity. However, Chakrabarty believes that the above opposition between abstract labor and life does not completely account for the diverse modes of being in modern capitalism. It is as if every time a Hegelian maneuver is made to bring two opposites together there remains another insurmountable outside. This outside-inside emerges in the relationship between History as capital, that is, as the abstract logic of capital, and the pasts that preceded it.

It is at this point that he introduces two different pasts in Marx's texts, which we have mentioned above: History 1 and History 2. History 1 is a "past posited by capital itself as its precondition," and it describes aspects that "contribute to the self-reproduction of capital."[33] From the perspective of History 1, time and history itself are produced by capital, which fundamentally mediates the way we see the world. Chakrabarty cites a passage from the *Grundrisse* to explain his point: "These 'conditions and presuppositions of the becoming and the arising of capital,' writes Marx, 'presuppose precisely that it is not yet in being but merely in becoming; they therefore disappear as real capital arises, capital which itself, on the basis of its own reality, posits the condition for its realization.'"[34]

The past ceases to be what it used to be once capitalism comes into being because of a new idea of temporality and history that develops with this new mode of production. Until this point in his chapter, Chakrabarty has been following a Hegelian model in thinking about two sides of an antinomy, but History 2 is not the dialectical Other of History 1 or histories posited by the logic of capital.

History 2 is a past that is "antecedent" to capital but cannot be completely reduced to the logic of capital. To use a Derridean metaphor, History 2 is something that the capitalist system cannot digest without remainder and consequently must eject.[35] In this sense it is life, but not life thought of in mere opposition to abstract labor. The textual basis for Chakrabarty's interpretation is somewhat confusing, since he relies on the following passage from the *Theories of Surplus Value*, where Marx writes: "In the course of its evolution, industrial capital must therefore subjugate these forms and transform them into derived or special functions of itself. It encounters these older forms in the epoch of its formation and development. It encounters them as antecedents, but not as antecedents established by itself, not as forms of its own life-process. In the same way as it originally finds the commodity already in existence, but not as its own product, and likewise finds money circulation, but not as an element in its own reproduction."[36] In this passage, Marx discusses how various practices such as commodity production and the use of money predated capitalism. In short, he suggests that industrial capitalism brings these existing practices into its own system, and we would usually think of such elements as being fairly well integrated into capitalism. Chakrabarty here performs something like an immanent critique of Marx. He contends that the above passage implies two histories: capital's own life process and the antecedent histories that precede it. Moreover, he concludes that capitalism will have to repeat this process completely. The subsumption of these remnants into capital can never be complete. By focusing on antecedents, Chakrabarty is highlighting a rupture in the temporality of capital. The remnants are in capital but of an earlier time. Unlike the opposition between use value and exchange value, there is a strange type of nonsynchronous synchronicity between History 1 and History 2.[37]

Although in the above passage Marx speaks of remnants such as commodities and money, which become central concepts of capital, Chakrabarty creatively reads the above passage to include feelings and modes of life, such as those of Guha's peasants, which become remnants that could potentially resist capital. Chakrabarty continues this reading by citing the following passage of the *Grundrisse*: "Bourgeois society is the most developed and the most complex historic organization of production. The categories that express its relations, the comprehension of its structure, thereby also allow insights into the structure and the relations of production of all the vanished social formations out of whose ruins and elements it built itself up, whose partly still unconquered remnants are carried along within it, whose mere nuances have developed explicit significance within it, etc."[38] Chakrabarty focuses on the idea of remnants and emphasizes that these are only partly conquered. Most readings of the above passage would conclude that Marx is discussing the early period of capitalism, when there are unconquered remnants and these will eventually be transformed. Indeed, the original text reads, "Noch unübergewundene Reste," which could also be rendered "not yet conquered remnants" and suggests a trajectory toward further incorporation but leaves open the possibility that full incorporation without remainder is impossible. Chakrabarty asks whether this incompleteness is a mere transitional moment or a more fundamental structural feature of capitalism. In the former case, the "not yet" would just be another version of the "waiting room" theory in which countries outside the history of capital must only wait until they are fully integrated into the logic of capital. Instead, he argues for the latter and calls these elements not reducible to capital's logic "History 2"; such elements can disrupt capital. In his words, "History 2s are thus not pasts separate from capital; they inhere in capital and yet interrupt and punctuate the run of capital's own logic."[39]

Chakrabarty leaps from elements that would become essential parts of capital, such as money and the commodity, to premodern remnants and various forms of life. History 2 represents the sides of the various feelings, attitudes, and comportments that people embody during their everyday lives but which cannot be directly connected to the reproduction of capital. Chakrabarty explains the relation between these two histories in this way: "One consists of *analytical* histories that, through the abstracting categories of capital, eventually tend to make all places exchangeable with another. History 1 is just that, analytical history. But the idea of History 2 beckons us to more *affective* narratives of human belonging where life-forms, although porous to one another, do not seem exchangeable through a third term of equivalence such as abstract labor."[40]

Chakrabarty moves away from the political-economic narrative of Marx, who focused on commodities and money, to phenomenological forms, such as those of belonging and identity. He explains how workers in the factory embody both of these types of history. A worker is of course producing surplus value for the capitalist, but on the other hand has a number of other histories, namely, History 2. These histories or narratives have an irreducible singularity and cannot be exchanged with one another like commodities on the market. Because of this singularity, they become potential sites of resistance against capital.

3. Phenomenology beyond Labor

However, such resistance is not based on brute life or labor. History 2 seems to be precisely not-labor. Indeed, Chakrabarty points out that as long as workers affirm their identity as workers or bearers of labor power, they are part of History 1, even or especially when they unionize to fight capital. "To the extent that both the distant and immediate pasts of the worker—including the work of unionization and citizenship—prepare him to be the figure posited by capital as its own condition and contradiction, those pasts do indeed constitute History 1."[41] This echoes Moishe Postone's argument that by affirming themselves as laborers, workers are deepening the logic of capitalism.[42]

Chakrabarty shows how capital constantly wants to turn the worker into sheer labor and make the worker part of its totality. The worker plays into this logic when she or he takes up the identity and practices of a worker. But this totalization can never be complete because there is always an excess, that which cannot be abstracted, a phenomenological remainder that cannot be reduced to labor. For this reason, Chakrabarty underscores that History 2 concerns the claim that "even in the very abstract and abstracting space of the factory that capital creates, ways of being human will be acted out in manners that do not lend themselves to the reproduction of the logic of capital."[43] This opens the space to rethink various forms of oppositional politics in relation to forms of identity other than the working class.

Chakrabarty's argument overlaps with a number of recent Marxist attempts to theorize labor. For example, Bruno Gullì recently contends that Marx has a third category of labor, called "neither-productive-nor-unproductive labor." He writes that this neutral labor is "able (that is, [has] the power of Potenza) to be what it is and what it wants to be, rather than being posited by capital as capital's disguised necessity."[44] Similar to Chakrabarty, Gullì separates that which is posited by capital and that which partially escapes its logic. He follows more orthodox Marxists in claiming that neutral creative labor is "always present within production, regardless of the mode of production."[45]

If Chakrabarty followed Gullì he would perhaps fall into what Postone objects to as criticizing capitalism from the standpoint of the transhistorical concept of labor.[46] Chakrabarty wants to avoid such recourse to labor; he would like to keep History 2 as something that interrupts capital, rather than something that produces history in general.

He rather connects the disruption of History 2 to phenomenology and global unevenness and writes:

> These pasts, grouped together in my analysis as History 2, may be under the institutional dominion of the logic of capital and exist in proximate relation to it, but they also do not belong to the "life process" of capital. They enable the human bearer of labor power to enact other ways of being in the world—other than, that is, being the bearer of labor power. We cannot ever hope to write a complete or full account of these pasts. They are partly embodied in the person's bodily habits, in unselfconscious collective practices, in his or her reflexes about what it means to relate to objects in the world as a human being and together with other human beings in his given environment.[47]

Chakrabarty makes two related points here. The first concerns the irreducibility of the human being in the world to the bearer of labor power or worker, which could have a number of implications.[48] However, second, by stressing the body and prereflective habits, Chakrabarty connects his narrative to phenomenology. The problem here is that there are two partially overlapping narratives of History 2, one stemming from Guha's analysis of peasant societies and the other stemming from phenomenologists, such as Martin Heidegger. The former narrative is one of remnants from previous modes of production of various practices, including modes of production and religious practices. The second narrative is phenomenological and more elusive, but also potentially universal. If it refers to a past, it is something like Maurice Merleau-Ponty's "past that was never present," an experience that has not been present in ordinary time but nonetheless fundamentally pierces one's subjectivity. Merleau-Ponty writes: "Hence reflection does not grasp itself in its full sense, unless it refers to its unreflective ground that it presupposes, from which it profits, and which constitutes for it an original past [*un passé originel*], a past that was never present [*un passé qui n'a jamais été présent*]."[49]

This original past, like History 2, could refer to the bodily habits that are prereflective and done before one is conscious of a present or time. Obviously, this phenomenology will be informed by the various remnants that emerge, but History 2 then is not structurally dependent on remnants of precapitalist modes of production. A worker's bodily habits might be inherited from his family members, whom one could perhaps eventually trace back to precapitalist times, but we would find no necessary hostility to capitalism in these forms of comportment. This would be different from the peasant, who feels his livelihood being threatened by various forms of indigenous and colonial domination and then revolts.

The key issue in both the phenomenological perspective and the discourse of unevenness concerns the incompleteness of capital's totalization. Because totalization cannot completely subsume human experience and values, Chakrabarty distinguishes between globalization and universalization in the final lines of the chapter, which again brings us back to the issue of unevenness: "But globalization of capital is not the same as capital's universalization. Globalization does not mean that History 1, the universal and necessary logic of capital so essential to Marx's critique has been realized. What interrupts and defers capital's self-realization are the various History 2s that always modify History 1 and thus act as our grounds for claiming historical difference."[50]

Here we return to a paradigm close to Guha's *Domination without Hegemony*, which Chakrabarty at times invokes. In another text, glossing Guha, Chakrabarty claims that capital and power should be considered as separate variables and therefore even though India has been incorporated into global capital, there remains a space for different types of politics, as is evidenced by the insurgent peasants. In short, the "global history of capital need not reproduce everywhere the same history of power."[51] At the same time, in *Provincializing Europe*, Chakrabarty articulates more universal theory that tries to grasp the structure of this difference. After all, History 1 and History 2 now work as universals connected to capital and are not merely limited to the Indian case.

Keeping this universality in mind, in the above passage, we might say that globalization works something like the formal subsumption under capital, where the original mode of production is not altered even when it is now used to make profit for capital. The universalization of capital could be tantamount to real subsumption, where the structure of labor changes and technological innovation and time discipline become essential components of capitalist production. This is a possible interpretation of Chakrabarty. History 2 at times appears to imply forms of life that are formally subsumed, as in Guha's peasants. Indeed this is perhaps a way of thinking about domination by capital and hegemony in a manner that does not rely on the bourgeoisie. The problem with this interpretation is that it would entail that if there is real subsumption, then History 2s would be gone.[52] However, we saw that there are History 2s going on even in the factory, which would appear to be an area of real subsumption.

Consequently, difference and transcendence or History 2's relation to capital is ambivalent. It is a remnant or a phenomenological experience of the everyday in an uneven capitalist and colonial system, but how these remnants or experiences will destabilize capitalism is unclear. In Chakrabarty's words, "Difference, in this account, is not something external to capital. Nor is it something subsumed into capital. It lives in intimate and plural relationships to capital, ranging from opposition to neutrality."[53]

Given the wide range of possible relations between History 2 and capitalism, we could say that we might need a new term to describe distinctions within History 2. Chibber suggests that there are two History 2s: History 2(1)s, which are indifferent to capitalism, and History 2(2)s, which pose a threat to capitalism.[54] We might want to add History 2(3), remnants that actually help to reproduce capital.[55] I am going to be more concerned with History 2(2) in what remains, but we should note that it bears some interesting structural differences from the other two in that, rather than being past or present oriented, it is future oriented. History 2 could be redescribed as religious and aesthetic visions that could be mobilized against capitalism to help envision new forms of community and being in the world.

One of the best examples of such History 2s is perhaps found in Michel Löwy's book *Redemption and Utopia*, which examines the work of a number of Jewish thinkers in central Europe during the Weimar period, including Franz Rosenzweig, Gustav Landauer, and Walter Benjamin. Following Löwy's analysis, we could argue that it was precisely a common Jewish History 2 that enabled a romantic resistance to capitalism. These History 2s may have included unconscious collective practices and shared ideas about dealing with humans and things. We could describe the process of Judaism becoming a modern religion as one in which History 1 attempts to incorporate a history that preexists capitalism, and such incorporation conflicted with some existing practices. The history of Judaism becomes incorporated within capitalism, but not without a remnant. Within capitalism, this remainder might offer possibilities of resistance. For example, Löwy claims that many Jewish intellectuals from central Europe mobilized Hebraic ideas such as "Tikkun" or the "restoration of the original harmony" to create romantic anti-capitalist visions.[56] Of course, here we are dealing with highly reflective appropriations of History 2s, and it is at least as much the moment of reflection as the inherited body of practices that help to constitute this particular form of romantic anti-capitalism. This reflection takes something that on face value appears to be a "restoration" and propels it not to a completely open future, but to a future beyond capitalism. We should note that reflection here is crucial because the type of reflection could change the nature of the movement. For example, we could argue that around the same time as the above messianic thinkers, Watsuji Tetsurō was elaborating his own conservative romantic anti-capitalism, drawing on various Asian traditions, including Buddhism and Bushidō (the way of the warrior). However, like many Japanese critics of modernity during this time, he ended up supporting Japanese imperialism and fascism.

In short, given that reflection is crucial to turning History 2s into a politics, by itself, even the History 2s that are potentially anti-capitalist risk being indeterminate. Indeed, this might be the revenge of Hegel since his critique of Schelling, namely, that he describes a night in which all cows are black seems to apply to History 2 as well. Moreover, given the history of various romantic anti-capitalisms, especially those like Heidegger's that were also antagonistic to the Enlightenment, we can immediately perceive the dangers. Therefore, it is not surprising that toward the end of his book, Chakrabarty returns to the necessary mediation by History 1 and the Enlightenment as a way to orient politics.

> In this history [History 1] inhere the Enlightenment universals. As moderns desirous of social justice and its attendant institutions, we, whether decisionist or historicist, cannot but have a shared commitment to it . . . It is through this commitment that is already built into our lives that our jousting with European thought begins. The project of provincializing Europe arises from this commitment. But this beginning does not define the project. The project has to be defined with reference to other pasts, that is to say, with reference to History 2s—pasts "encountered by capital as antecedents but not as belonging to its own life-process."[57]

Chakrabarty ends by claiming that he is finding within European thought and the Enlightenment impetus to provincialize and take our being in the world seriously. Indeed, Chakrabarty's History 2 commitment to autonomy from History 1 already implies some commitment to the Enlightenment.[58] So we must think of History 2 as part of a larger project to creatively rethink the ideals of the Enlightenment. However, to begin such a project, it becomes important to show how and what type of resistance History 2 entails or could entail. Chakrabarty himself notes that History 2's relation to capital could range from opposition to neutrality, but because History 2 remains indeterminate with respect to both the Enlightenment and with respect to capital, we have not been given a clear criterion as to how and when History 2 could count as resistance or what kinds of futures it could gesture toward. Chibber believes that there is a problem with the whole paradigm that Chakrabarty and other postcolonials use and therefore begins by interrogating the relationship between capitalism and the

Enlightenment. Through this critical gesture, we will come back to History 2 and its relation to capital in the final sections of this essay.

III. CHIBBER'S CRITIQUE OF CHAKRABARTY'S POSTCOLONIALISM

Chibber's criticism of postcolonialism is multidimensional; however, for the purposes of this essay, I will focus on two interrelated points: his defense of the Enlightenment and his emphasis on class, based on a restricted definition of capital. After dealing with these, I will further examine the significance of Chibber's discussion with respect to how to conceive of global capitalism. To some extent the restricted definition of capital allows him to affirm Chakrabarty's History 1 and History 2 without any problem. He does not believe that the existence of relatively autonomous cultural and phenomenological experiences is sufficient reason to give up Enlightenment values and indeed claims that the critique of capital requires the universal goals of the Enlightenment, including autonomy and equality.

Chibber's reading of the French and English experiences emerges as a response to Guha's reading of the Enlightenment and plays an important role in his critique of Chakrabarty's two histories. Because defending the Enlightenment from critics is part of Chibber's larger goal, his discussion of France is important for his general argument. Despite the difference between Guha and Chakrabarty, they are united in questioning the totality and universalization of capital and see the problem as the incompleteness of the Enlightenment project. As we shall see, Chibber will defuse their argument by deflating what he takes as their bloated conception of capitalism and their misunderstanding of French and English history.

Chibber distinguishes between the Enlightenment and capitalism by separating the French and English Revolutions and then showing that those who promoted the English revolution, especially the bourgeoisie supporters, were not interested in promoting universal rights and other Enlightenment principles. Consequently, he suggests that we need to rethink the historical significance of these revolutions. The following citation succinctly grasps Chibber's point: "The English Revolution could not be anti-feudal because it occurred after the transition to capitalism had already been completed. In France, capitalism had barely begun to sprout by 1789. Hence, there was every possibility for the revolution to be anti-feudal, and in fact, this was one of its defining characteristics. The problem is that it was not led by actors who in any sense could be identified as capitalists."[59]

One could say that before getting to the idea of History 2, he wants to show that History 1 has an internal rupture. In other words, capitalism and the Enlightenment, which are both supposed to be part of History 1, are now seen as separate and in tension with each other. At this point, Chibber draws on the work of Robert Brenner and Ellen Wood to show that the bourgeoisie is different in England and in France.[60]

Chibber's gesture here is interesting since it parallels Chakrabarty in creating a type of outside perspective to criticize capitalism. Indeed, even more than Chakrabarty's History 2, which is both inside and outside, Chibber's Enlightenment seems truly outside capital because it preceded capitalism. Drawing on William H. Sewell, Jr., and T. C. W. Blanning, Chibber explains that the term "bourgeoisie" in prerevolutionary France was vague and encompassed much more than just capitalists: "It is well understood in the historiography of the ancien régime that the term 'bourgeois' was a nebulous term, referring not to capitalists per se, but to a cluster of occupations that had in common only what they were not: neither peasant nor laborer, these persons belonged to moneyed strata outside the nobility. They could be industrialists, merchants, shopkeepers, urban professionals. In fact, the typical bourgeois in eighteenth-century France belong to the last category, simply because of its growing importance in the political economy."[61]

In this way, Chibber follows Wood in proposing a Marxist response to a huge range of historiography of the French Revolution, which attempted to understand the French Revolution as a bourgeois-capitalist revolution.[62] The separation between bourgeois and capitalist allows one to distinguish the historical trajectories of France and England, which in turn has implications for their respective intellectual histories. In Wood's view, the Enlightenment ideas of thinkers such as Rousseau and Condorcet both follow from these urban professionals and also bureaucrats, who are separate from the nobility but are not capitalists. One can hence begin to conceive an Enlightenment against capitalism. The logic of the Enlightenment involves a univer-salizing connected to the bureaucracy, which should be seen as sepa-rate from that of capitalism and its own ideologies. In particular, Wood argues that the Enlightenment ideals of equality predated capitalism and provide a contrast to the capitalist framework where everything is subordinated to productivity and profit. George Comninel applies the above differences to Marx and goes so far as to say that Marx was able to develop his critique of capitalism because he spent time in France, which provided him a standpoint related to the Enlightenment and outside of capitalist England.[63]

From this perspective, we could say that the Enlightenment should be added to the commodity and money as part of History 2.[64] Chakrabarty writes, "Marx recognizes the possibility that money and commodity, as relations, could have existed in history without neces-sarily giving rise to capital, they make up the kind of past that I have called History 2."[65] Bringing Wood and Chakrabarty together, one could argue that the Enlightenment is a History 2, which is even more antagonistic to capital than are either the commodity or money.

Note that with Chibber/Brenner/Wood capitalism has shrunk both conceptually and spatially. Capitalism is no longer what Chakrabarty claims is seen in terms of "the Hegelian idea of a totalizing unity."[66] Rather, Chibber explains his own more modest conception of capital-ism in the following manner: "Subalternist theorists work with an unduly expansive notion of what capitalism is supposed to universal-ize. We saw that the most defensible case is for a narrower conception, in which capitalist globalization amounts to the universalization of practices related to economic production."[67]

Capitalism has now become merely an economic form that does not entail any necessary relationship to Enlightenment values or other cultural practices; rather, it is about producing surplus value and even-tually relative surplus value. Chibber describes this process in the following manner:

> What capitalism universalizes then, is a particular strategy of economic reproduction. It compels economic units to focus single-mindedly on accumulating ever more capital. Economic managers internalize it as their goal because it is built into the structural

location of being a capitalist; it is not something capitalists have to be convinced to do. Wherever capitalism goes, so too does this impera-tive . . . Based on the new definition I have offered, we can accept that capital has universalized even if its political mission is not devoted to winning the consent of the laboring classes. By our criteria, the universalizing process is under way if agents' reproductive strategies shift toward market dependence.[68]

Chibber notes that the main point about capitalism concerns produc-ing only for exchange and profit, namely, the accumulation of capital and not merely for use. It is this logic that is universalized rather than any political structure. This is why when India becomes a capitalist society, it does not have to become a replica of England in terms of culture or politics. But Chibber continues to argue that because of market dependence and market competition, there are changes in intensity that primarily concern time, and this eventually leads to class struggle.

In short, as Chibber explains, the capitalist "has to induce his employees to produce more goods in the same amount of time, which translates into insisting that his employees work at the highest level of intensity that they can sustain."[69] As capitalists shift to producing rela-tive surplus value and resort to technological mediation, laborers will resist increases in productivity because it will "increase the likelihood of job loss, because as each worker is able to produce more goods in less time, the employer can afford to shed some of his labor force."[70] At the same time, even when their job is not in jeopardy, workers find that "the increasing intensity of labor comes at the cost of their well-being."[71] This discussion of course captures the famous dialogue between the worker and capitalist in Marx's chapter on the working day, but the concept of well-being is not an easily quantifiable concept and would be concerned with use values as opposed to exchange values. At the same time, Chibber would argue that the ideals of the Enlightenment, albeit abstract, could be mobilized by mass move-ments in order to secure greater well-being.

Chibber makes an important contribution by underscoring class and interest, especially movements involving the lower classes. Against Guha, Chibber argues that it is not the bourgeoisie who should be given credit for the spread of Enlightenment values in Europe, but the laboring classes and their movements that forced the upper classes to yield. This leaves open the question of whether, following Chakrabarty's logic, the workers were spreading the logic of capitalism as they caused the upper classes to yield. Here we may see the limitations of focusing on interests as a given, without a theory of how interests could be reconstituted toward a different future. It appears that all that is required for resistance to capitalism is a combination of interest and Enlightenment ideals.

Given Chibber's defense of the Enlightenment and of workers' resistance to capitalism, it is not surprising that he finds little use for Chakrabarty's abstract reading of capital or his reading of History 2, which he sees as irrelevant at best and possibly dangerous. Chibber rather says that the threat to capitalism comes from History 1. This "disruption" in capital comes from "the universal interest that working people have to protect their well-being from capitalist authority and abuse."[72] Here the idea of well-being is crucial to Chibber's argument and is another concept that plays a role something like Chakrabarty's History 2, since it is outside capital: "The interest in well-being is a fundamental source of instability to capital, simply because of its ubiquity—it is built into the psychology of social agents, regardless of culture or location. The very fact that cultures exist at all presupposes that social agents have a drive to protect their basic needs. But precisely because this interest is a component of human nature, it necessarily brings workers into conflict with the logic of accumulation, wherever and whenever it unfolds."[73]

Chibber's point about the drive echoes Spinoza's definition of the conatus. *Ethics*, Book III, Proposition 6 states: "Each thing as far as it is in itself, endeavors to persist in its being."[74] In Chibber's view, culture emerges out of this struggle for existence. While Chibber invokes human nature, he does not need this for his argument. His argument only requires a historically specific claim that workers and capitalists have mutually antagonistic conati at some level. Thus he could easily follow Marxists who contend that the idea of people following their individual interests emerges with capitalism, along with the idea that individuals are free and equal bearers of labor power, which they sell on the market.[75] But Chibber's contribution here is to bring class struggle into the abstract dichotomy between History 1 and History 2, which might offer a path to a more active History 2. Indeed, if one examines Chakrabarty's discourse, one finds no attempt to show how History 2s are mediated by class, such that capitalists' History 2s have a radically different texture than that of workers and so on. Perhaps the price that Chakrabarty had to pay when he generalized Guha's discourse of the Subalterns to the ontology of capital was that he had to be silent about class conflict. Capitalists might also be concerned for their well-being, but their role as capitalist involves the struggle to increase surplus value rather than merely to procure use values to promote one's personal well-being.[76]

Without getting into the issue of whether interests are in some sense universal, we need to take seriously the point that workers concerned for their well-being can cause a significant threat to capital and modify it. Although the specific struggles that Marx describes often occurred in Victorian England, "they have been played out all over the globe, whereever capital has established its rule. They are, to use Chakrabarty's language, a part of the universal and necessary history of capital, and hence of History 1."[77] However, by saying that the class struggle is part of the history of capital, he seems to be following Chakrabarty in subsuming class struggle into capitalism. In other words, class struggle would not point beyond capitalism but merely be incorporated into it.

As a partial answer to this problem, Chibber redefines what it means to "modify" the logic of capital and explains how and why struggles by the proletariat could modify the logic of capital. He argues that workers' struggle to shorten the working day could count as a modification of the logic of capitalism to the extent that it forces capitalists to move from absolute to relative surplus value, that is, to switch from merely exploiting labor power to focusing more on technological mediation.[78] Such a movement would of course not amount to overcoming the conditions of capitalism and hence is not yet a threat, but it does count as a modification of capitalism, and clearly a capitalism that is primarily based on relative surplus value is quite different from a capitalism based on absolute surplus value. In this way, we have seen how, using a new conception of the Enlightenment, Chibber has posed an alternative vision of the social universal to that of Chakrabarty.

However, in the end, neither Chibber nor Chakrabarty have been able to think of a vision beyond capitalism. While it might be the case that workers struggling for their interests helped to modify capitalism, such a logic seems fully compatible with the politics of capitalist social democracy. Chakrabarty at first seems to go further because he is attempting to find spaces beyond capitalism, but because he cannot show how such spaces would cause a threat to capitalism or be mobilized in such struggles, he retreats from the project of going beyond capitalism and appears to ask us to take solace in History 2s within capitalism.

IV. Rethinking Chibber and Chakrabarty in Light of Global Capitalism

Having seen in some detail Chakrabarty's attempt to launch an immanent critique of Marx and Chibber's immanent critique of postcolonial discourse, in the next two sections I am going to begin an immanent critique of Chakrabarty and Chibber to shed light on the possibilities of a postcapitalist future. I separate this part of the essay into three sections because there are three aspects to my immanent critique: (A) determining the conditions of the possibility of the object of critique, namely, Chibber and Chakrabarty's respective discourses, in capital, which leads to (B) theorizing the relationship between capital and the nation-state. Finally, (C) I make some remarks about how the logic of capital, which is also the object of Chibber and Chakrabarty's respective critiques, could point toward a different future. None of these are simple tasks, and therefore, the next sections can only consist of preliminary sketches.

A. Bringing History 1 and 2 together: Rethinking the logic of capital

When discussing History 1 and 2, Chibber makes a provocative statement about Chakrabarty's conception of capital, which points toward an immanent critique of his own work and Chakrabarty's: "Chakrabarty's argument amounts to the rather absurd view that universalization requires the subordination of all practices to the dictates of capitalism, to the 'logic of capital.' Yet I am unaware of any theorist outside of the domain of postcolonial studies who would defend this view, nor do I see any justification for it."[79] Interestingly, this conception of capital as a totalizing dynamic that encompasses all modes of life is not only close to Chakrabarty's position but perhaps, more accurately, describes the position of Moishe Postone. Postone's reinterpretation of Marxism is relevant here not only because it represents a conception of capital that Chibber finds in Chakrabarty, and has been recently mobilized against Chakrabarty,[80] but because it will pave the way to ground History 1 and 2 as part of capital. Although Postone's Marxist project has little to do with provincializing Europe, in this section we will see how, far from leading to Eurocentrism, Marxism allows us to provincialize Europe in a more fundamental sense—that is, by showing how the logic of capital itself creates differences between Europe and Asia. Moreover, capital's relation to regions and nations can change over time, as is evidenced in the transformations of China and Brazil since the 1970s.

The first conceptual move is to separate capital from Europe. The former is an abstract dynamic that is logically prior to regions such as Europe and Asia. In other words, as Chakrabarty suggests, Europe invades Asia because of the logic of capital and the uneven world that it creates. In this context, Postone's framework appears to allow one to criticize Chakrabarty not for being too Hegelian but for not being Hegelian enough. Instead of arguing that History 2 is outside of capital, from this reading of Marx, one could suggest that History 1 as Enlightenment and History 2 as phenomenological feeling and concrete modes of belonging are both products of the commodity form and logic of capital. Such a reading would complement Chakrabarty's view of the Enlightenment, explaining how it is connected to capital and also offering some suggestions concerning how to deal with History 2. On this reading of Marx, the key to grounding History 1 and 2 lies in locating these forms in the logic of the commodity.

In the first chapter of volume 1 of *Capital*, Marx explains that the commodity has two sides: exchange value, which reduces the various commodities in the world to a common measure, and use value, which represents the particular way in which one can use a commodity. From the latter perspective, a commodity is a particular thing that can be used. The use of a computer is different from that of a table and so on.

However, from the standpoint of exchange value, the various commodities lose their particular concrete existence and come to represent a number, which is generally construed as the socially necessary labor time required to produce a given commodity and is eventually represented as the commodity's price. Although the two sides of the commodity appear in the same object, once exchange value appears as money, people experience the two sides of the commodity form, the abstract and the concrete, as separate. Because the value of a commodity is eventually embodied in an external object as money, people in capitalist society immediately experience exchange value and use value separately. This separation allows for various forms of consciousness. Now let us examine the extent to which we can ground History 1 and History 2 in capital, using the above framework.

Turning to History 1 and the Enlightenment, we might ground these concepts in the commodity. One might immediately accept the homology between the abstraction of the commodity form and Enlightenment abstractions, such as the idea of equality. However, we would need to do more work before we could conclude that abstractions such as equality are grounded in the exchange value side of the commodity form. This is especially the case if we follow Chibber in concluding that France was not capitalist during the French Revolution. Recall that Wood attempted to connect the ideals of the likes of Condorcet not to capital, but to the state.

William Sewell has recently made a strong argument for the applicability of the categories of the first chapter of volume 1 of *Capital* to eighteenth-century France. Sewell suggests that the ideas of "civil equality" during the French Revolution could have emerged through market exchange. He contends that "eighteenth-century French commercial capitalist development fostered a vigorous growth of abstract forms of social relations and that the growing experience of such abstraction in daily life helped make the notion of civic equality both conceivable and attractive by the 1780s."[81] He does not place the emphasis on class but focuses on Chapter 1 of Marx's *Capital*, which is about production for the market and exchange. Sewell's point allows one to ground the Enlightenment in the commodity and market exchange and dovetails with Jacques Bidet's comments about how market exchange presupposes concepts of equality and freedom.

Bidet claims that the concept of capital does not really emerge until the fourth chapter of volume 1 of *Capital*, which, as the title suggests, deals with the transformation of money into capital.[82] Before this point, the concept of wage labor has not actually been introduced and interestingly this point might be relevant to France in the eighteenth century. As Sewell explains, "although the textile producers were generally quite poor and were exploited very effectively by the merchants who supplied them with raw materials and marketed the products, they were not actually wage-workers."[83] So although we do not have capitalism in its developed form, we do have the relations outlined in the first three chapters of *Capital*, which presupposes the ideas of equality and freedom, and through participation in the market, these elements become part of the structures of feeling of commoners. The key issue here is that the so-called economic practices that Chibber highlights entail cultural and intellectual dimensions, including ideas of equality and freedom.

Bringing Postone, Sewell, and Bidet together, we can also more fully ground Ellen Wood's insight, which connected the idea of equality to the state and bureaucracy. The meta-structure of the market, namely, the ideas of free and equal individuals exchanging commodities, must be backed by some type of legal structure, which implies the state. Following Sewell, one could conclude that the state during eighteenth-century France embodies this contradiction of on the one hand supporting market equality, at least in some places, and on the other reproducing an extremely hierarchical system. Although it might be the lower classes and state functionaries who would draw on the above ideals more than the aristocracy, there is no logical connection between such ideals and any particular class—they are not merely products of a capitalist class. In some sense, this discussion has grounded Chibber's understanding of Enlightenment and Chakrabarty's History 1 in a theory of the commodity and market exchange. The above analysis shows that Marx's example of capital finding money and commodities preexisting it, far from being History 2, actually tends to produce History 1. Now we can return to grounding History 2 in capitalism, which is a more difficult task.

Chakrabarty's History 2 is clearly polysemic. In the above discussion we have seen that it could mean phenomenological experience,

concrete religious feelings of belonging related to unevenness, especially between places in the center and the periphery, but also more
generally experiences that could potentially resist or provide temporary transcendent vantage points on capitalist society. In addition to
all of this, there is a temporal dimension to History 2 both because it is
a "history" and because it emerges in capitalism as something that has
always already been. So although one can assert that History 2 is
concrete, one still needs to think about how to deal with the temporality and spatiality of History 2 in relation to capitalism and dominant
forms of political belonging.

In the context of dealing with forms of belonging, we need to
inquire into how History 2 could be understood in the interface
between the nation-state and capital. In a footnote to his discussion of
capitalism and the nation-state, Chibber invokes Manu Goswami's
emphasis on the "material basis of national consciousness" in colonial
India, which suggests some ways to deal with History 2 as unevenness.[84] In particular, Goswami contends that History 1 and History 2
are both produced by the dynamic of capital. She writes:

> A conception of global space-time as hierarchical and differentiated
> rather than unified and homogenous foregrounds the ongoing crea-
> tion of unevenness (economic and cultural, spatial and temporal) as
> the internal supplement of the universalizing orientation of capital.
> It suggests that the universalizing dynamic of capital develops
> unevenly across space and time and that it actively generates new
> forms of sociospatial and sociocultural unevenness. From this
> perspective, History 2 represents an internal dimension of History
> 1, not an absolute outside that episodically interrupts the suppos-
> edly homogenous, linear progression of an abstract logic of capital
> as such."[85]

In such a framework, we can understand History 1 and 2 in a world in
which the dynamic of capital along with the logic of territorialization
continually reproduces the ideal of equality and real inequality,
unevenness, and domination. Goswami explains how the "interpene-
tration of socioeconomic processes, during this period, was part and
parcel of the consolidation of Britain's global hegemony as defined by

its welding together, as Giovanni Arrighi argues, of 'territorialist and capitalist logics of power' on a historically novel world-wide scale."[86]

Although they are "welded together," Arrighi analytically separates territorial and capitalist logics, and, as we have seen, Chibber makes a similar distinction in his discussion of India and Korea. The basic insight here is that the organizational, social, and political infrastructures that help to reproduce capital are by no means expressions of the capitalist social relations.[87] To the extent that History 2 involves narrative and feelings of belonging, we could connect them to the logic of territoriality. At this point we come to the problem of nationalism to which I alluded earlier. Drawing on Henri Lefebvre, Neil Brenner succinctly summarizes the issue of nationalism and the state in the following manner:

> Lefebvre argues, the relation of national states to multinational capital is never predetermined but is the object and expression of nearly continual sociopolitical contestation, conflict and struggle. If the risk persists that the state might be subordinated to the demands of global corporations, so too, according to Lefebvre, does the possibility of a state controlled by an anti-imperialist, popular democratic coalition oriented toward radically anti-productivist goals. Although Chibber does not cite Lefebvre, his book is fundamentally concerned with the extent to which people could mobilize the nation-state against capital, especially in the initial stages of the struggle for socialism.[88]

B. Nationalism against capitalism?

Chapter 10 of Chibber's book is called "The Nation Unmoored" and explicitly argues for the idea of a Third World nationalism as potentially destabilizing capitalism. The major aim of this chapter is to criticize Chatterjee's conception of nationalism in a number of his writings. However, Chibber's major aim is to potentially separate nationalism from capitalism, which is part of his project to separate the Enlightenment/modernity from capitalism. We can now deal further with this major rift between the postcolonials and Chibber as we move toward rethinking capital and the possibilities of its determinate negation in relation to nationalism.

Chibber promotes a modernizing anti-colonial nationalism against Chatterjee's more spiritual version. While Chatterjee does not use the term "History 2," we can see similar themes in the following citation:

> By my reading, anti-colonial nationalism creates its own domain of sovereignty within colonial society well before it ever begins its political battle with the imperial power. It does this by dividing the work of social institutions and practices into two domains—the material and the spiritual. The material is the domain of the "outside," of the economy and of statecraft, of science and technology, a domain where the West had proved its superiority and the East had succumbed . . . The spiritual, on the other hand, is an "inner" domain bearing the "essential" marks of cultural identity . . . This formula is, I think, a fundamental feature of anti-colonial nationalism.[89]

In this passage, many of the things associated with History 1, such as the Enlightenment and capital, are not part of anti-colonial nationalism. We could read Chatterjee as outlining one possible political use of History 2.[90] The problem with the above description is that anti-colonialist nationalism ends up being like Hegel's "beautiful soul," which is beautiful only as long as it does not enter reality.[91] Unfortunately, in a global capitalist world of nation-states, anti-colonial nationalists eventually have to enter this reality and end up mixing Chatterjee's categories of outer and inner. Hence, they can be criticized for eventually becoming modernizers. Chatterjee's critique of the nationalism of Gandhi and others involves this maneuver.

Chibber, on the other hand, sees a hope in this anti-colonial nationalism and claims that not only did they not follow the above model, they should not have. He mentions Mao Zedong, Amical Cabral, and Ho Chi Minh as some of the nationalists who openly embraced the modernizing model and were critical of their own traditions.[92] The question is, What role could such a nationalism play in creating a future beyond capitalism? If one separates the logic of territoriality from the logic of accumulation à la Arrighi or market from organization à la Bidet, it would be logically possible to think of a type of nationalism that was not capitalist. This is a controversial interpretation of capital and the state but followed by a number of Marxists on whom Chibber draws, so let us assume that we can make this analytical separation. In this case, we would need to specify further how such a noncapitalist nation-state could play a role in promoting a wider movement not just against capitalism, but toward socialism. After all, even Althusser-influenced Marxists such as Jacques Bidet and Gerard Duménil argue that actually existing socialist regimes used organization to overcome the market mechanisms of capitalism, but ended up reproducing many of the same phenomena, including domination and alienation.[93]

Marx hinted at the potentialities of unevenness in his letter to Vera Zasulich. Zasulich asked whether Russia had to go through the same stage of capitalism as Western Europe and dissolve its earlier communal forms of life. Marx suggests that there may be areas where earlier forms of communal life continue by being articulated into a capitalist world. The question concerns to what extent these forms of life could be drawn on to imagine and even realize a future beyond capitalism. Marx wrote many drafts of his response, but the basic idea is grasped in the following remarks: "My answer is that, thanks to the unique combination of circumstances in Russia, the rural commune, which is still established on a national scale, may gradually shake off its primitive characteristics and directly develop an element of collective production on a national scale. Precisely because it is contemporaneous with capitalist production, the rural commune may appropriate all its positive achievements without undergoing its [terrible] frightful vicissitudes. Russia does not live in isolation from the modern world, and nor has it fallen prey, like the East Indies, to a conquering foreign power."[94]

For our purposes, one of the key issues here is the "contemporaneity" of Russia with the world of capitalist production, which makes notions such as backward and forward irrelevant when discussing the development of nation-states. The discussion also intimates History 2, because the communes are contemporary with global capitalism, but still different. Harry Harootunian has recently connected the above case to the issue of formal subsumption. In his view, Marx's point is that countries on the periphery of the global capitalist system could "utilize residues of prior modes of production to create either a new register of formal subsumption or bypass capitalism altogether."[95] This is an extremely tempting position that combines anti-imperialist nationalism on the periphery of global capitalism and the hope for socialism. However, unless it can eventually move beyond nationalism, one may find oneself reproducing the problem of the beautiful soul that has to keep from being contaminated by a capitalist reality. This will only aggravate the organizational controls that attempt to purge such contamination from the nation.[96]

C. Contradictions of capitalism: Deriving "ought" from "is"

Although they are both in some sense supporting Third World nationalisms, Chibber would probably not approve of Harootunian's use of the Zasulich letters or his endorsement of the peasant communes. Moreover, Chibber asserts that it is only the conflict between labor and capitalism that constitutes a potential threat to capitalism, while the structural crisis of capitalism only leads to its spatial expansion.[97] However, Chibber overlooks another aspect of the crisis of capitalism that is temporal and would be an important part of an immanent critique of capitalism. We can now return to the problem of immanent critique, which Postone calls locating the "ought" in actually existing capitalism. If the Vera Zasulich narrative stresses History 2, we need a more dynamic notion of how History 1 actually provides a possibility beyond itself. One needs to show how the existent society itself points beyond itself toward a postcapitalist society. The spatial crisis that Chibber delineates gets us only halfway there. Many Marxists have pointed out that the expansion of capitalism causes capital to exhaust the resources of nature, which consequently will eventually threaten the human species.[98] This, along with the ways in which capitalism oppresses and dominates people in various ways, might not give us an "ought," but it does provides us with an explanation of how this "ought" is possible. Chakrabarty had already touched on the passage that showed this possibility but did not dwell on its implications.

> Capital itself is the moving contradiction [in] that it presses to reduce labour time to a minimum, while it posits labour time, on the other side, as sole measure and source of wealth. Hence it diminishes labour-time in the necessary form so as to increase it in the superfluous form; hence it posits the superfluous in growing measure as a

condition—question of life and death—for the necessary. On the one side, then, it calls to life all the powers of science and of nature, as of social combination and of social intercourse in order to make the creation of wealth. On the other side, it wants to use labour time as the sole measuring rod for the giant social forces thereby created, and to confine them within the limits required to maintain the already created value as value.[99]

This passage shows a contradiction between living and dead labor, where it is actually dead labor that makes living labor cease to be the prime creator of wealth. Put simply, although many Marxists, including Chibber, focus on the contradiction between labor and capital, therefore emphasizing living labor, they overlook that it is the potentiality of dead labor that could make a new society possible. In other words, the increase of machines and technological mediation makes living labor obsolete for the creation of actual use values. At the same time, as long as society remains capitalist, capital will continue to exploit labor to create value, regardless of the extent of technological mediation. The result will be various forms of crises and unemployment, of which the history of capitalism has provided ample evidence.

This brings us back to points made, respectively, by Gullì and Chakrabarty, namely, that workers have histories other than being bearers of labor power. In the above context, this problem is not just one about the subjectivity of the worker but concerns the logic of capitalism as well. In advanced capitalism, workers do not need to do as much work to produce wealth, but the problem concerns how they could turn their daydreams and movements toward the creation of a society where wage labor does not dominate our existence.

This goal or vision of the future provides the tools for us to rethink working-class movements in order to realize this goal.[100] This is what Postone has in mind when he writes: "If a movement, concerned with workers, were to point beyond capitalism, it would have to defend workers' interests and have to participate in their transformation—for example, by calling into question the given structure of labor, not identifying any longer in terms of that structure, and participating in rethinking those interests."[101]

As with Chibber, worker movements begin with interests, but they must rethink these interests. In some ways, Postone also anticipates Chakrabarty and Gulli, since the above passage implies separating a workers' interest qua worker and his or her interest qua being in the world. The issue is not to oppose working-class politics with the politics of belonging or other forms of politics but to try to think of both these politics together in relation to the struggle for a postcapitalist world. For this reason, Postone does not use the term "working-class movement" but rather "a movement concerned with workers," which involves a politics of naming to avoid reifying the identity of the working class. The concern with workers is separate from the identity of workers as workers, which enables us to conceive of a movement dealing with workers that potentially transcends working-class identity. This is where the solidarity between working-class movements and the subaltern movements could come into play.

In short, a serious politics that wanted to challenge capitalism would have to take into consideration the above temporal dynamic of capitalism while at the same time drawing on interests and various dimensions of History 2 and then connecting with various movements on the periphery of capitalism, which might offer ideals of community but will not be able to be realized without a larger global transformation. In this context, we can return to the problem of History 2.

V. CONCLUSION: A CRITIQUE OF PURE ROMANTIC ANTI-CAPITALISM

The hope to realize capitalism by drawing on History 2s or remnants is clearly a form of romantic capitalism, because it posits resistance to capitalism without grounding this impulse in contradictory social relations and dynamics. In this sense, one could say that I have proposed a critique of pure romantic capitalism. But when the critique of romantic anticapitalism goes to an extreme, we become incapable of imagining a future beyond capitalism. In this context, romantic anticapitalism, and Löwy's discussion in particular, might have something to offer.[102]

In addition to the above philosophical reasoning, there are structural reasons to attempt a synthesis of romantic anti-capitalism with more concrete visions of politics and analysis. In particular, the temporal dynamic of capitalism toward greater levels of productivity does not imply a homogeneous world of capitalism. On the contrary, as Alex Callinicos points out, socially necessary labor time is radically different in various regions of the world, and this difference is structurally reproduced.[103]

In this context, scholars such as Vijay Prashad have documented the struggles in the peripheries of global capitalism, such as the Chiapas and other movements in Latin America, Asia, and Africa, which entail "local resistance against transnational firms."[104] David McNally sympathetically examines worker movements in various societies on the periphery of capitalism, especially those in Latin America.[105] The immediate goals of these movements are often not something in the distant future, such as a postcapitalist society, but connected to subsistence and land relations. Hence it would be inaccurate to claim that such forms of peasant and worker resistance directly point beyond capitalism. However, perhaps the inspiration that we can continue to take from Maoism is the attempt to connect these issues of the everyday, which at some level are confronting global capitalism, to the hope and practices for a world beyond capitalism. The revolutions of the twentieth century were clearly faced with such a question, and it was clear to most socialists that the various movements on the periphery would not succeed without some attempt to create alliances with "movements concerned with workers" both in their own region and elsewhere.

However, there is often mutual hostility between leaders of peasant movements and more mainstream communist parties, such as we see in the contemporary Maoist movement in India.[106] Such examples show that, even in one nation, it is difficult to unite movements closer to History 1 (mainstream Communist parties) and those that to different degrees resist aspects of the Enlightenment. At a global level, the spatial dynamics of capital and the state make transnational unity more difficult, especially for the lower classes, whose mobility is more restricted. For such a unity to begin and for it to move in a direction beyond existing paradigms of social democracy, we must transcend narrow perceptions of identity and interest. While one cannot be optimistic today about the future of socialist movements, we can hope that

Mao will be correct when he said in 1945: "The path has many twists and turns, but the future is bright."[107] The twentieth century has already proved the first part of this statement true, perhaps for reasons that Mao could not have realized. Although theory perhaps cannot completely outline a practice to create a brighter future, it could inspire political practice by showing how the contradictions of capitalism make a better future possible.

Credits

1. "Subaltern Studies and *Capital*," Partha Chatterjee, *Economic and Political Weekly*, Vol. 48, No. 37, September 14, 2013. Available at www. epw.in/journal/2013/37/notes/subaltern-studies-and-capital. html#sthash.LQoW8gBy.dpuf

2. "Subaltern Studies Revisited: A Response to Partha Chatterjee," Vivek Chibber, *Revisiting Subaltern Studies*, Vol. 49, No. 9, March 1, 2014. Available at www.epw.in/journal/2014/9/discussion/revisiting-subaltern-studies.html#sthash.vK3YKubZ.dpuf
Extended version available at http://sociology.fas.nyu.edu/docs/IO/225/SubalternStudies-Revisited.pdf

3. "Postcolonial Theory and the Specter of Capital," Gayatri Chakravorty Spivak, *Cambridge Review of International Affairs*, Vol. 27, No. 1, 2014, pp. 184–98.

4. "Making Sense of Postcolonial Theory: A Response to Gayatri Chakravorty Spivak," Vivek Chibber, *Cambridge Review of International Affairs*, Vol. 27, No. 3, 2014, pp. 617–24.

5. "Subaltern-Speak," Bruce Robbins, *n+1*, Issue 18, Winter 2013. Available at https://nplusonemag.com/issue-18/reviews/subaltern/

6. "Reply to Bruce Robbins," Vivek Chibber, *n+1*, January 9, 2014. Available at https://nplusonemag.com/online-only/online-only/response-to-vivek-chibber/

7. "Introduction: Review Symposium on Vivek Chibber's *Postcolonial Theory and the Specter of Capital*," Ho-fung Hung, *Journal of World-Systems Research*, Vol. 20, No. 2, July 2014, p. 281.

8. "On Vivek Chibber's *Postcolonial Theory and the Specter of Capital*," William H. Sewell, Jr., *Journal of World-Systems Research*, Vol. 20, No. 2, July 2014, p. 300.

9. "Back to Basics? The Recurrence of the Same in Vivek Chibber's *Postcolonial Theory and the Specter of Capital*," Bruce Cumings, *Journal of World-Systems Research*, Vol. 20, No. 2, July 2014, p. 289.

10. "On the Articulation of Marxist and Non-Marxist Theory in Colonial Historiography," George Steinmetz, *Journal of World-Systems Research*, Vol. 20, No. 2, July 2014. Available at http://jwsr.pitt.edu/ojs/index.php/jwsr/article/view/558

11. "Capitalist Development, Structural Constraint and Human Agency in the Global South: An Appreciation of Vivek Chibber's *Postcolonial Theory and the Specter of Capital*," Michael Schwartz, *Journal of World-Systems Research*, Vol. 20, No. 2, July 2014. Available at http://jwsr.pitt.edu/ojs/index.php/jwsr/article/view/562/574

12. "Minding Appearances: The Labor of Representation in Vivek Chibber's *Postcolonial Theory and the Specter of Capital*," David Pedersen, *Journal of World-Systems Research*, Vol. 20, No. 2, July 2014. Available at http://jwsr.pitt.edu/ojs/index.php/jwsr/article/view/559/571

13. "Confronting Postcolonial Theory: A Response to Critics," Vivek Chibber, *Journal of World-Systems Research*, Vol. 20, Winter 2014, pp. 308–14. Available at http://jwsr.pitt.edu/ojs/index.php/jwsr/article/view/561/573

14. "Subaltern Stakes," Timothy Brennan, *New Left Review*, Vol. 89, September/October 2014. Available at https://newleftreview.org/II/89/timothy-brennan-subaltern-stakes

15. "*Postcolonial Theory and the Specter of Capital*, Review Essay," Stein Sundstøl Eriksen, *Forum for Development Studies*, Vol. 42, No. 3, 2015, pp. 579–87. Available at www.tandfonline.com/doi/abs/10.1080/0803 9410.2015.1042279

16. "Looking for Resistance in All the Wrong Places? Chibber, Chakrabarty, and a Tale of Two Histories," Viren Murthy, *Critical Historical Studies*, Vol. 2, No. 1, Spring 2015, pp. 113–53. Published by the University of Chicago Press on behalf of the Chicago Center for Contemporary Theory. Available at www.jstor.org/stable/10.1086/680928

References

1. SUBALTERN STUDIES AND *CAPITAL*

Chakrabarty, Dipesh, *Rethinking Working-Class History: Bengal 1890–1940*, Princeton: Princeton University Press, 1989.

Chakrabarty, Dipesh, *Provincializing Europe: Postcolonial Thought and Historical Difference*, Princeton: Princeton University Press, 2000.

Chatterjee, Partha, *Nationalist Thought and the Colonial World: A Derivative Discourse?*, London: Zed Books, 1986.

Chatterjee, Partha, *Bengal 1920–47: The Land Question*, Calcutta: K. P. Bagchi, 2012, first published 1984.

Chibber, Vivek, *Postcolonial Theory and the Specter of Capital*, London: Verso; New Delhi: Navayana, 2013.

Guha, Ranajit, *Dominance without Hegemony: History and Power in Colonial India*, Cambridge, MA: Harvard University Press, 1997, first published 1989.

Kaviraj, Sudipta, "An Outline of a Revisionist Theory of Modernity," *Archives européennes de sociologie* 46: 3, 2005, 497–526.

Laclau, Ernesto, and Chantal Mouffe, *Hegemony and Socialist Strategy: Towards a Radical Democratic Politics*, trans. Winston Moore and Paul Cammack, London: Verso, 1985.

Marx, Karl, ed., *Theories of Surplus Value*, vol. 3, Moscow: Progress Publishers, 1979.

Marx, Karl, *Capital*, vol. 1, trans. Ben Fowkes, London: Penguin, 1990.

Prakash, Gyan, "Subaltern Studies as Post-Colonial Criticism," *American Historical Review* 99: 5, December 1994, 1475–90.

Sanyal, Kalyan, *Rethinking Capitalist Development: Primitive Accumulation, Governmentality and Post-Colonial Capitalism*, New Delhi and New York: Routledge, 2007.

Sen, Amartya, *A Theory of Justice*, London: Penguin, 2009.

Spivak, Gayatri Chakravorty, "Subaltern Studies: Deconstructing Historiography," in Ranajit Guha, ed., *Subaltern Studies IV*, Delhi: Oxford University Press, 1987, 338–63.

Spivak, Gayatri Chakravorty, "Can the Subaltern Speak?" in Cary Nelson and Lawrence Grossberg, eds, *Marxism and the Interpretation of Culture*, Urbana, IL: University of Illinois Press, 1988.

2. SUBALTERN STUDIES REVISITED

Brown, Michael, "Cultural Relativism 2.0," *Current Anthropology* 49: 3, June 2008, 363–83.

Chakrabarty, Dipesh, *Rethinking Working-Class History: Bengal 1890–1940*, Princeton: Princeton University Press, 1989.

Chatterjee, Partha, *The Nation and Its Fragments*, Princeton: Princeton University Press, 1993.

Chatterjee, Partha, "Agrarian Relations and Communalism in Bengal, 1926–1935," in *Subaltern Studies I*, Oxford: Oxford University Press, 1982, 9–38.

Chibber, Vivek, *Postcolonial Theory and the Specter of Capital*, London: Verso; New Delhi: Navayana, 2013.

Gintis, Herbert, Samuel Bowles, Robert Boyd, and Ernst Fehr, eds, *Moral Sentiments and Material Interests: The Foundations of Cooperation in Economic Life*, Cambridge, MA: MIT Press, 2005.

Guha, Ranajit, *Dominance without Hegemony: History and Power in Colonial India*, Cambridge, MA: Harvard University Press, 1997, first published 1989.

Gurven, Michael, "The Evolution of Contingent Cooperation," *Current Anthropology* 47: 1, February 2006, 185–92.

Gurven, Michael, and Jeffrey Winking, "Collective Action in Action: Prosocial Behavior in and out of the Laboratory," *American Anthropologist* 110: 2, June 2008, 179–90.

Price, Michael, "Pro-community Altruism and Social Status in a Shuar Village," *Human Nature* 14: 2, 2003, 191–208.

Runciman, Walter Garrison, "Stone-Age Sociology," *Journal of the Royal Anthropological Institute* 11: 1, March 2005, 129–42.

3. *POSTCOLONIAL THEORY AND THE SPECTER OF CAPITAL*

Ahmad, Aijaz, *In Theory: Classes, Nations, Literatures*, New York: Verso, 1992.

Amin, Shahid, "Gandhi as Mahatma: Gorakhpur District, Eastern UP, 1921–2," *Subaltern Studies* 3, 1984, 1–61.

Anderson, Benedict, *Imagined Communities: Reflections on the Origin and Spread of Nationalism*, New York: Verso, 1982.

Banerjee, Sumanta, "Gandhi's Flexible Non-violence," *Economic and Political Weekly* 48: 31, 2013, 4.

Benjamin, Walter, "Theses on the Philosophy of History," *Illuminations*, trans. Harry Zohn, New York: Schocken, 1968, 253–64.

Bhabha, Homi K., "DissemiNation: Time, Narrative and the Margins of the Modern Nation," in *The Location of Culture*, London: Routledge, 1994, 139–70.

Birla, Ritu, *Stages of Capital: Law, Culture, and Market Governance in Late Colonial India*, Durham, NC: Duke University Press, 2009.

Chakrabarty, Dipesh, *Provincializing Europe: Postcolonial Thought and Historical Difference*, Princeton: Princeton University Press, 2000.

Chatterjee, Partha, "Gandhi and the Critique of Civil Society," *Subaltern Studies* 3, 1984, 153–95.

Chatterjee, Partha, *Nationalist Thought and the Colonial World: A Derivative Discourse*, Minneapolis: University of Minnesota Press, 1993.

Chaudhuri, K. N., *Asia before Europe: Economy and Civilization of the Indian Ocean from the Rise of Islam to 1750*, Cambridge, UK: Cambridge University Press, 1991.

Collins, Kathleen, *Clan Politics and Regime Transition in Central Asia*, Cambridge, UK: Cambridge University Press, 2006.

Du Bois, W. E. B., "The Negro Mind Reaches Out," in Alain Locke, ed., *The New Negro: An Interpretation*, New York: Athenaeum Press, 1968, 385–414.

Du Bois, W. E. B., *Black Reconstruction in America*, New York: Free Press, 1998.

Gramsci, Antonio, *Selections from the Prison Writings*, trans. Quentin Hoare and Geoffrey Nowell Smith, New York: International, 1971.

Guha, Ranajit, *A Rule of Property for Bengal: An Essay on the Idea of Permanent Settlement*, Paris: Mouton, 1963.

Guha, Ranajit, *Elementary Aspects of Peasant Insurgency in Colonial India*, Delhi: Oxford University Press, 1983.

Guha, Ranajit, *Dominance without Hegemony: History and Power in Colonial India*, Cambridge, MA: Harvard University Press, 1997, first published 1989.

Guha, Ranajit, *The Small Voice of History*, Ranikhet: Permanent Black,2009.

Guha, Ranajit, and Gayatri Chakravorty Spivak, *Selected Subaltern Studies*, Oxford: Oxford University Press, 1988.

Hardiman, David, "Gandhi's Adaptable Non-violence," *Economic and Political Weekly* 48: 33, 2013, 4–5.

Honneth, Axel, *Reification: A New Look at an Old Idea*, Oxford: Oxford University Press, 2012.

Kant, Immanuel, "The Metaphysics of Morals," *Political Writings*, trans. H. B. Nisbet, Cambridge, UK: Cambridge University Press, 1991, 139.

Kosambi, Damodar Dharmanand, *An Introduction to the Study of Indian History*, Mumbai: Popular Prakashan, 1975.

Lévinas, Emmanuel, *Otherwise than Being, or, Beyond Essence*, trans. Alphonso Lingis, Pittsburgh: Duquesne University Press, 1998.

Luxemburg, Rosa, *The Essential Rosa Luxemburg: Reform or Revelation and Mass Strike*, Chicago: Haymarket Books, 2007.

Marx, Karl, *The German Ideology*, Moscow: Progress Publishers, 1976.

Marx, Karl, *Capital: A Critique of Political Economy*, vol. 1, trans. Ben Fowkes, London: Penguin Books, 1990.

Said, Edward W., *Orientalism*, New York: Pantheon, 1978.

Said, Edward W., "Permission to Narrate," *Journal of Palestine Studies* 13: 3, 1984, 27–48.

Sen, Amartya, *Poverty and Famines: An Essay on Entitlements and Deprivation*, Oxford: Oxford University Press, 1981.

Spivak, Gayatri Chakravorty, *Readings*, ed. Lara Choksey, Calcutta: Seagull, 2014.

Thompson, John, *Studies in the Theory of Ideology*, London: Polity Press, 1985.

Van Dijk, Teun, *Discourse and Power*, New York: Palgrave Macmillan, 2008.

Wong, Susan M. L., "China's Stock Market: A Marriage of Capitalism and Socialism," *Cato Journal* 26: 3, 2006, 389–424.

4. Making Sense of Postcolonial Theory

Chibber, Vivek, "What Is Living and What Is Dead in the Marxist Theory of History," *Historical Materialism* 19: 2, 2011, 60–91.

Chibber, Vivek, *Postcolonial Theory and the Specter of Capital*, London: Verso; New Delhi: Navayana, 2013.

Chibber, Vivek, "Revisiting Postcolonial Studies," *Economic and Political Weekly* 9, March 2014, 82–5.

7. Review Symposium

Afary, Janet, and Kevin B. Anderson, *Foucault and the Iranian Revolution: Gender and the Seduction of Islamism*, Chicago: Chicago University Press, 2005.

Habermas, Jürgen, "Modernity: An Incomplete Project," *New German Critique* 22, 1981, 3–15.

8. On Vivek Chibber's *Postcolonial Theory and the Specter of Capital*

Chakrabarty, Dipesh, *Rethinking Working-Class History: Bengal 1890–1940*, Princeton: Princeton University Press, 1989.

Chakrabarty, Dipesh, *Provincializing Europe: Postcolonial Thought and Historical Difference*, Princeton: Princeton University Press, 2000.

Guha, Ranajit, *Dominance without Hegemony: History and Power in Colonial India*, Cambridge, MA: Harvard University Press, 1997, first published 1989.

9. Back to Basics?

Chakrabarty, Dipesh, *Provincializing Europe: Postcolonial Thought and Historical Difference*, Princeton: Princeton University Press, 2000.

Chibber, Vivek, *Postcolonial Theory and the Specter of Capital*, London: Verso; New Delhi: Navayana, 2013.

Guha, Ranajit, *Dominance without Hegemony: History and Power in Colonial India*, Cambridge, MA: Harvard University Press, 1997, first published 1989.

Habermas, Jürgen, *The Philosophical Discourse of Modernity*, trans. Frederick Lawrence, Cambridge, MA: MIT Press, 1987.

Harootunian, Harry D., *Overcome by Modernity: History, Culture, and Community in Interwar Japan*, Princeton: Princeton University Press, 2002.

Nietzsche, Friedrich, *Beyond Good and Evil*, New York: Cambridge University Press, 2002.

Nietzsche, Friedrich, *Untimely Meditations*, New York: Cambridge University Press, 1983.

Rueschemeyer, Dietrich, Evelyne Huber Stephens, and John D. Stephens, *Capitalist Development and Democracy*, Chicago: University of Chicago Press, 1992.

Weber, Max, *General Economic History*, trans. Frank H. Knight, New Brunswick, NJ: Transaction Books, 1981.

White, Stephen K., "Reason, Modernity and Democracy," in *The Cambridge Companion to Habermas*, New York: Cambridge University Press, 1995, 3–16.

10. ON THE ARTICULATION OF MARXIST AND NON-MARXIST THEORY

Berridge, Kent C., "Pleasure, Unconscious Affect and Irrational Desire," in A. S. R. Manstead, N. H. Frijda, and A. H. Fischer, eds, *Feelings and Emotions: The Amsterdam Symposium*, New York: Cambridge University Press, 2004, 43–62.

Berridge, Kent C., and Piotr Winkielman, "What Is an Unconscious Emotion? (The Case for Unconscious Liking)," *Cognition and Emotion* 17: 2, 2000, 181–211.

Bhabha, Homi K., *The Location of Culture*, London and New York: Routledge, 1994.

Blackbourn, David, and Geoff Eley, *The Peculiarities of German History*, New York: Oxford University Press, 1985.

Braverman, Harry, *Labor and Monopoly Capital. The Degradation of Work in the Twentieth Century*, New York: Monthly Review Press, 1974.

Bourdieu, Pierre, *Sur l'état: cours au Collège de France 1989–1992*, Paris: Seuil, 2012.

Bourdieu, Pierre, "Séminaires sur le concept de champ, 1972–1975," *Actes de la recherche en sciences sociales* 200, 2013, 4–37.

Chakrabarty, Dipesh, *Provincializing Europe: Postcolonial Thought and Historical Difference*, Princeton: Princeton University Press, 2000.

Chibber, Vivek, *Postcolonial Theory and the Specter of Capital*, London: Verso; New Delhi: Navayana, 2013.

Cooper, Frederick, *Decolonization and African Society*, Cambridge: Cambridge University Press, 1996.

Gandhi, Leela, *Affective Communities: Anti-Colonial Thought, Fin-de-Siècle Radicalism, and the Politics of Friendship*, Durham, NC: Duke University Press, 2006.

Gandhi, Leela, *Postcolonial Theory*, New York: Columbia University Press, 1998.

Jessop, Robert, "Zur Relevanz von Luhmanns Staatstheorie und von Laclau und Mouffes Diskursanalyse für die Weiterentwicklung der marxistischen Staatstheorie" in Joachim Hirsch, John Kannakulam, and Jens Wissel, eds, *Der Staat der bürgerlichen Gesellschaft*, Frankfurt: Nomos, 2008, 157–79.

Laclau, Ernesto, and Chantal Mouffe, *Hegemony and Socialist Strategy: Towards a Radical Democratic Politics*, London: Verso, 1985.

Lukács, Georg, *Die Zerstörung der Vernunft*, vol. 1, Darmstadt: Luchterhand, 1973, first published 1954.

Mamdani, Mahmood, *Citizen and Subject: Contemporary Africa and the Legacy of Late Colonialism*, Princeton: Princeton University Press, 1996.

Parsons, Talcott, "Sociological Elements of Economic Thought," *Quarterly Journal of Economics* 49: 3, 1934, 511–45.

Postone, Moishe, *Time, Labor and Social Domination: A Reinterpretation of Marx's Critical Theory*. New York: Cambridge University Press, 1993.

Said, Edward W., *Orientalism*, New York: Pantheon, 1978.

Said, Edward W., *Culture and Imperialism*, New York: Knopf, 1993.

Spivak, Gayatri Chakravorty, "Can the Subaltern Speak?" in Cary Nelson and Lawrence Grossberg, eds, *Marxism and the Interpretation of Culture*, Urbana, IL: University of Illinois Press, 1988.

Spivak, Gayatri Chakravorty, *In Other Worlds: Essays in Cultural Politics*, New York: Routledge, 1998.

Steinmetz, George, "German Exceptionalism and the Origins of Nazism: The Career of a Concept," in Ian Kershaw and Moshe Lewin, eds, *Stalinism and Nazism: Dictatorships in Comparison*, Cambridge: Cambridge University Press, 1997, 251–84.

Steinmetz, George, "Critical Realism and Historical Sociology," *Comparative Studies in Society and History* 40: 1, 1998, 170–86.

Steinmetz, George, "Decolonizing German Theory: An Introduction," *Postcolonial Studies* 9: 1, 2006, 3–13.

Steinmetz, George, *The Devil's Handwriting: Precoloniality and the German Colonial State in Qingdao, Samoa, and Southwest Africa*, Chicago: University of Chicago Press, 2007.

Steinmetz, George, "Charles Tilly, Historicism, and the Critical Realist Philosophy of Science," *American Sociologist* 41: 4, 2010, 312–36.

Steinmetz, George, "État-mort, État-fort, État-empire," *Actes de la recherche en sciences sociales* 201, 2014, 112–19.

Winkielman, Piotr, and Kent C. Berridge, "Unconscious Emotion," *Current Directions in Psychological Sciences* 13: 3, 2004, 120–3.

11. CAPITALIST DEVELOPMENT, STRUCTURAL CONSTRAINT

Anderson, Perry, *Arguments within English Marxism*, New York: New Left Books, 1980.

Chibber, Vivek, *Postcolonial Theory and the Specter of Capital*, London: Verso; New Delhi: Navayana, 2013.

Engels, Friedrich, *Anti-Dühring*, New York: International Publishers, 1972.

Goodwin, Jeff, *No Other Way Out: States and Revolutionary Movements, 1945–1991*, New York: Cambridge University Press, 2001.

Paige, Jeffrey M., *Agrarian Revolution*, New York: Free Press, 1978.

Williams, Richard, *Hierarchical Structures and Social Value: The Social Construction of Black and Irish Identities in the U.S.*, New York: Cambridge University Press, 1990.

12. Minding Appearances

Ascher, William, and Barbara Hirschfelder-Ascher, *Revitalizing Political Psychology: The Legacy of Harold D. Lasswell*, Mahwah, NJ: Erlbaum, 2003.

Bhaskar, Roy, *Scientific Realism and Human Emancipation*, New York: Verso, 1986.

Chakrabarty, Dipesh, "Marx after Marxism: History, Subalternity, and Difference," in Makdisi, Saree, Cesare Casarino, and Rebecca Karl, eds, *Marxism Beyond Marxism*, New York: Routledge, 1995.

Chibber, Vivek, *Postcolonial Theory and the Specter of Capital*, London: Verso; New Delhi: Navayana, 2013.

Coronil, Fernando, "Beyond Occidentalism: Toward Nonimperial Geohistorical Categories," *Cultural Anthropology* 11: 1, 1996, 51–87.

Derrida, Jacques, *Specters of Marx: The State of the Debt, the Work of Mourning and the New International*, New York: Routledge, 1995.

Köpping, Klaus Peter, *Adolf Bastian and the Psychic Unity of Mankind: The Foundations of Anthropology in Nineteenth-Century Germany* (History and Theory of Anthropology/Geschichte und Theorie der Ethnologie), Berlin: LIT Verlag, 2005.

Lowe, Lisa, and David Lloyd, eds, *The Politics of Culture in the Shadow of Capital*, Durham: Duke University Press, 1997.

Sprinker, Michael, ed., *Ghostly Demarcations: A Symposium on Jacques Derrida's Specters of Marx*, New York: Verso, 2008.

Stocking, Jr., George W., *The Shaping of American Anthropology, 1883–1911: A Franz Boas Reader*, New York: Basic Books, 1984.

Taylor, Chris, "Not Even Marxist: On Vivek Chibber's Polemic against Postcolonial Theory," April 29, 2013, available at http://clrjames.blogspot.com/2013/04/not-even-marxist-on-vivek-chibbers.html.

Trouillot, Michel-Rolph, "Anthropology and the Savage Slot: The Poetics and Politics of Otherness," in Richard G. Fox, ed., *Recapturing Anthropology: Working in the Present*, Santa Fe, NM: School of American Research Press, 1991, 17–44.

13. Confronting Postcolonial Theory

Chibber, Vivek, *Postcolonial Theory and the Specter of Capital*, London: Verso; New Delhi: Navayana, 2013.

Warren, Bill, *Imperialism: Pioneer of Capitalism*, London: Verso, 1980.

14. SUBALTERN STAKES

Almond, Ian, *The New Orientalists: Postmodern Representations of Islam from Foucault to Baudrillard*, London and New York: I. B. Tauris, 2007.

Andersson, Axel, "Obscuring Capitalism: Vivek Chibber's Critique of Postcolonial Theory," *Los Angeles Review of Books*, November 6, 2013.

Auerbach, Erich, "Einleitung," in Giambattista Vico, *Die neue Wissenschaft*, Munich: Walter de Gruyter, 1924.

Badiou, Alain, *Deleuze: The Clamor of Being*, Minneapolis: University of Minnesota Press, 2000.

Bataille, Georges, *The Accursed Share: An Essay on General Economy*, vol. 1, New York: Zone Books, 1988, first published 1949.

Bataille, Georges, *The Accursed Share: An Essay on General Economy*, vols. 2 and 3, New York: Zone Books, 1993, first published 1976.

Benjamin, Walter, *The Arcades Project*, ed. Rolf Tiedemann, Cambridge, MA, and London: Harvard University Press, 1999.

Brass, Tom, "Moral Economists, Subalterns, New Social Movements and the (Re-) Emergence of a (Post-) Modernized (Middle) Peasant," in Vinayak Chaturvedi, ed., *Mapping Subaltern Studies and the Postcolonial*, London and New York: Verso, 2000, 127–62.

Brennan, Timothy, "Humanism, Philology, and Imperialism," in *Wars of Position: The Cultural Politics of Left and Right*, New York: Columbia University Press, 2006.

Brennan, Timothy, "Edward Said as a Lukácsian Critic: Modernism and Empire," *College Literature* 40: 4, Fall 2013.

Brennan, Timothy, *Borrowed Light: Vico, Hegel and the Colonies*, Stanford: Stanford University Press, 2014.

Centre for Studies in Social Sciences, Workshop on Gramsci and South Asia at the Calcutta 1987, repr. *Economic and Political Weekly*, January 30, 1988.

Chakrabarty, Dipesh, *Provincializing Europe: Postcolonial Thought and Historical Difference*, Princeton: Princeton University Press, 2000.

Chibber, Vivek, *Locked in Place: State-Building and Late Industrialization in India* Princeton: Princeton University Press, 2003.

Chibber, Vivek, *Postcolonial Theory and the Specter of Capital*, London: Verso; New Delhi: Navayana, 2013.

Coronil, Fernando, "Can Postcoloniality Be Decolonized? Imperial Banality and Postcolonial Power," *Public Culture* 5: 1, Fall 1992.

Damiani, Alberto Mario, *La dimensión política de la "Scienza Nuova" y otros estudios sobre Giambattista Vico*, Buenos Aires: Editorial Universitaria de Buenos Aires, 1998.

Fisch, Max Harold, and Thomas Goddard Bergin, "Introduction," in *The Autobiography of Giambattista Vico*, Ithaca and London: Cornell University Press, 1944.

Ganguly, Keya, "Temporality and Postcolonial Critique," in Neil Lazarus, ed., *The Cambridge Companion to Postcolonial Literary Studies*, Cambridge: Cambridge University Press, 2004, 162–82.

Gopal, Priyamvada, "Reading Subaltern History," in Neil Lazarus, ed., *The Cambridge Companion to Postcolonial Literary Studies*, Cambridge: Cambridge University Press, 2004, 139–61.

Gramsci, Antonio, *Quaderni del carcere*, vol. 2, ed. Valentino Gerratana, Turin: Einaudi, 1975.

Guha, Ranajit, ed., *Subaltern Studies V*, Delhi: Oxford University Press, 1987.

Guha, Ranajit, *Dominance without Hegemony: History and Power in Colonial India*, Cambridge, MA: Harvard University Press, 1997, first published 1989.

Hung, Ho-fung, "Introduction: Review Symposium on Vivek Chibber's *Postcolonial Theory and the Specter of Capital*," *Journal of World-Systems Research* 20: 2, July 2014.

Husserl, Edmund G., *Phenomenology and the Crisis of Philosophy*, New York: Harper and Row, 1965, first published 1935.

Jani, Pranav, "Marxism and the Future of Postcolonial Theory," *International Socialist Review* 92, Spring 2014.

Kaiwar, Vasant, *The Postcolonial Orient: The Politics of Difference and the Project of Provincialising Europe*, Leiden, The Netherlands, and Boston: Brill, 2014.

Kojève, Alexandre, *Introduction to the Reading of Hegel*, Ithaca: Cornell University Press, 1969.

Lafargue, *Le déterminisme économique de Karl Marx: Recherches sur l'origine des idées de justice, du bien, de l'âme et de Dieu*, Paris: V. Giard et E. Brière, 1911.

Marx, Karl, *Grundrisse*, London: Penguin, 1973.

Marx, Karl, *Capital*, vol. 1, London: Penguin, 1990.

Marx, Karl, *Collected Works*, vol. 41, Moscow: Progress Publishers, 1985.

Murphet, Julian, "No Alternative," *Cambridge Journal of Postcolonial Literary Inquiry* 1: 1, March 2014.

Nietzsche, Friedrich, *The Complete Works of Friedrich Nietzsche*, ed. Oscar Levy, London, J. Foulis, 1909–13.

O'Brien, Susie, and Imre Szeman, "Introduction: The Globalization of Fiction/the Fiction of Globalization," *South Atlantic Quarterly* 100: 3, 2001.

Parry, Benita, *Postcolonial Studies: A Materialist Critique*, London and New York: Routledge, 2004.

Roldán, David, "La recepción filosófica de Vico y sus aporías filológicas: El caso del marxismo occidental," *Pensamiento* 68: 253, 2012.

Roy, M. N., *The Communist International*, Bombay: Radical Democratic Party, 1943.

Said, Edward, *Culture and Imperialism*, New York: Vintage, 1993.

Sarkar, Sumit, "The Decline of the Subaltern in *Subaltern Studies*," in Vinayak Chaturvedi, ed., *Mapping Subaltern Studies and the Postcolonial*, London and New York: Verso, 2000, 300–23.

Simon, Lawrence H., "Vico and Marx: Perspectives on Historical Development," *Journal of the History of Ideas* 42: 2, 1981.

Sorel, Georges, *Études sur Vico et autres textes*, ed. Anne-Sophie Menasseyre, Paris: H. Champion, 2007.

Sutherland, Keston, "Marx in Jargon," *World Picture* 1, Spring 2008.

Thompson, Edward Palmer, *The Poverty of Theory and Other Essays*, New York: Monthly Review Press, 1978.

15. Review Essay

Chakrabarty, Dipesh, *Rethinking Working-Class History: Bengal 1890–1940*, Princeton: Princeton University Press, 1989.

Chakrabarty, Dipesh, *Provincializing Europe: Postcolonial Thought and Historical Difference*, Princeton: Princeton University Press, 2000.

Chatterjee, Partha, "Agrarian Relations and Communalism in Bengal 1926–35," in Ranajit Guha, ed., *Subaltern Studies I*, Delhi: Oxford University Press, 1982, 9–38.

Chibber, Vivek, *Postcolonial Theory and the Specter of Capital*, London: Verso; New Delhi: Navayana, 2013.

Guha, Ranajit, *Dominance without Hegemony: History and Power in Colonial India*, Cambridge, MA: Harvard University Press, 1997, first published 1989.

16. Looking for Resistance in All the Wrong Places?

Arthur, Christopher J., *The New Dialectic and Marx's Capital*, Leiden: Brill, 2004.

Baker, Keith Michael, *Essays on the Political Culture in the Eighteenth Century*, Cambridge: Cambridge University Press, 1990.

Bensaïd, Daniel, *Marx for Our Times: Adventures and Misadventures of a Critique*, trans. Gregory Elliott, London: Verso, 2002.

Bidet, Jacques, *Explication et reconstruction du Capital*, Paris: Presses Universitaires de France, 2004.

Bidet, Jacques, *L'État-monde: Libéralisme, socialisme et communisme à l'échelle globale*, Paris: Presses Universitaires de France, 2011.

Bidet, Jacques, and Gérard Duménil, *Altermarxisme: Un autre marxisme pour un autre monde*, Paris: Presses Universitaires de France, 2007.

Blanning, T. C. W., *The French Revolution: Aristocrats versus Bourgeois?*, London: Macmillan, 1987.

Brenner, Neil, "Henri Lefebvre's Critique of State Productivism," in *Space, Difference and Everyday Life: Reading Henri Lefebvre*, ed. Kanishka Goonewardena, Stefan Kipfer, Richard Milgram, and Christian Schmid, London: Routledge, 2008, 231–49.

Brenner, Robert, "Agrarian Class Structure and Economic Development in Pre-Industrial Europe" and "The Agrarian Roots of European Capitalism" in T. H. Aston and C. H. E. Philpin, eds, *The Brenner Debate: Agrarian Class Structure and Economic Development in Pre-industrial Europe*, Cambridge: Cambridge University Press, 1985.

Callinicos, Alex, *Imperialism and Global Political Economy*, London: Polity, 2009.

Chakrabarty, Dipesh, *Habitations of Modernity: Essays in the Wake of Subaltern Studies*, Chicago: University of Chicago Press, 2002.

Chakrabarty, Dipesh, *Provincializing Europe: Postcolonial Thought and Historical Difference*, Princeton: Princeton University Press, 2000.

Chatterjee, Partha, *The Nation and Its Fragments: Colonial and Postcolonial Histories*, Princeton: Princeton University Press, 1993.

Chibber, Vivek, "The Return of Imperialism to Social Science," *Archives de Europeenes de Sociologie/European Journal of Sociology* 45, December 2004.

Chibber, Vivek, "Response to Clemens, Paige and Panitch," *Comparative and Historical Sociology* 18, 2007.

Chibber, Vivek, *Postcolonial Theory and the Specter of Capital*, London: Verso; New Delhi: Navayana, 2013.

Clemens, Elizabeth, "The Lessons of Failure," *Comparative and Historical Sociology* 18, Spring 2007.

Comninel, George C., "Marx's Context," *History of Political Thought* 21, 2000, 467–83.

Day, Alex, "The End of the Peasant? The New Rural Reconstruction in China," *Boundary* 2, Summer 2008, 49–73.

Derrida, Jacques, and R. Klein, "Economimesis," in "The Ghost of Theology: Readings of Kant and Hegel," special issue, *Diacritics* 11: 2, Summer 1981, 2–25.

Duara, Prasenjit, *Rescuing History from the Nation: Questioning Narratives of Modernity in China and India*, Chicago: University of Chicago Press, 1995.

Furet, François, and Denis Richet, *La Révolution Française*, Paris: Fayard/Pluriel, 2010, first published 1965.

Goswami, Manu, *Producing India: From Colonial Economy to National Space*, Chicago: University of Chicago Press, 2004.

Guha, Ranajit, *Dominance without Hegemony: History and Power in Colonial India*, Cambridge, MA: Harvard University Press, 1997, first published 1989.

Guha, Ranajit, *Elementary Aspects of Peasant Insurgency in Colonial India*, Durham, NC: Duke University Press, 1999.

Gullì, Bruno, *Labor of Fire: The Ontology of Labor between Culture and Economy*, Philadelphia: Temple University Press, 2005.

Hairong, Yan, and Chen Yiyuan, "Debating the Rural Cooperative Movement in China, the Past and the Present," *Journal of Peasant Studies* 40: 6, 2013, 955–81, 963.

Harootunian, Harry, "Remembering the Historical Present," *Critical Inquiry* 33, 2007, 471–94.

Harootunian, Harry, "Who Needs Postcoloniality: A Reply to Linder," *Radical Philosophy* 164, November/December 2010.

Harvey, David, *The Limits to Capital*, London: Verso, 2006.

Hegel, G. W. F., *Phänemonologie des Geistes*, Frankfurt am Main: Suhrkamp, 1992.

Hobsbawm, Eric, *Primitive Rebels: Studies in Archaic Forms of Social Movement in the 19th and 20th Centuries*, New York: W. W. Norton, 1959.

Kaiwar, Vasant, "Towards Orientalism and Nativism: The Impasse of Subaltern Studies," *Historical Materialism* 12: 2, 2004, 189–247.

Kosík, Karel, *The Crises of Modernity and Other Essays and Observations from the 1968 Era*, ed. James Shatterwhite, Lanham, MD: Rowman & Littlefield, 1995.

Kymlicka, Will, *Multicultural Citizenship: A Liberal Theory of Minority Rights*, Oxford: Oxford University Press, 2000.

Larsen, Neil, "Literature, Immanent Critique and the Problem of Standpoint," *Mediations* 24, Spring 2009, 48–65, 57.

Löwy, Michael, *Redemption and Utopia: Jewish Libertarian Thought in Central Europe: A Study of Elective Affinity*, trans. Hope Heany, Stanford, CA: Stanford University Press, 1988.

Marx, Karl, *Grundrisse der Kritik der Politischen Ökonomie*, Berlin: Dietz Berlin, 1953.

Marx, Karl, *Theories of Surplus Value*, Moscow: Progress Publishers, 1978.

Marx, Karl, *Late Marx and the Russian Road: Marx and "The Peripheries of Capitalism,"* ed. Theodor Shanin, New York: Monthly Review Press, 1983.

Marx, Karl, *Grundrisse*, trans. Martin Nicolaus, London: Penguin, 1993.

McNally, David, *The Global Slump*, Oakland, CA: PM Press, 2011.

Merleau-Ponty, Maurice, *Phénoménologie de la perception*, Paris: Gallimard, 1967.

Merleau-Ponty, Maurice, *Phenomenology of Perception*, trans. Colin Smith, London: Routledge, 1989. Translation amended by the author.

Nussbaum, Martha, "Human Functioning and Social Justice: In Defense of Aristotelian Essentialism," *Political Theory* 20: 2, 1992, 202–46.

Postone, Moishe, *Time, Labor and Social Domination: A Reinterpretation of Marx's Critical Theory*, Cambridge: Cambridge University Press, 1993.

Prashad, Vijay, *The Poorer Nations: A Possible History of the Global South*, London: Verso, 2012.

Sandel, Michael, *Liberalism and the Limits of Justice*, Cambridge, MA: Cambridge University Press, 1982.

Sandel, Michael, *Democracy's Discontents: America's Search for a Public Philosophy*, New York: Belknap Press, 1996.

Sayre, Robert, and Michael Löwy, "Figures of Romantic Anti-Capitalism," *New German Critique* 32, 1984, 42–92.

Sewell Jr., William H., *A Rhetoric of Bourgeois Revolution: The Abbé Sieyès and What Is the Third Estate?*, Durham, NC: Duke University Press, 1994.

Sewell Jr., William H., "Connecting Capitalism to the French Revolution: The Parisian Promenade and the Origins of Civic Equality in Eighteenth-Century France," *Critical Historical Studies* 1, Spring 2014, 5–47.

Spinoza, Baruch, *Ethics, Treatise on the Emendation of the Intellect and Selected Letters*, trans. Samuel Shirley, ed. Seymour Feldman, Indianapolis: Hackett, 1992.

Taylor, Chris, "Not Even Marxist: On Vivek Chibber's Polemic against Postcolonial Theory," April 29, 2013, available at http://clrjames.blogspot.com/2013/04/not-even-marxist-on-vivek-chibbers.html.

Tetsurō, Watsuji, "Gendai nihon to Chonin Konjō" [Contemporary Japan and the nature of the cities] in *Keizoku nihon seishin shi* [A continuation of a history of the Japanese spirit], in *Watsuji Tetsurō*, vol. 4, Tokyo: Iwanami shoten, 1976, 435–505.

Thompson, Edward Palmer, "Time, Work-Discipline and Industrial Capitalism," in *Essays in Social History*, ed. M. W. Flinn and T. C. Smout, Oxford: Clarendon, 1974.

Tiejun, Wen, *Jiegou xiandai xing: Wen Tiejun Jiangyan lv* [Deconstruction of modernization: A collection of speeches by Wen Tiejun], Guangzhou: Guangdong renmin chubanshe, 2004.

Walker, Gavin, "The World of Principle, or Pure Capitalism: Exteriority and Suspension in Uno Kōzō," *Journal of International Economic Studies* 26, 2012, 15–37.

Weil, Robert, *Is the Torch Passing: Resistance and Revolution in China and India*, Delhi: Setu Prakashani, 2013.

Wright, Eric, "What Is Analytical Marxism?" in *Rational Choice Marxism*, ed. Terrell Carver and Paul Thomas, University Park: Pennsylvania University Press, 1995, 11–31.

Wood, Ellen Meiksins, *The Pristine Culture of Capitalism: A Historical Essay on Old Regimes and Modern States*, London: Verso, 1996.

Wood, Ellen Meiksins, "Capitalism or Enlightenment?," *History of Political Thought* 21, 2000, 405–26.

Zedong, Mao, "Chonqing tanpan," in *Mao Zedong xuanji*, Beijing: Renmin chubanshe, 1991.

Notes

The Chibber Debate: An introduction—Achin Vanaik

1 Perry Anderson, "Modernity and Revolution" in C. Nelson and L. Grossberg (eds), *Marxism and Interpretations of Culture*, Chicago: University of Illinois Press, 1988. Modernity exists where there is a "still usable classical past, a still indeterminate technical present, and a still unpredictable political future." Again, modernity is at the junction between "a semi-aristocratic ruling order, a semi-industrialised capitalist economy, and a semi-emergent . . . labour movement" (pp. 317–38, esp. p. 326). As a characterization of colonial and postcolonial India, this would hardly be out of place where the hierarchies of caste have always been even more important than those of "royal blood."

2 This discourse of Multiple Modernities may have been initiated at the turn of the millennium by S. N. Eisenstadt. "Multiple Modernities," *Daedalus* 129, 2000, 1–29. But a number of Indian origin contributors have implicitly or explicitly endorsed this paradigm shift, such as S. Kaviraj, "An Outline of a Revisionist Theory of Modernity," *European Journal of Sociology* 46: 3, 2005, 497–526, and H. Mukhia, "Subjective Modernities," Occasional Papers in *History and Society*, New Delhi: Nehru Memorial Museum and Library, 2013, 1–20. Another school is also characterized by an unbalanced culturalism but is critical of MM, deeming it methodologically incapable of developing a genuine post-Western global historical sociology. This is the "Connected Histories" approach, whose key figures include Professor S. Subramanyam at the University of California, Los Angeles, and Professor G. Bhambra at Warwick University in Coventry, England. See G. Bhambra, "Talking Among Themselves? Weberians and Marxist Historical Sociologies as Dialogue without 'Others'," *Millennium*, March 2011; "Historical Sociology, Modernity and Postcolonial Critique," *American Historical Review* 16: 3, 2011; "The Possibilities of, and for, Global Sociology: A Postcolonial Perspective," *Postcolonial Sociology, Political Power and Social Theory* 24, 2013, 295–314.

3 See Terry Eagleton, *After Theory*, New York: Basic Books, 2003, esp. Chapter 5 on "Truth, Virtue and Objectivity."

1. SUBALTERN STUDIES AND *CAPITAL*—PARTHA CHATTERJEE

1 Ranajit Guha, *Dominance without Hegemony: History and Power in Colonial India*, Cambridge, MA: Harvard University Press, 1997, first published 1989.
2 Ibid., 13–30.
3 Ibid., 15.
4 Vivek Chibber, *Postcolonial Theory and the Specter of Capital*, London: Verso; New Delhi: Navayana, 2013, 84.
5 As a matter of fact, although Guha does not cite them, his use of the concept is perfectly consistent with Laclau and Mouffe's interpretation of the Gramscian concept of hegemony, with the proviso that hegemony is constructed on the plane of the fundamental classes and that the hegemonic center ceases to hold in periods of organic crisis. Ernesto Laclau and Chantal Mouffe, *Hegemony and Socialist Strategy: Towards a Radical Democratic Politics*, trans. Winston Moore and Paul Cammack, London: Verso, 1985, 136–8.
6 Chibber, *Postcolonial Theory and the Specter of Capital*, 111.
7 Ibid., 125.
8 Ibid., 139.
9 Ibid., 143.
10 Ibid., 139.
11 Karl Marx, *Capital*, vol. 1, trans. Ben Fowkes, London: Penguin, 1990, 275.
12 Dipesh Chakrabarty, *Rethinking Working-Class History: Bengal 1890–1940*, Princeton: Princeton University Press, 1989.
13 Ibid., 217.
14 Chibber, *Postcolonial Theory and the Specter of Capital*, 153.
15 Ibid., 166.
16 Ibid., 162.
17 Partha Chatterjee, *Nationalist Thought and the Colonial World: A Derivative Discourse?*, London: Zed Books, 1986.
18 Partha Chatterjee, *Bengal 1920–47: The Land Question*, Calcutta: K. P. Bagchi, 2012, first published 1984.
19 Chibber, *Postcolonial Theory and the Specter of Capital*, 191.
20 Ibid., 197.
21 Ibid., 231.
22 Ibid., 197.
23 Ibid., 201–2.
24 Ibid., 200.
25 Amartya Sen, *A Theory of Justice*, London: Penguin, 2009.
26 Chatterjee, *Nationalist Thought and the Colonial World*.
27 Chibber, *Postcolonial Theory and the Specter of Capital*, 275.
28 Dipesh Chakrabarty, *Provincializing Europe: Postcolonial Thought and Historical Difference*, Princeton: Princeton University Press, 2000.
29 Karl Marx, ed., *Theories of Surplus Value*, vol. 3, Moscow: Progress Publishers, 1979, 491–2.

30 Sudipta Kaviraj, "An Outline of a Revisionist Theory of Modernity," *Archives européennes de sociologie* 46: 3, 2005, 497–526.

31 Kalyan Sanyal, *Rethinking Capitalist Development: Primitive Accumulation, Governmentality and Post-Colonial Capitalism*, New Delhi and New York: Routledge, 2007.

32 Chibber, *Postcolonial Theory and the Specter of Capital*, 202.

33 Gayatri Chakravorty Spivak, "Subaltern Studies: Deconstructing Historiography," in Ranajit Guha, ed., *Subaltern Studies IV*, Delhi: Oxford University Press, 1987, 338–63; Spivak, "Can the Subaltern Speak?" in Cary Nelson and Lawrence Grossberg, eds, *Marxism and the Interpretation of Culture*, Urbana, IL: University of Illinois Press, 1988.

34 Gyan Prakash, "Subaltern Studies as Post-Colonial Criticism," *American Historical Review* 99: 5, December 1994, 1475–90.

2. Subaltern Studies Revisited: A Response to Partha Chatterjee

1   Vivek Chibber, *Postcolonial Theory and the Specter of Capital*, London: Verso; New Delhi: Navayana, 2013, 44–5, 91–2.

2   Partha Chatterjee, "Subaltern Studies and *Capital*," Chapter 1 of this volume, 32.

3   Ranajit Guha, *Dominance without Hegemony*, Cambridge, MA: Harvard University Press, 1997, 19, emphasis added.

4   Ibid., 6–11.

5   Ibid., 6–7.

6   Ibid., 7.

7   Ibid., 13, emphasis added.

8   Ibid.

9   Ibid.

10 Ibid.

11 Ibid., 17, emphasis added.

12 Ibid.

13 Ibid., 18.

14 Ibid., 19.

15 Ibid., 5.

16 Ibid., xi–xiii, 3–5.

17 Ibid., 4–5.

18 Ibid., 38, emphasis added.

19 Ibid., 130–1.

20 Ibid., 133.

21 Ibid.

22 Ibid., 134, emphasis added.

23 Ibid., 135.

24 Ibid., 95, emphasis added.

25 Ibid., 95–6, emphasis added.

26 Chatterjee, "Subaltern Studies and *Capital*," 38.
27 See Dipesh Chakrabarty, *Rethinking Working-Class History: Bengal 1890–1940*, Princeton: Princeton University Press, 1989, 225–6. These are the only pages on which Chakrabarty actually discusses abstract labor.
28 Chatterjee, "Subaltern Studies and *Capital*," 38.
29 Chibber, *Postcolonial Theory and the Specter of Capital*, ch. 8.
30 Chatterjee, "Subaltern Studies and *Capital*," 39.
31 I will not directly address Chatterjee's rather amusing objection to my use of "psychology" to refer to subaltern consciousness. I did so only because it is common parlance in social science and philosophy. Readers made anxious by concepts like "psychology" may rest assured that the two words refer to the same object.
32 Chatterjee, "Subaltern Studies and *Capital*," ooo[[x-ref]]***.
33 Partha Chatterjee, *The Nation and Its Fragments*, Princeton: Princeton University Press, 1993, 163.
34 Ibid., 163–4. Also see Chibber, *Postcolonial Theory and the Specter of Capital*, 162.
35 Partha Chatterjee "Agrarian Relations and Communalism in Bengal, 1926–1935," in *Subaltern Studies I*, Oxford: Oxford University Press, 1982, 9–38, quotation on p. 37.
36 Chibber, *Postcolonial Theory and the Specter of Capital*, 157–66.
37 Ibid., ch.7, sections 4 and 5.
38 Ibid., 172–4.
39 There is another such resort to authority, which I will not address at any length. Briefly: Chatterjee defends Chakrabarty's culturalist argument—the target of my criticism in Chapter 8 of *PTSC*—by pointing to its "solid Marxist provenance" in Hegel's *Philosophy of Right* (Chatterjee, "Subaltern Studies and *Capital*," 42). Only three points need be made: first, its being found in Hegel is a bizarre basis for calling it Marxist; second, even if it can be found in Marx, this has no bearing on whether or not it is a defensible position; and third, I address the very distinction to which he alludes, criticize Chakrabarty's use of it, and provide actual arguments in favor of my view in *PTSC* (Chibber, *Postcolonial Theory and the Specter of Capital*, ch. 8, particularly pp. 187–200). I do not reject his argument on the grounds that it is a deviation from Marx. In fact, I never make any claim about its lineage one way or another, since it is of no relevance in assessing its soundness. Chatterjee's appeal to authority is therefore not only a little sad, but also utterly irrelevant.
40 See Michael Brown, "Cultural Relativism 2.0," *Current Anthropology* 49: 3, June 2008, 363–83, and the ensuing discussion.
41 The research on this subject is enormous. Some of it is summarized in Herbert Gintis, Samuel Bowles, Robert Boyd, and Ernst Fehr, eds, *Moral Sentiments and Material Interests: The Foundations of Cooperation in Economic Life*, Cambridge, MA: MIT Press, 2005. See also Michael Gurven, "The Evolution of Contingent Cooperation," *Current Anthropology* 47: 1, February 2006, 185–92; Michael Gurven and Jeffrey Winking, "Collective Action in Action: Prosocial Behavior in and out of the Laboratory," *American Anthropologist* 110: 2, June 2008,

179–90; Walter Garrison Runciman, "Stone-Age Sociology," *Journal of the Royal Anthropological Institute* 11: 1, March 2005, 129–42; Michael Price, "Pro-community Altruism and Social Status in a Shuar Village," *Human Nature* 14: 2, 2003, 191–208.

42 Chibber, *Postcolonial Theory and the Specter of Capital*, 281–3.

3. *POSTCOLONIAL THEORY AND THE SPECTER OF CAPITAL*

1 Cry of the children as the effigy of Guy Fawkes, the guardian of the gunpowder, was burnt on November 5th, the anniversary of the Gunpowder Plot (1605) to blow up the English House of Lords with King James I of England in it. Since Ranajit Guha, at ninety, is our "old guy," and Vivek Chibber burns him for misreading the English Revolution, this child's cry seemed an appropriate title.

2 I have long wanted to admit that I forgot this lesson when I was in my thirties twice (with reference to Jürgen Habermas and James Wolfensohn) and have bitterly regretted it. For consciousness-raised ideologically bound feminist readers of this review, of a book that has no feminist concern, I mention that part of this forgetfulness was because I felt unself-consciously obliged to prove to my then partner that I was not a "bourgeois proto-fascist" (his repeated phrase). This book is by a resolutely non-identitarian South-Asian American. The personal may be political.

3 Vivek Chibber, *Postcolonial Theory and the Specter of Capital*, London: Verso; New Delhi: Navayana, 2013, 296.

4 Edward W. Said, *Orientalism*, New York: Pantheon, 1978.

5 John Thompson, *Studies in the Theory of Ideology*, London: Polity Press, 1985.

6 Ranajit Guha and Gayatri Chakravorty Spivak, *Selected Subaltern Studies*, Oxford: Oxford University Press, 1988.

7 Aijaz Ahmad, *In Theory: Classes, Nations, Literatures*, New York: Verso, 1992.

8 Partha Chatterjee, *Nationalist Thought and the Colonial World: A Derivative Discourse*, Minneapolis: University of Minnesota Press, 1993, vii.

9 Chibber, *Postcolonial Theory and the Specter of Capital*, 80.

10 Ibid., 101.

11 Ibid., 81.

12 Ranajit Guha, *A Rule of Property for Bengal: An Essay on the Idea of Permanent Settlement*, Paris: Mouton, 1963.

13 Ranajit Guha, *The Small Voice of History*, Ranikhet: Permanent Black, 2009.

14 Compare Kirti Chaudhuri's impatience: "While it is possible to criticize Braudel's works on matters of factual detail or interpretation, to do so is rather like standing in front of Michelangelo's statue of David in Piazza Signoria in Florence or looking up at his paintings in the Sistine Chapel in Rome and saying that the artist's grasp of the human anatomy was all wrong" (K. N. Chaudhuri, *Asia before Europe: Economy and Civilization of the Indian Ocean from the Rise of Islam to 1750*, Cambridge, UK: Cambridge University Press, 1991, 6, emphasis mine).

15 Ranajit Guha, *Dominance without Hegemony: History and Power in Colonial India*, Cambridge, MA: Harvard University Press, 1997, first published 1989.

16 Ibid., 6, emphasis added.

17 Karl Marx, *The German Ideology*, Moscow: Progress Publishers, 1976.

18 Chibber, *Postcolonial Theory and the Specter of Capital*, 109.

19 Ibid., 280.

20 Ibid., 217.

21 Ibid., 233.

22 Ibid., 125.

23 Ibid., 250.

24 Ibid., 6.

25 Ibid., 6.

26 W. E. B. Du Bois, "The Negro Mind Reaches Out," in Alain Locke, ed., *The New Negro: An Interpretation*, New York: Athenaeum Press, 1968, 385–414.

27 Chibber, *Postcolonial Theory and the Specter of Capital*, 8.

28 Kathleen Collins, *Clan Politics and Regime Transition in Central Asia*, Cambridge, UK: Cambridge University Press, 2006.

29 Chibber, *Postcolonial Theory and the Specter of Capital*, 200–2.

30 Emmanuel Lévinas, *Otherwise than Being, or, Beyond Essence*, trans. Alphonso Lingis, Pittsburgh: Duquesne University Press, 1998, 27–48.

31 Edward W. Said, "Permission to Narrate," *Journal of Palestine Studies* 13: 3, 1984, 27–48.

32 Amartya Sen, *Poverty and Famines: An Essay on Entitlements and Deprivation*, Oxford: Oxford University Press, 1981. His work was enriched by Esther Bostrup's work on famines since the 60s.

33 Karl Marx, *Capital: A Critique of Political Economy*, vol. 1, trans. Ben Fowkes, London: Penguin Books, 1990.

34 Rosa Luxemburg, *The Essential Rosa Luxemburg: Reform or Revelation and Mass Strike*, Chicago: Haymarket Books, 2007.

35 Guha, *Dominance without Hegemony*, 35.

36 Ibid., 119.

37 Chibber, *Postcolonial Theory and the Specter of Capital*, 52.

38 Ibid., 291.

39 Damodar Dharmanand Kosambi, *An Introduction to the Study of Indian History*, Mumbai: Popular Prakashan, 1975.

40 Chibber, *Postcolonial Theory and the Specter of Capital*, 291.

41 Kosambi, *An Introduction to the Study of Indian History*, 1.

42 Chibber, *Postcolonial Theory and the Specter of Capital*, 286, emphasis in original.

43 W. E. B. Du Bois, *Black Reconstruction in America*, New York: Free Press, 1998.

44 Chibber, *Postcolonial Theory and the Specter of Capital*, 275.

45 Guha, *Dominance without Hegemony*, 37.

46 Unpublished conversation, 1989; I cannot reproduce his persuasive and thunderous accent, alas.

47 Shahid Amin, "Gandhi as Mahatma: Gorakhpur District, Eastern UP, 1921–2," *Subaltern Studies* 3, 1984, 1–61; Partha Chatterjee, "Gandhi and the Critique of Civil Society," *Subaltern Studies* 3, 1984, 153–95.

48 Sumanta Banerjee, "Gandhi's Flexible Non-violence," *Economic and Political Weekly* 48: 31, 2013, 4.

49 David Hardiman, "Gandhi's Adaptable Non-violence," *Economic and Political Weekly* 48: 33, 2013, 4–5.

50 Chibber, *Postcolonial Theory and the Specter of Capital*, 287.

51 Ibid., 140, emphasis in original.

52 Marx, *Capital*.

53 Axel Honneth, *Reification: A New Look at an Old Idea*, Oxford: Oxford University Press, 2012.

54 Antonio Gramsci, *Selections from the Prison Writings*, trans. Quentin Hoare and Geoffrey Nowell Smith, New York: International, 1971.

55 Ibid., 52.

56 Chibber, *Postcolonial Theory and the Specter of Capital*, 268.

57 Teun Van Dijk, *Discourse and Power*, New York: Palgrave Macmillan, 2008.

58 Chibber, *Postcolonial Theory and the Specter of Capital*, 75.

59 Ibid., 54.

60 Ibid., 152–3.

61 Ibid., 79.

62 Susan M. L. Wong, "China's Stock Market: A Marriage of Capitalism and Socialism," *Cato Journal* 26: 3, 2006, 389–424.

63 Chibber, *Postcolonial Theory and the Specter of Capital*, 220.

64 Walter Benjamin, "Theses on the Philosophy of History," *Illuminations*, trans. Harry Zohn, New York: Schocken, 1968, 253–64.

65 Ibid., 255, 261.

66 Gayatri Chakravorty Spivak, *Readings*, ed. Lara Choksey, Calcutta: Seagull, 2014.

67 Dipesh Chakrabarty, *Provincializing Europe: Postcolonial Thought and Historical Difference*, Princeton: Princeton University Press, 2000, 17.

68 Chibber, *Postcolonial Theory and the Specter of Capital*, 89.

69 Ibid., 178.

70 Guha, *Dominance without Hegemony*, 3.

71 Ritu Birla, *Stages of Capital: Law, Culture, and Market Governance in Late Colonial India*, Durham, NC: Duke University Press, 2009.

72 Ranajit Guha, *Elementary Aspects of Peasant Insurgency in Colonial India*, Delhi: Oxford University Press, 1983.

73 Chibber, *Postcolonial Theory and the Specter of Capital*, 98.

74 Kant, Immanuel, "The Metaphysics of Morals," *Political Writings*, trans. H. B. Nisbet, Cambridge, UK: Cambridge University Press, 1991, 139.

4. MAKING SENSE OF POSTCOLONIAL THEORY

1 Vivek Chibber, *Postcolonial Theory and the Specter of Capital*, London: Verso; New Delhi: Navayana, 2013.

2 This essay is the author's response to a review previously published by the *Cambridge Review of International Affairs* (Chapter 3 of this volume).

3 Both concepts originate in Gramsci's *Prison Notebooks*.
4 Chapter 1 of this volume.
5 See Chapter 1. For a rebuttal of Chatterjee, see Chapter 2 of this volume, where I provide detailed textual evidence against his claims.
6 Chapter 3 of this volume, 79.
7 Ibid., 74.
8 Chapter 3, 80–2.
9 Chapter 3, 75.
10 Chibber, *Postcolonial Theory and the Specter of Capital*, 130.
11 Vivek Chibber, "What Is Living and What Is Dead in the Marxist Theory of History," *Historical Materialism* 19: 2, 2011, 60–91.

7. INTRODUCTION: REVIEW SYMPOSIUM

1 Chapters 7–13 emerged from a symposium on *Postcolonial Theory and the Specter of Capital*.
2 Jürgen Habermas, "Modernity: An Incomplete Project," *New German Critique* 22, 1981, 3–15.
3 Janet Ajary and Kevin B. Anderson, *Foucault and the Iranian Revolution: Gender and the Seduction of Islamism*, Chicago: Chicago University Press, 2005.

8. ON VIVEK CHIBBER'S *POSTCOLONIAL THEORY AND THE SPECTER OF CAPITAL*

1 Dipesh Chakrabarty, *Provincializing Europe: Postcolonial Thought and Historical Difference*, Princeton: Princeton University Press, 2000.
2 Ranajit Guha, *Dominance without Hegemony: History and Power in Colonial India*, Cambridge, MA: Harvard University Press, 1997, first published 1989.
3 Dipesh Chakrabarty, *Rethinking Working-Class History: Bengal 1890–1940*, Princeton: Princeton University Press, 1989.
4 Chakrabarty, *Provincializing Europe*, 27, 40.
5 Ibid., 250, 71.
6 Ibid., 66.

9. BACK TO BASICS?

1 Vivek Chibber, *Postcolonial Theory and the Specter of Capital*, London: Verso; New Delhi: Navayana, 2013, 295.
2 Ibid., quoted on p. 8.
3 For example, see ibid., p. 87.

4 Dietrich Rueschemeyer, Evelyne Huber Stephens, and John D. Stephens, *Capitalist Development and Democracy*, Chicago: University of Chicago Press, 1992.

5 Ranajit Guha, *Dominance without Hegemony: History and Power in Colonial India*, Cambridge, MA: Harvard University Press, 1997, first published 1989.

6 Ibid., 35.

7 Ibid.

8 Chibber, *Postcolonial Theory and the Specter of Capital*, 292.

9 Ibid., quoted on page 13.

10 See my *Parallax Visions: Making Sense of American–East Asian Relations*, Durham, NC, and London: Duke University Press, 2002, ch. 6.

11 Dipesh Chakrabarty, *Provincializing Europe: Postcolonial Thought and Historical Difference*, Princeton: Princeton University Press, 2000.

12 Chibber, *Postcolonial Theory and the Specter of Capital*, 291.

13 Ibid., 108.

14 Friedrich Nietzsche, *Beyond Good and Evil*, New York: Cambridge University Press, 2002, 48.

15 Harry D. Harootunian, *Overcome by Modernity: History, Culture, and Community in Interwar Japan*, Princeton: Princeton University Press, 2002.

16 Chibber, *Postcolonial Theory and the Specter of Capital*, 25.

17 Ibid., 49.

18 Ibid., 80–1.

19 Ibid., 176.

20 Ibid., 206.

21 Ibid., 212.

22 Friedrich Nietzsche, *Untimely Meditations*, New York: Cambridge University Press, 1983, 128.

23 Jürgen Habermas, *The Philosophical Discourse of Modernity*, trans. Frederick Lawrence, Cambridge, MA: MIT Press, 1987, 367.

24 Stephen K. White, "Reason, Modernity and Democracy," in *The Cambridge Companion to Habermas*, New York: Cambridge University Press, 1995, 9.

25 Max Weber, *General Economic History*, trans. Frank H. Knight, New Brunswick, NJ: Transaction Books, 1981, 312–14.

10. On the Articulation of Marxist and Non-Marxist Theory

1 See, for example, Ernesto Laclau and Chantal Mouffe, *Hegemony and Socialist Strategy: Towards a Radical Democratic Politics*, London: Verso, 1985.

2 See, for example, Moishe Postone, *Time, Labor and Social Domination: A Reinterpretation of Marx's Critical Theory*, New York: Cambridge University Press, 1993.

3 See, for example, Robert Jessop, "Zur Relevanz von Luhmanns Staatstheorie und von Laclau und Mouffes Diskursanalyse für die Weiterentwicklung der marxistischen Staatstheorie" in Joachim Hirsch, John Kannakulam, and Jens

Wissel, eds, *Der Staat der bürgerlichen Gesellschaft*, Frankfurt: Nomos, 2008, 157–79.

4 On neo-historicist social epistemology see my "Charles Tilly, Historicism, and the Critical Realist Philosophy of Science," *American Sociologist* 41: 4, 2010, 312–36; on critical realism in this context see my "Critical Realism and Historical Sociology," *Comparative Studies in Society and History* 40: 1, 1998, 170–86.

5 Edward W. Said, *Orientalism*, New York: Pantheon, 1978, and *Culture and Imperialism*, New York: Knopf, 1993.

6 Gayatri Chakravorty Spivak, "Can the Subaltern Speak?" in Cary Nelson and Lawrence Grossberg, eds, *Marxism and the Interpretation of Culture*, Urbana, IL: University of Illinois Press, 1988, and *In Other Worlds: Essays in Cultural Politics*, New York: Routledge, 1998.

7 Homi K. Bhabha, *The Location of Culture*, London and New York: Routledge, 1994.

8 Leela Gandhi, *Affective Communities: Anti-Colonial Thought, Fin-de-Siècle Radicalism, and the Politics of Friendship*, Durham, NC: Duke University Press, 2006.

9 For an excellent overview see Leela Gandhi, *Postcolonial Theory*, New York: Columbia University Press, 1998.

10 George Steinmetz, "Decolonizing German Theory: An Introduction," *Postcolonial Studies* 9: 1, 2006, 3–13.

11 Vivek Chibber, *Postcolonial Theory and the Specter of Capital*, London: Verso; New Delhi: Navayana, 2013, 217.

12 Ibid., 123.

13 David Blackbourn and Geoff Eley, *The Peculiarities of German History*, New York: Oxford University Press, 1985. Lukács (*Die Zerstörung der Vernunft*, vol. 1, Darmstadt: Luchterhand, 1973, 41) claimed that the German bourgeoisie from the sixteenth century onward was "characterized by a servility, pettiness, baseness, and miserabilism" which distinguished it from other European bourgeoisies. See George Steinmetz, "German Exceptionalism and the Origins of Nazism: The Career of a Concept," in Ian Kershaw and Moshe Lewin, eds, *Stalinism and Nazism: Dictatorships in Comparison*, Cambridge: Cambridge University Press, 1997, 251–84.

14 Chibber, *Postcolonial Theory and the Specter of Capital*, 112, 123.

15 Ibid., 123. A similar criticism can be made of Bourdieu's state theory, which twists the stick too far in the direction of symbolic domination (Pierre Bourdieu, *Sur l'état: cours au Collège de France 1989–1992*, Paris: Seuil, 2012). See George Steinmetz, "État-mort, État-fort, État-empire," *Actes de la recherche en sciences sociales* 201, 2014, 112–19.

16 Chibber, *Postcolonial Theory and the Specter of Capital*, 144.

17 *Pace* Harry Braverman, *Labor and Monopoly Capital: The Degradation of Work in the Twentieth Century*, New York: Monthly Review Press, 1974.

18 Dipesh Chakrabarty, *Provincializing Europe: Postcolonial Thought and Historical Difference*, Princeton: Princeton University Press, 2000.

19 Chibber, *Postcolonial Theory and the Specter of Capital*, 123.

20 Ibid., 125.

21 Ibid., 224.

22 Ibid., 226.

23 Ibid., 230.

24 Ibid., 233.

25 Ibid.

26 Ibid., 239.

27 Pierre Bourdieu, "Séminaires sur le concept de champ, 1972–1975," *Actes de la recherche en sciences sociales* 200, 2013, 4–37.

28 Kent C. Berridge and Piotr Winkielman, "What Is an Unconscious Emotion? (The Case for Unconscious Liking)," *Cognition and Emotion* 17: 2, 2000, 181–211; Kent C. Berridge, "Pleasure, Unconscious Affect and Irrational Desire," in A. S. R. Manstead, N. H. Frijda, and A. H. Fischer, eds, *Feelings and Emotions: The Amsterdam Symposium*, New York: Cambridge University Press, 2004, 43–62; and Piotr Winkielman and Kent C. Berridge, "Unconscious Emotion," *Current Directions in Psychological Sciences* 13: 3, 2004, 120–3.

29 Mahmood Mamdani, *Citizen and Subject: Contemporary Africa and the Legacy of Late Colonialism*, Princeton: Princeton University Press, 1996.

30 I provide evidence of efforts to limit capital's universalization in various colonial contexts in *The Devil's Handwriting: Precoloniality and the German Colonial State in Qingdao, Samoa, and Southwest Africa*, Chicago: University of Chicago Press, 2007. The British and French colonial development policies after World War II were the result of a particular political-economic conjuncture and cannot be seen as the inevitable breakthrough of capital exerting its universalizing power. Frederick Cooper, *Decolonization and African Society*, Cambridge: Cambridge University Press, 1996.

31 Chibber, *Postcolonial Theory and the Specter of Capital*, 125.

32 Ibid., 227.

33 Talcott Parsons, "Sociological Elements of Economic Thought," *Quarterly Journal of Economics* 49: 3, 1934, 446.

11. Capitalist Development, Structural Constraint

1 Friedrich Engels, *Anti-Dühring*, New York: International Publishers, 1972, 10.

2 Vivek Chibber, *Postcolonial Theory and the Specter of Capital*, London: Verso; New Delhi: Navayana, 2013, 286–93, 285.

3 In particular, ibid., ch. 9.

4 Ibid., 174.

5 Ibid., 132–4.

6 Ibid., 145.

7 Ibid., 232.

8 Richard Williams, *Hierarchical Structures and Social Value: The Social Construction of Black and Irish Identities in the U.S.*, New York: Cambridge University Press, 1990.

9 Chibber, *Postcolonial Theory and the Specter of Capital*, 250.

10 Jeffrey M. Paige, *Agrarian Revolution*, New York: Free Press, 1978.

11 Another building block toward this analysis can be found in Jeff Goodwin, *No Other Way Out: States and Revolutionary Movements, 1945–1991*, New York: Cambridge University Press, 2001.

12 Chibber, *Postcolonial Theory and the Specter of Capital*, 285.

13 Perry Anderson, *Arguments within English Marxism*, New York: New Left Books, 1980, 20.

12. MINDING APPEARANCES

1 Vivek Chibber, *Postcolonial Theory and the Specter of Capital*, London: Verso; New Delhi: Navayana, 2013, xii.

2 See Bruce Robbins's review, "Subaltern-Speak," Chapter 5 of this volume, and the online post by Chris Taylor of the University of Chicago, "Not Even Marxist: On Vivek Chibber's Polemic against Postcolonial Theory," April 29, 2013, available at http://clrjames.blogspot.com/2013/04/not-even-marxist-on-vivek-chibbers.html.

3 On the significance of "specters" with respect to both the figure of Marx and his work, see Jacques Derrida's *Specters of Marx: The State of the Debt, the Work of Mourning and the New International*, New York: Routledge, 1995, delivered in 1993 as the plenary address for a conference at the University of California, Riverside's Center for Ideas and Society. Nine critical commentaries on the book and Derrida's response to them are collected in *Ghostly Demarcations: A Symposium on Jacques Derrida's Specters of Marx*, New York: Verso, 2008, edited by the late Michael Sprinker.

4 I borrow this term from Roy Bhaskar (*Scientific Realism and Human Emancipation*, New York: Verso, 1986) as a way to refer to the combined task of explaining the workings of capitalism and the falsity of its necessary self-representation.

5 Klaus Peter Köpping, *Adolf Bastian and the Psychic Unity of Mankind: The Foundations of Anthropology in Nineteenth-Century Germany* (History and Theory of Anthropology/Geschichte und Theorie der Ethnologie), Berlin: LIT Verlag, 2005.

6 George W. Stocking, Jr., *The Shaping of American Anthropology, 1883–1911: A Franz Boas Reader*, New York: Basic Books, 1984, 14. Bastian was Boas's senior advisor at the Ethnographic Museum in Berlin.

7 William Ascher and Barbara Hirschfelder-Ascher, *Revitalizing Political Psychology: The Legacy of Harold D. Lasswell*, Mahwah, NJ: Erlbaum, 2003.

8 In a presentation on Chibber's book later published in *Economic and Political Weekly* (see Chapter 1 of this volume), Partha Chatterjee suggested that "political psychology" was not an appropriate category, because it had never been used by the Subaltern Studies authors, particularly Ranajit Guha.

9 Chibber, *Postcolonial Theory and the Specter of Capital*, 153.

10 Ibid., 154.

11 Ibid., 185.

12 Ibid., 196.

13 Ibid., 199.

14 Ibid., 197.

15 Ibid., 198.

16 Ibid., 200.

17 Lisa Lowe and David Lloyd, eds, *The Politics of Culture in the Shadow of Capital*, Durham: Duke University Press, 1997.

18 Chibber cites an essay that I co-authored on the relevance of Marx's value-theoretic inquiries for the anthropological study of capitalism. He includes our piece along with others that he claims make the error of interpreting "abstract" labor as referring to the empirical homogeneity of actual laboring people. However, our only reference to "homogeneous" was the same as Chibber's on page 135 in his book where he draws on the famous quotation from *Capital*, vol. 1, on the oddity of the objectification of abstract labor that is specific to capitalism: "Let us look at the residue of the products of labor . . . they are merely congealed quantities of homogeneous labor." In the introduction to my book *American Value, Migrants, Money and Meaning in El Salvador and the United States*, I make the same critique of Lowe and Lloyd as Chibber.

19 Dipesh Chakrabarty, "Marx after Marxism: History, Subalternity, and Difference," in Saree Makdisi, Cesare Casarino, and Rebecca Karl, eds, *Marxism Beyond Marxism*, New York: Routledge, 1995, 60.

20 There are at least two compelling critiques of this project written by anthropologists: Fernando Coronil's "Beyond Occidentalism: Toward Nonimperial Geohistorical Categories," *Cultural Anthropology* 11: 1, 1996, 51–87, and Michel Rolph Trioullout's "Anthropology and the Savage Slot: The Poetics and Politics of Otherness," in Richard G. Fox, ed., *Recapturing Anthropology: Working in the Present*, Santa Fe, NM: School of American Research Press, 1991, 17–44.

13. Confronting Postcolonial Theory

1 I offer a more elaborate explanation for my decision to focus on Subaltern Studies in Chapter 4 of this volume, which I do not want to repeat here.

2 Vivek Chibber, *Postcolonial Theory and the Specter of Capital*, London: Verso; New Delhi: Navayana, 2013, 228–9.

3 Ibid., 229.

4 Bill Warren, *Imperialism: Pioneer of Capitalism*, London: Verso, 1980.

5 See Chibber, *Postcolonial Theory and the Specter of Capital*, 125 fn. 39, 144–5, 145 fn. 31.

6 Ibid., 183–200, particularly 193–6.

14. SUBALTERN STAKES

1 Friedrich Nietzsche, *The Complete Works of Friedrich Nietzsche*, ed. Oscar Levy, London: J. Foulis, 1909–13, 12. Nietzsche loathed subalterns, denouncing Socratic dialectics for placing the lower classes at center stage.

2 I would like to thank Keya Ganguly for her help with this essay.

3 Vivek Chibber, *Postcolonial Theory and the Specter of Capital*, London: Verso; New Delhi: Navayana, 2013.

4 For a sense of how "theory" affected the reading of Gramsci in India, see the proceedings of a workshop on Gramsci and South Asia at the Centre for Studies in Social Sciences, Calcutta 1987, repr. *Economic and Political Weekly*, January 30, 1988.

5 Princeton: Princeton University Press, 2003.

6 Chibber, *Postcolonial Theory and the Specter of Capital*, 3.

7 Chibber, *Locked in Place*, 85.

8 Among the most balanced and informative discussions of the book is Pranav Jani's "Marxism and the Future of Postcolonial Theory," *International Socialist Review* 92, Spring 2014. For a highly informed scholarly treatment, see the Ho-fung Hung roundtable, featuring George Steinmetz, Bruce Cumings, and other social scientists, in "Review Symposium on Vivek Chibber's *Postcolonial Theory and the Specter of Capital*," *Journal of World-Systems Research* 20: 2, July 2014. For critiques of Chibber from the Left that demonstrate real familiarity with postcolonial theory—many reviews do not—see, for example, Julian Murphet, "No Alternative," *Cambridge Journal of Postcolonial Literary Inquiry* 1: 1, March 2014, and Axel Andersson, "Obscuring Capitalism: Vivek Chibber's Critique of Postcolonial Theory," *Los Angeles Review of Books*, November 6, 2013. For a defense of Subaltern Studies against Chibber, see Partha Chatterjee's "Subaltern Studies and *Capital*," Chapter 1 of this volume, and Gayatri Spivak (cited below).

9 For instance, Tom Brass, "Moral Economists, Subalterns, New Social Movements and the (Re-) Emergence of a (Post-) Modernized (Middle) Peasant" and Sumit Sarkar, "The Decline of the Subaltern in *Subaltern Studies*," in Vinayak Chaturvedi, ed., *Mapping Subaltern Studies and the Postcolonial*, London and New York: Verso, 2000, 127–62, 300–23.

10 Chibber, *Postcolonial Theory and the Specter of Capital*, 5.

11 Susie O'Brien and Imre Szeman, "Introduction: The Globalization of Fiction/ the Fiction of Globalization," *South Atlantic Quarterly* 100: 3, 2001.

12 Edward Said, *Culture and Imperialism*, New York: Vintage, 1993, xix.

13 M. N. Roy, in a familiar kind of criticism, rightly excoriated the Third International for its "defective understanding of the situation in other countries," and for "projecting Russian problems" onto their realities (*The Communist International*, Bombay: Radical Democratic Party, 1943, 42–3). But like others, he recognized that the International created networks, devised rhetorical weapons, and gave material assistance that became models for postwar decolonization.

14 Friedrich Nietzsche, *The Complete Works of Friedrich Nietzsche*, ed. Oscar Levy, London: J. Foulis, 1909–13, vol. 9, 215–17; vol. 10, 78; vol. 12, 196; vol. 13, 224.

15 Edmund G. Husserl, *Phenomenology and the Crisis of Philosophy*, New York: Harper and Row, 1965, first published 1935, 149–92.

16 Published during the first surge of postwar decolonization, Bataille's *The Accursed Share* (vol. 1, New York: Zone Books, 1988, first published 1949; vols. 2 and 3, New York: Zone Books, 1993, first published 1976), seized upon the watchwords of the independence movements—freedom, political representation, development—in order to explode them from within. Alluding to the new "world situation" of decolonization—and his own fear of its Sovietization (vol. 1, 147–68)—his study took as its central term "sovereignty," which he wrested away from its associations with the independence movements so that it came to mean rather the cruelty of sexual freedom.

17 Alexandre Kojève, *Introduction to the Reading of Hegel*, Ithaca: Cornell University Press, 1969, 160–1.

18 I make this argument more fully in "Humanism, Philology, and Imperialism" (in *Wars of Position: The Cultural Politics of Left and Right*, New York: Columbia University Press, 2006) and in "Edward Said as a Lukácsian Critic: Modernism and Empire," *College Literature* 40: 4, Fall 2013.

19 Chibber's argument would have benefited from exploring the bases of subaltern essentialism in the broader circles of "theory" itself. See Ian Almond's provocative study *The New Orientalists: Postmodern Representations of Islam from Foucault to Baudrillard*, London and New York: I. B. Tauris, 2007.

20 Erich Auerbach, "Einleitung," in Giambattista Vico, *Die neue Wissenschaft*, Munich: Walter de Gruyter, 1924, 23 (my translation).

21 Antonio Gramsci, *Quaderni del carcere*, vol. 2, ed. Valentino Gerratana, Turin: Einaudi, 1975, Q11, §25, 1429 (my translation).

22 Walter Benjamin, *The Arcades Project*, ed. Rolf Tiedemann, Cambridge, MA, and London: Harvard University Press, 1999, 476.

23 Keston Sutherland, "Marx in Jargon," *World Picture* 1, Spring 2008.

24 Alain Badiou, *Deleuze: The Clamor of Being*, Minneapolis: University of Minnesota Press, 2000, 55.

25 Lafargue, *Le déterminisme économique de Karl Marx: Recherches sur l'origine des idées de justice, du bien, de l'âme et de Dieu*, Paris 1911; Sorel, *Études sur Vico et autres textes*, ed. Anne-Sophie Menasseyre, Paris: H. Champion, 2007.

26 Edward Palmer Thompson, *The Poverty of Theory and Other Essays*, New York: Monthly Review Press, 1978.

27 Marx refers to Vico at least three times in his writings, although what is Vichian about his thought—as later commentators observed—has more to do with its systematic parallels to Vico borne out in common sources (Varro on Roman Law, for instance [*Grundrisse*, London: Penguin, 1973, 834]), and by way of Hegel, whose Vichian influences have been well marked. See *Capital*, vol. I (London: Penguin, 1990, 493), and the letter to Ferdinand Lassalle (*Collected Works*, vol. 41, Moscow: Progress Publishers, 1985, 355), where Marx praises Vico and observes that he was at "the foundation of comparative philology." For

more on this tradition, see Timothy Brennan, *Borrowed Light: Vico, Hegel and the Colonies*, Stanford: Stanford University Press, 2014.

28 For example, Max Harold Fisch and Thomas Goddard Bergin in their brilliant introduction to *The Autobiography of Giambattista Vico* (Ithaca and London: Cornell University Press, 1944), where they point out that the attribution is as old as Georges Sorel's *Études sur Vico*; a more contemporary example, one of many, can be found in Lawrence H. Simon, "Vico and Marx: Perspectives on Historical Development," *Journal of the History of Ideas* 42: 2, 1981.

29 The Vichian lineages of Marxism have been enthusiastically discussed, at least, outside the Anglo-American academy. See, for example, David Roldán, "La recepción filosófica de Vico y sus aporías filológicas: El caso del marxismo occidental," *Pensamiento* 68: 253, 2012; Alberto Mario Damiani, *La dimensión política de la "Scienza Nuova" y otros estudios sobre Giambattista Vico*, Buenos Aires: Editorial Universitaria de Buenos Aires, 1998.

30 Respectively, Benita Parry, *Postcolonial Studies: A Materialist Critique*, London and New York: Routledge, 2004, 36; Fernando Coronil, "Can Postcoloniality Be Decolonized? Imperial Banality and Postcolonial Power," *Public Culture* 5: 1, Fall 1992.

31 Chibber, *Postcolonial Theory and the Specter of Capital*, 4. The work of Vasant Kaiwar is very interesting in this context. From 2004 onwards he anticipated many of Chibber's later lines of attack, demonstrating peculiar strengths missing in the latter's efforts: for example, wider reference to previous scholarship, exhibiting a feel for the textures and flavors of everything from Bengali *adda* to the holistic blend of sociology and literature that animates the best postcolonial work. He too attributes to Guha an "orientalist enthusiasm," criticizing him for sidestepping the Muslim question and for expressing views that at times come uncomfortably close to the "organicist fantasies of the contemporary Hindu right about 'tradition'": *The Postcolonial Orient: The Politics of Difference and the Project of Provincializing Europe*, Leiden, The Netherlands, and Boston: Brill, 2014.

32 See Priyamvada Gopal's "Reading Subaltern History" (in Neil Lazarus, ed., *The Cambridge Companion to Postcolonial Literary Studies*, Cambridge: Cambridge University Press, 2004, 139–61), which I follow here. The quotation is from Guha's "Chandra's Death," in Guha, ed., *Subaltern Studies V*, Delhi: Oxford University Press, 1987, 141.

33 Guha, *Dominance without Hegemony: History and Power in Colonial India*, Cambridge, MA: Harvard University Press, 1997, first published 1989, 14–16.

34 Dipesh Chakrabarty, *Provincializing Europe: Postcolonial Thought and Historical Difference*, Princeton: Princeton University Press, 2000, 243. The appropriation is derived from Homi Bhabha, as Keya Ganguly has pointed out in "Temporality and Postcolonial Critique," *The Cambridge Companion to Postcolonial Literary Studies*, 174. Quotations from Bloch are from this essay.

35 Kaiwar, *The Postcolonial Orient*; Gayatri Chakravorty Spivak, "Review of *Postcolonial Theory and the Specter of Capital*," Chapter 3 of this volume.

15. REVIEW ESSAY

1 Vivek Chibber, *Postcolonial Theory and the Specter of Capital*, London: Verso; New Delhi: Navayana, 2013, 150.
2 Ibid., 250.
3 Ibid., 288–9.
4 Ranajit Guha, *Dominance without Hegemony: History and Power in Colonial India*, Cambridge, MA: Harvard University Press, 1997, first published 1989, 134.
5 Ibid., 14.
6 Dipesh Chakrabarty, *Provincializing Europe: Postcolonial Thought and Historical Difference*, Princeton: Princeton University Press, 2000.
7 Ibid., 63–4.
8 Chibber, *Postcolonial Theory and the Specter of Capital*, 145, fn 31.
9 Ibid., 291.
10 Partha Chatterjee, "Subaltern Studies and *Capital*," Chapter 1 of this volume.

16. LOOKING FOR RESISTANCE IN ALL THE WRONG PLACES?

1 I would like to thank Dipesh Chakrabarty, Nandini Chandra, Ron Radano, Saul Thomas, Max Ward, and especially two anonymous reviewers and the editors at Critical Historical Studies for reading and discussing this essay with me. Any mistakes that remain are of course my own responsibility.
2 In a review of Chibber's book, Gayatri Spivak takes Chibber to task for not exhaustively looking at the postcolonial corpus: "In a 306-page book full of a repeated and generalized account of the British and French revolutions, and repeated cliches about how capitalism works, and repeated boyish moments of 'I have disproved arguments 1, 2, 3, therefore Guha (or Chakrabarty, or yet Chatterjee) is wrong, and therefore subaltern studies is a plague and a seduction, and must be eradicated, although it will be hard because careers will be ruined, etc., there could have been some room for these references to describe the range, roots and ramifications of postcolonial studies, so that the book's focused choice could have taken its place in Verso's protective gestures towards the preservation of 'Little Britain Marxism', shared to some degree by the journal Race and Class. Aijaz Ahmad's *In Theory* (1992) was such an attempt. Postcolonial theory is the blunter instrument, and its attempt to disregard the range of postcolonial studies in order to situate subaltern studies—confined to three texts—as its representative can mislead students more effectively" (Gayatri Spivak, Review of *Postcolonial Theory and the Specter of Capital*, Chapter 3 of this volume). Spivak is correct to say that Chibber only looks at three authors and ignores African and Latin American postcolonialists. However, he has honed in on three extremely influential postcolonial theorists and has clearly read some of their representative texts carefully. Perhaps the best critical essay

so far on Chibber's work is Timothy Brennan's piece "Subaltern Stakes," Chapter 14 of this volume. Brennan accepts the force of many of Chibber's arguments but contends that he fails to deal seriously with culture.

3 Chris Taylor, "Not Even Marxist: On Vivek Chibber's Polemic against Postcolonial Theory," April 29, 2013, available at http://clrjames.blogspot.com/2013/04/not-even-marxist-on-vivek-chibbers.html.

4 Vivek Chibber, *Postcolonial Theory and the Specter of Capital*, London: Verso; New Delhi: Navayana, 2013, 5.

5 Neil Larsen, "Literature, Immanent Critique and the Problem of Standpoint," *Mediations* 24, Spring 2009, 48–65, 57.

6 Moishe Postone, *Time, Labor and Social Domination: A Reinterpretation of Marx's Critical Theory*, Cambridge: Cambridge University Press, 1993, 87.

7 Elizabeth Clemens, "The Lessons of Failure," *Comparative and Historical Sociology* 18, Spring 2007, 6.

8 Vivek Chibber, "Response to Clemens, Paige and Panitch," *Comparative and Historical Sociology* 18, 2007, 9.

9 Chibber, *Postcolonial Theory and the Specter of Capital*, 286.

10 Chibber, "Response to Clemens, Paige, and Panitch," 9. In his analysis of imperialism as well, he separates capital from geopolitics. "American planners in the decade following World War II propped up rival empires where it might have been expected to shove them aside—Southeast Asia, Africa, and especially the Middle East—sometimes against the wishes of US capitalists, who saw a golden opportunity to move in. This is difficult to explain except through a framework which accords a great deal more autonomy to policy planners than Lenin and Luxemburg seemed to." Vivek Chibber, "The Return of Imperialism to Social Science," *Archives de Europeenes de Sociologie/European Journal of Sociology* 45, December 2004, 430.

11 Compare Jacques Bidet's distinction between the functionaries of the state and the capitalists, *Explication et reconstruction du Capital*, Paris: Presses Universitaires de France, 2004, 228, and *L'État-monde: Libéralisme, socialisme et communisme à l'échelle globale*, Paris: Presses Universitaires de France, 2011, 10.

12 Partha Chatterjee, *The Nation and Its Fragments: Colonial and Postcolonial Histories*, Princeton: Princeton University Press, 1993, 163. Cited in Chibber, *Postcolonial Theory and the Specter of Capital*, 158.

13 Michael Sandel, *Liberalism and the Limits of Justice*, Cambridge, MA: Cambridge University Press, 1982, and *Democracy's Discontents: America's Search for a Public Philosophy*, New York: Belknap Press, 1996.

14 Watsuji Tetsurō, "Gendai nihon to Chonin Konjō" [Contemporary Japan and the nature of the cities] in *Keizoku nihon seishin shi* [A continuation of a history of the Japanese spirit], in *Watsuji Tetsurō zenshū*, vol. 4, Tokyo: Iwanami shoten, 1976, 435–505.

15 Mao Zedong, cited in Yan Hairong and Chen Yiyuan, Hairong, Yan, and Chen Yiyuan, "Debating the Rural Cooperative Movement in China, the Past and the Present," *Journal of Peasant Studies* 40: 6, 2013, 955–81, 963.

16 Wen Tiejun has become something of a phenomenon in Chinese peasant studies, especially because of his critique of modernity. For an introduction to his work, see Wen Tiejun, *Jiegou xiandai xing: Wen Tiejun Jiangyan lv*

[Deconstruction of modernization: A collection of speeches by Wen Tiejun], Guangzhou: Guangdong renmin chubanshe, 2004. For a sympathetic discussion of Wen's work in English, see Alex Day, "The End of the Peasant? The New Rural Reconstruction in China," *Boundary* 2, Summer 2008, 49–73.

17 Chibber, *Postcolonial Theory and the Specter of Capital*, 165. Compare Ranajit Guha, *Elementary Aspects of Peasant Insurgency in Colonial India*, Durham, NC: Duke University Press, 1999, 190.

18 The text in question here is Eric Hobsbawm, *Primitive Rebels: Studies in Archaic Forms of Social Movement in the 19th and 20th Centuries*, New York: W. W. Norton, 1959. Chibber contends that Guha misreads this text, but I will not address this issue.

19 Guha, *Elementary Aspects*, 225.

20 Dipesh Chakrabarty, *Provincializing Europe: Postcolonial Thought and Historical Difference*, Princeton: Princeton University Press, 2000, 13.

21 Compare Guha, *Elementary Aspects*, 99.

22 Chakrabarty, *Provincializing Europe*, 49.

23 Ibid., 48; Edward Palmer Thompson, "Time, Work-Discipline and Industrial Capitalism," in *Essays in Social History*, ed. M. W. Flinn and T. C. Smout, Oxford: Clarendon, 1974, 66, 61.

24 Chakrabarty, *Provincializing Europe*, 50.

25 Bidet, *Explication*, 165.

26 Moreover, he also provides a way to historicize the issue of individual interests, since capitalism posits individuals selling their labor power and consequently pursuing their interests. To the extent that colonial India was incorporated into capitalism, we should not be surprised that peasants in colonial India are pursuing individual interests. In this way, Chakrabarty can avoid the question that Chibber poses about whether people in precapitalist societies pursued their individual interests.

27 Chakrabarty, *Provincializing Europe*, 54.

28 Ibid., 55.

29 Ibid., 60.

30 Ibid.

31 Ibid. Here Chakrabarty's reading overlaps with that of the Japanese Marxist Uno Kōzō. Gavin Walker writes: "This is what Uno referred to as the 'mantra' of Capital (*Shihonron no 'nembutsu'*): the 'impossibility' of 'nihil reason' of the commodification of labor power (*rōdōryoku shōhinka no 'muri'*)." See Gavin Walker, "The World of Principle, or Pure Capitalism: Exteriority and Suspension in Uno Kōzō," *Journal of International Economic Studies* 26, 2012, 15–37, 17.

32 Chakrabarty, *Provincializing Europe*, 60–1.

33 Ibid., 63–4.

34 Ibid., 63.

35 Jacques Derrida and R. Klein, "Economimesis," in "The Ghost of Theology: Readings of Kant and Hegel," special issue, *Diacritics* 11: 2, Summer 1981, 2–25, 21.

36 Karl Marx, *Theories of Surplus Value*, Moscow: Progress Publishers, 1978, 3:468. Compare Chakrabarty, *Provincializing Europe*, 63–4.

37 One could of course read use-value as having a different temporality, but I am not going to pursue this line of argument here.

38 Karl Marx, *Grundrisse der Kritik der Politischen Ökonomie*, Berlin: Dietz Berlin, 1953, 25–6, and *Grundrisse*, trans. Martin Nicolaus, London: Penguin, 1993, 105.

39 Chakrabarty, *Provincializing Europe*, 64.

40 Ibid., 71.

41 Ibid., 67.

42 Postone, *Time, Labor and Social Domination*.

43 Chakrabarty, *Provincializing Europe*, 67.

44 Bruno Gullì, *Labor of Fire: The Ontology of Labor between Culture and Economy*, Philadelphia: Temple University Press, 2005, 63.

45 Ibid., 12.

46 Of course, Gullì himself would like to avoid merely being transhistorical and contends that "this transhistoricality must be understood not as a realm outside of history but, rather as history itself, as what in history sustains and makes possible the coming to be and passing away of stages, ages and modes." Gullì here expands the History 2–like description of labor such that it creates not only History 1, but even history before and after capitalism. Ibid., 12.

47 Chakrabarty, *Provincializing Europe*, 66.

48 As Gullì writes, "even when the worker is working, he or she is also not working, also not a worker. Concretely, during the labor process the worker may choose to spend time daydreaming, organizing the next struggle, implementing an act of sabotage against production itself." Gullì, *Labor of Fire*, 18.

49 Maurice Merleau-Ponty, *Phénoménologie de la perception*, Paris: Gallimard, 1967, 280; *Phenomenology of Perception*, trans. Colin Smith, London: Routledge, 1989. Translation amended by the author.

50 Chakrabarty, *Provincializing Europe*, 71.

51 Chakrabarty, *Habitations of Modernity: Essays in the Wake of Subaltern Studies*, Chicago: University of Chicago Press, 2002, 13. Ranajit Guha, *Dominance without Hegemony: History and Power in Colonial India*, Cambridge, MA: Harvard University Press, 1997, first published 1989.

52 One could of course say that total real subsumption is never complete, as does Harry Harootunian, and in this way, History 2s would always exist. However, Chakrabarty does not take this road. See Harry Harootunian, "Remembering the Historical Present," *Critical Inquiry* 33, 2007, 471–94, 474–5.

53 Chakrabarty, *Provincializing Europe*, 66.

54 Chibber, *Postcolonial Theory and the Specter of Capital*, 233.

55 We could think here of religious subjectivities that support capitalist practices, such as Weber's famous discussion of Protestantism.

56 Michael Löwy, *Redemption and Utopia: Jewish Libertarian Thought in Central Europe: A Study of Elective Affinity*, trans. Hope Heany, Stanford, CA: Stanford University Press, 1988, 16.

57 Chakrabarty, *Provincializing Europe*, 250.

58 In the Canadian context, we can think of liberals such as Will Kymlicka's multiculturalism as protecting the History 2s of the Quebecois, indigenous people

among others. If one wanted to push History 2 in a liberal direction, one might propose a "right to one's History 2." This is not an argument I will address, but see Will Kymlicka, *Multicultural Citizenship: A Liberal Theory of Minority Rights*, Oxford: Oxford University Press, 2000.

59 Chibber, *Postcolonial Theory and the Specter of Capital*, 67.

60 In a footnote, Chibber writes: "My understanding of not only the English case, but also the contrasting French experience, owes an enormous debt to Brenner's pathbreaking scholarship" (Chibber, *Postcolonial Theory and the Specter of Capital*, 57 fn 6). See Robert Brenner, "Agrarian Class Structure and Economic Development in Pre-Industrial Europe" and "The Agrarian Roots of European Capitalism" in T. H. Aston and C. H. E. Philpin, eds, *The Brenner Debate: Agrarian Class Structure and Economic Development in Pre-industrial Europe*, Cambridge: Cambridge University Press, 1985. Chibber also cites Ellen Wood's *The Pristine Culture of Capitalism*, which is largely inspired by Brenner's work (Chibber, *Postcolonial Theory and the Specter of Capital*, 70 fn 37). See Ellen Wood, *The Pristine Culture of Capitalism: A Historical Essay on Old Regimes and Modern States*, London: Verso, 1996.

61 Chibber, *Postcolonial Theory and the Specter of Capital*, 69–70. Chibber draws on William H. Sewell, Jr., *A Rhetoric of Bourgeois Revolution: The Abbé Sieyès and What Is the Third Estate?*, Durham, NC: Duke University Press, 1994; and T. C. W. Blanning, *The French Revolution: Aristocrats versus Bourgeois?*, London: Macmillan, 1987.

62 Wood responds to conservative scholars such as François Furet. See François Furet and Denis Richet, *La Révolution Française*, Paris: Fayard/Pluriel, 2010, first published 1965. See also Keith Michael Baker, *Essays on the Political Culture in the Eighteenth Century*, Cambridge: Cambridge University Press, 1990.

63 George C. Comninel, "Marx's Context," *History of Political Thought* 21, 2000, 467–83. Ellen Wood, "Capitalism or Enlightenment?," *History of Political Thought* 21, 2000, 405–26.

64 I would like to thank Max Ward for mentioning this formulation to me.

65 Chakrabarty, *Provincializing Europe*, 64.

66 Ibid., 47.

67 Chibber, *Postcolonial Theory and the Specter of Capital*, 224.

68 Ibid., 111.

69 Ibid., 116.

70 Ibid.

71 Ibid.

72 Ibid., 231.

73 Ibid., 231–2.

74 Baruch Spinoza, *Ethics, Treatise on the Emendation of the Intellect and Selected Letters*, trans. Samuel Shirley, ed. Seymour Feldman, Indianapolis: Hackett, 1992, 108.

75 Compare Jacques Bidet, *Explication*. With this I am admittedly trying to side-step an issue, namely, Chibber's commitment to rational choice Marxism, which has been criticized by a number of Marxists from different perspectives. I am

not going to delve into these criticisms here due to limitations of space. However, a brief look at the literature shows that proponents and critics often understand different things by "rational choice" or "analytical" Marxism. Part of the problem is that the critics often do not grasp the range of analytic Marxism. For example, Daniel Bensaïd has a perceptive critique of much analytical Marxism in Chapter 5 of his *Marx for Our Times: Adventures and Misadventures of a Critique*, trans. Gregory Elliott, London: Verso, 2002. But much of his critique is geared against those who use Rawls and ideas of justice, which is not so relevant to the issue at hand. Critics of rational choice Marxism, such as Ellen Wood, seem to exempt Eric Wright from scrutiny because they believe that his conception of rational choice is fairly thin. Eric Wright himself makes the following disclaimer with respect to individualism: "This identification of Analytical Marxism with methodological individualism is, I believe mistaken. Indeed, a number of Analytical Marxists have been explicitly critical of methodological individualism and have argued against the exclusive reliance on models of the abstract rationalism as a way of understanding human action. What is true, however, is that most Analytical Marxists take quite seriously the problem of understanding the relationship between individual choice and social processes" (Eric Wright, "What Is Analytical Marxism?" in *Rational Choice Marxism*, ed. Terrell Carver and Paul Thomas, University Park: Pennsylvania University Press, 1995, 11–31, 21). Perhaps because Chibber uses an approach similar to Wright's, he acknowledges the importance of building solidarity, and while he sees the pursuit of interest as universal, he does not deny mediation by other factors. This approach has problems and entails a number of questionable conclusions, including the rejection of dialectics. However, this would require a separate paper to deal with.

76 By stressing universal interests in well-being, Chibber draws on scholars such as Martha Nussbaum. See Nussbaum, "Human Functioning and Social Justice: In Defense of Aristotelian Essentialism," *Political Theory* 20: 2, 1992, 202–46. Chibber explicitly cites Nussbaum in *Postcolonial Theory and the Specter of Capital*, 197.

77 Chibber, *Postcolonial Theory and the Specter of Capital*, 232.

78 Ibid., 232.

79 Ibid., 224.

80 Vasant Kaiwar, "Towards Orientalism and Nativism: The Impasse of Subaltern Studies," *Historical Materialism* 12: 2, 2004, 189–247.

81 William H. Sewell, Jr., "Connecting Capitalism to the French Revolution: The Parisian Promenade and the Origins of Civic Equality in Eighteenth-Century France," *Critical Historical Studies* 1, Spring 2014, 5–47, 11.

82 Bidet, *Explication*, esp. chs. 1–3.

83 Sewell, "Connecting Capitalism," 10.

84 See Chibber, *Postcolonial Theory and the Specter of Capital*, 263 fn 24.

85 Manu Goswami, *Producing India: From Colonial Economy to National Space*, Chicago: University of Chicago Press, 2004, 40.

86 Ibid., 41. Manu Goswami does not follow Arrighi in separating state from capital but premises her arguments on the doubled character of space-time matrices

produced by capital as a global formation. This would be another interesting avenue of research, which I will address in another essay.

87 David Harvey, *The Limits to Capital*, London: Verso, 2006, 399. Harvey goes on to argue that the circulation of capital supports certain infrastructures rather than others (399). But at the same time, the state is a general field of class struggle, which again shows that its relation to the capitalist social relations is underdetermined.

88 Neil Brenner, "Henri Lefebvre's Critique of State Productivism," in *Space, Difference and Everyday Life: Reading Henri Lefebvre*, ed. Kanishka Goonewardena, Stefan Kipfer, Richard Milgram, and Christian Schmid, London: Routledge, 2008, 231–49, 239.

89 Chatterjee, *The Nation and Its Fragments*, 6, cited in Chibber, *Postcolonial Theory and the Specter of Capital*, 278.

90 This might be too antagonistic for Chakrabarty, but it might be what has to happen when one mobilizes History 2.

91 G. W. F. Hegel, *Phänemonologie des Geistes*, Frankfurt am Main: Suhrkamp, 1992, 491, para. 668.

92 Chibber, *Postcolonial Theory and the Specter of Capital*, 279.

93 Jacques Bidet and Gérard Duménil, *Altermarxisme: Un autre marxisme pour un autre monde*, Paris: Presses Universitaires de France, 2007, 161.

94 Karl Marx, *Late Marx and the Russian Road: Marx and "The Peripheries of Capitalism,"* ed. Theodor Shanin, New York: Monthly Review Press, 1983, 105–6.

95 Harry Harootunian, "Who Needs Postcoloniality: A Reply to Linder," *Radical Philosophy* 164, November/December 2010, 43.

96 This point supports Prasenjit Duara's thesis that some separation between inside and outside is implied by all nationalisms, not merely anti-colonial nationalism. For this reason, fear of contamination could be a possibility in any nationalism. See Prasenjit Duara, *Rescuing History from the Nation: Questioning Narratives of Modernity in China and India*, Chicago: University of Chicago Press, 1995.

97 Chibber, *Postcolonial Theory and the Specter of Capital*, 232.

98 See, e.g., Christopher J. Arthur, *The New Dialectic and Marx's Capital*, Leiden: Brill, 2004, 77.

99 Marx, *Grundrisse*, trans. Nicolaus, 706. Compare Chakrabarty, *Provincializing Europe*, 62.

100 Karel Kosík points out how a conception of the future influences the forms in which movements are organized in the present. See his discussion of the future as an "incomplete happening" in Karel Kosík, *The Crises of Modernity and Other Essays and Observations from the 1968 Era*, ed. James Satterwhite, Lanham, MD: Rowman & Littlefield, 1995, 131.

101 Postone, *Time, Labor and Social Domination*, 371–2.

102 See Löwy, *Redemption and Utopia*. See also Robert Sayre and Michael Löwy, "Figures of Romantic Anti-Capitalism," *New German Critique* 32, 1984, 42–92.

103 Alex Callinicos, *Imperialism and Global Political Economy*, London: Polity, 2009, 89.

104 Vijay Prashad, *The Poorer Nations: A Possible History of the Global South*, London: Verso, 2012, 239.

105 See David McNally, *The Global Slump*, Oakland, CA: PM Press, 2011.

106 For a sympathetic discussion of the Maoist movement in India, see Robert Weil, *Is the Torch Passing: Resistance and Revolution in China and India*, Delhi: Setu Prakashani, 2013.

107 Mao Zedong, "Chonqing tanpan," in *Mao Zedong xuanji*, Beijing: Renmin chubanshe, 1991, 4:1163.

Printed in the United States
by Baker & Taylor Publisher Services